The Late Age of Print

The Late Age of Print

EVERYDAY BOOK CULTURE
FROM CONSUMERISM TO CONTROL

Ted Striphas

COLUMBIA UNIVERSITY PRESS | NEW YORK

Columbia University Press
Publishers Since 1893
New York   Chichester, West Sussex

Library of Congress Cataloging-in-Publication Data

Striphas, Theodore G.
   The late age of print : everyday book culture from consumerism to
control / Ted Striphas.
        p. cm.
   Includes bibliographical references and index.
   ISBN 978-0-231-14814-6 (alk. paper)
   1. Book industries and trade—United States. 2. Books and
reading—United States. 3. Publishers and publishing—United
States. 5. Electronic publishing—United States. 6. Internet
bookstores—United States. I. Title.

   Z471.S85   2009
   381'.45002—dc22

Designed by Lisa Hamm

References to Internet Web sites (URLs) were accurate at the time
of writing. Neither the author nor Columbia University Press is
responsible for URLs that may have expired or changed since the
manuscript was prepared.

For Phaedra

Contents

Acknowledgments

HAVING TAUGHT COURSES on the history and cultural politics of electronic media for the better part of a decade, in the fall of 2006 I decided to shift gears a bit. I designed a new undergraduate course called "The Cultures of Books and Reading," hoping it would dovetail with a book—this book—I was working on at the time. As excited as I was about the subject matter, I couldn't help but harbor some doubt. Would the class attract enough students to avoid preemptive cancellation by the university registrar? After all, experience had taught me that undergraduates, most of whom are between the ages of eighteen and twenty-two, would be enthusiastic to learn about cutting-edge digital media and would also have plenty to say about increasingly "old-fashioned" technologies, such as television. But would a class about book culture, offered not in a literature but in a communication department, spark their interest? Or would it seem too out of touch, too frumpy, too analog? Some days it's easy to believe books won't be around much longer. My worst fear, perhaps, was that something as mundane as a lack of interest in my class would simultaneously lend credence to this belief and effectively undercut a main argument I make here, namely, that reports announcing the death of books have been greatly exaggerated.

As it turns out, I shouldn't have second-guessed myself. To my surprise and delight, the course enrollment was one student shy of the maximum. The group was savvy about what's been happening lately—and, in some cases, not so lately—in the book world. Many students professed to being avid book readers, well beyond what they were assigned. Some even finished a few pages of what seemed to be pleasure reading in the moments before our class periods began. Granted, this course was an elective; the extent to which their knowledge and interests can be described as typical of their peers is thus difficult to judge. Even so, I should have known better than to assume my undergraduate students hadn't found a meaningful place for books in their everyday lives.

Like these students, many people have caused me to clarify my own assumptions about everyday book culture during the long process of conceiving, researching, writing, revising, and finally publishing this book. The list of those I wish to thank must begin with Lawrence Grossberg. Larry helped nurture this project from its inception, displaying his characteristic generosity of time, spirit, and intellect. I owe a profound debt to him, one I have no hope of repaying, except perhaps by mentoring my students as skillfully and patiently as he mentored me.

I wish to extend my heartfelt gratitude to the following teachers who supported my research during my years as a graduate student in communication studies at the University of North Carolina, Chapel Hill: Marcus Breen for helping me to find my bearings as a media historian; Michael Hardt for his rigorous reading of Marxism and contemporary theory, which runs like a thread throughout this book; Vicky Johnson for first prompting me to imagine how television relates to books; Della Pollock for consistently reminding me that good faith and good humor are key to making critical intellectual work engaging for all involved; and Jan Radway for demonstrating how to make cultural studies and book history harmonize. Collectively you were—and are—my dream team.

I also want to acknowledge the contributions, both tangible and intangible, of mentor, teacher, and friend John Nguyet Erni. It was John who first introduced me to cultural studies. In doing so, he forever affected how I think about the everyday objects that surround us. Other friends and colleagues deserve special recognition for assisting me at various stages of this project. Kembrew McLeod, John Durham Peters, Jonathan Sterne, and Siva Vaidhyanathan provided the advice, perspective, and support I needed precisely when I needed it. My gratitude extends to the Conjunctures group for offering a safe space in which to try out new ideas. Charles Acland, Marty Allor, Anne Balsamo, Briankle Chang, Melissa Deem, Ron Greene, James Hay, Lisa Henderson, Gil Rodman, Greg Seigworth, Mehdi Semati, Jennifer Slack, Charlie Stivale, and Greg Wise have been especially helpful in this regard. Thanks are also due to Henry A. Giroux, Gary Hall, and Julia T. Wood for the confidence they've displayed in my work, and to Tony Falzone for helping me to navigate the murky waters of permission culture.

While working on this book I've enjoyed the company of bright and talented colleagues at two universities. Greg Waller, my department chair at Indiana University, and Barb Klinger, my faculty mentor, provided both practical and intellectual guidance. I also want to thank my research assistant, Brian Ruh, for his diligence and exceptional organizational skills. Stephen Berrey, Ilana Gershon, Mary Gray, Michael Kaplan, John Lucaites, Josh Malitsky, Yeidy Rivero, Cynthia Duquette Smith, and Robert Terrill each deserve a shout-out not only for their friendship but also for forwarding pertinent materials on book culture whenever they happened upon them. At Ohio University I benefited from Michael Arrington's camaraderie, Greg Shepherd's counsel, and Jeff St. John's well-tempered bibliophilia. An Ohio University summer research grant helped support my work on this book.

I'm grateful to the publishers, editors, and reviewers of three scholarly journals who allowed me to audition some of the arguments I now share here in substantially revised and extended form. Chapter 1 draws heavily on my essay "Disowning Commodities: Ebooks, Capitalism, and Intellectual Property Law," *Television and New Media* 7, no. 3 (August 2006): 231–60. Chapter 3 includes material that originally appeared in "Cracking the Code: Technology, Historiography, and the 'Back Office' of Mass Culture," *Social Epistemology* 19, nos. 2–3 (April–September 2005): 261–82. Lastly, a portion of chapter 4 was published as "A Dialectic with the Everyday: Communication and Cultural Politics on Oprah Winfrey's Book Club," *Critical Studies in Media Communication* 20, no. 3 (September 2003): 295–316. I wish to acknowledge Sage Publications, Taylor & Francis, Ltd. (http://www.tandf.co.uk/journals), and the National Communication Association for granting me permission to reproduce portions of this work in modified form.

My gratitude extends to all those at Columbia University Press who have had a hand in bringing this book to life. I especially wish to single out my editor, Philip Leventhal, not only for believing in this book but also for championing some of the principles it stands for. He facilitated its release in both hardbound form and as a Creative Commons–licensed electronic edition. It's a testament to Philip's vision, and to the vision of Columbia University Press, that they've permitted this book to deliver on one of the most compelling aspects of the late age of print.

My mother, Sue Striphas, instilled in me a passion for language and taught me how to read—foundational life lessons too often overlooked, without which this book certainly wouldn't exist. Her contributions to this volume, however indirect, are nonetheless profound. For their support and encouragement I thank my sister, Anne Striphas; my mom's "main squeeze," Rick Patterson; my godmother, Jean Frangos; my uncle, Jim Frangos; my cousins, George and Alexandra Frangos; and the Courtsunis family (John, Chris, George, and Gus); my in-laws, Carmen and Vincent Pezzullo; my extended family, particularly Jinny and Jerry Alpaugh; all my Goshen peeps; and my four-legged family members, Neptune and Ecco.

The most important person I wish to acknowledge is my partner and muse, Phaedra Pezzullo. The idea for this book first took shape long ago in the form of a conversation with her. She generously pored over the text countless times and was instrumental in helping me to craft a more pointed book out of a sprawling manuscript draft. Beyond all that, it is Phaedra who shows me why the everyday is "what is humble and solid." Each day she affirms for me the joy of beginning again anew. I dedicate this book to her, with love, respect, and gratitude.

The Late Age of Print

Introduction: The Late Age of Print

"AN IMMINENT CULTURAL CRISIS." That's how the National Endowment for the Arts (NEA) summarized the findings of its 2004 report on the health of reading in the United States.[1] What precipitated the agency's grim prognosis was a dramatic, 10 percent dip it had discovered in the number of literature readers—defined as readers of novels, short stories, plays, or poetry.[2] In 1982 almost 57 percent of adults reported having read at least one literary work for pleasure in the preceding year. By 2002 that figure had tumbled to roughly 45 percent and showed no sign of rebounding.[3] With fewer than half of all adults in the United States reading literature, the clichéd conversation starter, "Have you read any good books lately?" was now more likely to elicit a shrug than a verbal response. Perhaps even more troubling than this shift was the NEA's other main discovery: about twenty million people who in 1982 reportedly had read one or more literary works no longer claimed to have read any at all in 2002.[4] In other words, adults seemed to be abandoning books at the alarming rate of one million people per year. Were the trend to continue, the NEA observed, adults in the United States would all but forsake the leisurely reading of literature in just fifty years.[5]

Little wonder, then, why the NEA titled its report *Reading at Risk*. Like an "at risk" child, reading seemed to be vulnerable, corruptible, and consequently in need of immediate intervention. The 2007 sequel to the report, *To Read or Not to Read: A Question of National Consequence*, rounded out the picture. The agency correlated reading interest and proficiency with larger patterns of academic, economic, cultural, and civic achievement among Americans of all ages.[6] It found, for example, that literary readers were almost three times as likely to engage in volunteer or charity work than nonreaders, and that voting likelihood correlated positively with reading ability. On the other hand, the NEA also found poor reading skills among the underemployed, those who failed to finish high school, and the prison population.[7] The implication was hardly subtle: without an interest in literary reading—which is to say of a particular type of book reading—the United States would end up a nation of deadbeats, dropouts, and criminals.

To be sure, the NEA's reports were jarring, but how surprising were they, really?[8] For decades scholars, journalists, critics, educators, and book industry insiders have been sounding alarm bells about the well-being of reading, not to mention of books and book culture generally. Titles such as "The Last Book," "The Bookless Future," *The Gutenberg Elegies*, and *The Last Days of Publishing* tend to paint a bleak picture signaling the decline of printed books and book reading.[9] Author John Updike summarized these concerns pointedly in his address at the 2006 book industry trade gathering BookExpo America: "Book readers and writers are approaching the condition of holdouts, surly hermits refusing to come out and play in the electronic sunshine of the post-Gutenberg village."[10] Ours, evidently, is an age in which the buzz of electronic media predominates. Amid the incessant flow of twenty-four-hour radio and television, the visual and sonic entropy of digitally enhanced cinema, the dizzyingly connective Internet maze, the kaleidoscopic intensity of digital gaming, and the frenetic pace at which new media of all stripes seem to shape the patterns of our daily lives, it seems difficult to imagine books shouldering much world-historical responsibility anymore.

The familiar story of the morbidity and decline of printed books is not, however, the one driving this book. While it would be a mistake to ignore these and other changes in book culture, there's ample evidence to suggest that books have played—and will continue to play—an important role in shaping the syntax of everyday life. Indeed, books arguably have enjoyed something of a renewal of late. In the last fifty years or so retail bookselling has reached unprecedented proportions. Innovative systems for coding, cataloging, distributing, and tracking books have been implemented. Book clubs have enjoyed a resurgent public profile. Moreover, the book trade has globalized more intensively than ever before. In this book I question commonsense understandings of a crisis of book culture. Books aren't as imperiled as some critics believe, and in some ways they might even be thriving. They continue to serve—sometimes in new ways, sometimes in traditional ones—as "equipment for living," to quote Kenneth Burke's memorable phrase.[11] In other words, books remain key artifacts through which social actors articulate and struggle over specific interests, values, practices, and worldviews.

Still, critics on all sides seem to agree that something *has* changed. The culture of books has been shifting—and continues to shift—under our collective feet. The relatively small and genteel publishing houses of the early twentieth century seem quaint compared to the cutthroat multimedia conglomerates that now control an estimated 80 percent (and counting) of the book trade in the United States.[12] The so-called paperback revolution of the 1950s seems to have lost much of its revolutionary fervor, given the ubiquity of paperback publishing today. Local independent bookstores seem imperiled by their geographically promiscuous corporate counterparts. Television personalities command unprecedented authority to make or break books. Whether one believes the relationship between printed books and other media to be contrary, complementary, or some combination of both, books exist in a more densely mediated landscape than ever before.

This dynamic chapter in book history—in which books remain a vital if slippery and perhaps not quite as central a force in the shaping of dominant and emergent ways of life—deserves a name. Jay David Bolter dubs it the "late age of print." While I'm reluctant to use this phrase to describe an epoch or historical totality, it does capture the odd, simultaneously conspicuous and elusive character of books today. The late age of print, Bolter explains, consists of "a transformation of our social and cultural attitudes toward, and uses of, this familiar technology. Just as late capitalism is still vigorous capitalism, so books and other printed materials in the late age of print are still common and enjoy considerable prestige."[13] A refreshingly modest concept, the late age of print underscores the enduring role of books in shaping habits of thought, conduct, and expression. At the same time, it draws attention to the ways in which the social, economic, and material coordinates of books have been changing in relation to other media, denser forms of industrial organization, shifting patterns of work and leisure, new laws governing commodity ownership and use, and a host of other factors. The phrase points up the tense interplay of persistence and change endemic to today's everyday book culture without necessarily presuming a full-blown crisis exists. More to the point, the phrase underscores the fact that we're living in a period of transition in which books and book culture seem the same, only they are somehow different.

I'm neither prepared to write an elegy for printed books, nor am I prepared to make the claim that little has changed—or should have changed—

in the cultures of books over the past twenty-five, fifty, hundred, or five hundred years. I genuinely value books, especially printed ones. I'm surrounded by them as I write these words. Nevertheless, the purpose of *The Late Age of Print* isn't to make a fetish of books. A substantial number of books about books have been published over the last decade or so, many of which rhapsodize about book collecting and care, the inveterate passion for reading, the wonder of libraries and bookstores, the highs imparted by the smell and texture of printed books—in a word, what Nicholas A. Basbanes admiringly calls "bibliomania."[14] This book isn't one of them, at least not in any straightforward way. Singularly affirmative narratives about books, though often personally moving and poetic, can obscure book history's more sinister side. One person's bibliomania often depends indirectly on the exploitation of another's labor. It may also depend on potentially damaging forms of social and epistemological exclusion that flow from privileging the printed word over other, more fully embodied forms of expression.[15]

By the same token, I'm not cynical enough to suggest that printed books are anachronisms whose longevity only hampers our achieving a sublime digital future.[16] Anachronisms aren't things. They're performative utterances whose force empowers people to sidestep difficult questions about the being of time and to install themselves as gatekeepers of temporal propriety. Hence, there are no anachronisms, only ways of seeing things as anachronisms. Whenever common sense tells us that printed books are dusty holdovers from the pre-electronic, analog era, we would do well to change our frame of reference. Books are artifacts with a deep and abiding history that belong in and to our own age—no more and no less so than flat-screen televisions, MP3 players, computers, and other so-called cutting-edge technologies.

If this book neither declares that there is a crisis nor denies major historical shifts, if it neither rejoices in printed books nor aspires to bid them a fond farewell, then what, exactly, is its intention? First, it explores the history and conditions by which books have become ubiquitous and mundane social artifacts in and of our time. It's worth remembering that as recently as the mid-nineteenth century many people living in the West still considered books to be rarities. According to Raymond Williams, "It is only in our own century [the twentieth], and still in incomplete ways, that books began to come with any convenience to the majority of people."[17] Particular books may be noteworthy—even precious—for one reason or another, but for many of us today books are also ubiquitous, accessible, and comparatively mundane things. How did we get from there to here?[18] As Williams well knew, the everydayness of books belies a long, complicated, and still unfinished history, one intimately bound up with all of the following: a changed and changing mode of production; new technological products and processes; shifts in law and jurisprudence; the proliferation of culture and the rise of cultural politics; and a host of sociological transformations, among many other factors. This book is about the prevalent and pedestrian character of books today and, more important, about a broad set of conditions leading to their constitution as such.

This first story largely turns on the relationship of the past to the present. The second story, which overlaps partially with the first, concerns the relationship of the present to the future. The everyday character of books has emerged gradually, unevenly, and in some respects paradoxically, for it has occurred alongside a general loosening of what Williams calls "the dominant relations of print."[19] By this I assume he means something along the lines of the late age of print, for he acknowledges "the new cultural period we have already entered."[20] But what, exactly, are this period's conditions of possibility? What are its defining characteristics beyond the persistence of printed books and people's changing attitudes toward them? The challenge in answering these questions stems from what, I contend, is this period's diffuseness. The late age of print encompasses both dominant and emergent values, practices, and worldviews.[21] As such, it continues to take shape in the present even as it opens out onto the future. In this book I attempt to glimpse the contours of the late age of print in some of the most prosaic activities characteristic of book culture today: browsing around a large retail bookstore; selling books online; scanning a book's bar code at the checkout counter; reading and discussing a popular work with a group; waiting on a line to buy a hotly anticipated best seller; and creating spin-offs based on popular literary characters, to name just a few.

From electronic books and book superstores to online bookselling, and from Oprah Winfrey's book club to Harry Potter, this book moves among some of the most prominent—indeed, commonplace—aspects of everyday book culture today. Its aim is not only to map the prevalent and pedestrian character of books but also to explore what their everydayness might tell us about a gathering configuration of politics, economics, law, culture, sociality, and technology. More specifically, I argue that books were integral to the making of a modern, connected consumer culture in the twentieth century, and that today they form a key part of consumer capitalism's slow slide into what I call, following Henri Lefebvre, a "society of controlled consumption."[22]

Bottom Lines

The connection between books and people's everyday economic activities is a critically important one. Yet for a large number of people outside the book industry—and even for some insiders—the link may be somewhat dubious. People buy and sell books all the time. They've done so for generations. Still, conventional wisdom says there's something more to them—something that sets books apart from, say, light bulbs, DVDs, automobiles, and other mass merchandise for which people pay good money. Laura J. Miller sums up the matter succcinctly: "Books, as storehouses of ideas and as a perceived means to human betterment, have long been viewed as a kind of 'sacred product.'"[23] The value of books would seem to lie, first and foremost, in their capacity for moral, aesthetic, and intellectual development, and only secondarily—if at all—in the marketplace. What makes a "good" book good—or, rather, what makes *books* good—is their purported ability to transcend vulgar economic considerations for the sake of these loftier goals.[24]

The notion that books belong at a significant remove from the realm of economic necessity is one of the most entrenched myths of contemporary book culture. By "myth" I don't mean a falsehood but rather a particularly generative type of communication that trades on common sense.[25] For example, several book industry insiders have suggested that an unremitting concern for the economic bottom line took hold in their trade in the 1960s or 1970s, following a spate of mergers and acquisitions that brought some of the most esteemed publishing houses under corporate control. Before that ideas and artistry led the way.[26] What's important about these accounts is not that they're inaccurate but rather that they're inadequate. It may be true that the publishing industry of today pays more attention to profits and losses than the industry of forty or fifty years ago, but this statement can hardly be taken to mean that the book industry had subordinated economics up to that point. Rather, it registers the degree to which certain economic realities of the book trade have come to be seen as so customary, so banal, as to be overlooked almost entirely today.[27]

It may be that the "crisis" of books is linked not only to purported decreases in the amount of reading but also to people's misgivings about—or, more accurately, their lack of historical perspective on—the economic organization of the book trade. The work of Lucien Febvre and Henri-Jean Martin is particularly instructive in this regard. In their pathbreaking study *The Coming of the Book* they paint a detailed portrait of the intimate and enduring relationship between capitalist economics and book culture, writing that "from its earliest days printing existed as an industry, governed by the same rules as any other industry." They add that most of those who have been involved in the production, distribution, and sale of printed books have tended to treat them—if not in theory then most certainly in practice—as "piece[s] of merchandise which [they] produced before anything else to earn a living."[28] Books may connote and sometimes even provide for leisureliness, erudition, and a modicum of distance from the exigencies of daily life. That said, one mustn't lose sight of the fact that they've long been tied to people's immediate economic realities.

This point holds true even for those not in the book industry's employ. Book publishing was one of the first large-scale industries to coalesce as such, and it did so in part by pioneering the rationalization and standardization of mass-production techniques. Its voluminous output—as many as twenty million books in the age of incunabula alone—depended not only on the successful implementation, diffusion, and uptake of a new technology (print) but also on new ways of organizing labor practices, class relations, and bodily habits within and beyond the print shop.[29] To wit, the book industry was among the first to embrace what was, even as late as the seventeenth century, a relatively novel form of compensation: hourly wage labor. Coupled with a more efficient production process, the move toward an hourly wage effectively boosted the creation of surplus value for master printers and their financiers. At the same time, it constrained seriously the socioeconomic mobility of journeymen and apprentices, eventually—and not without resistance—proletarianizing members of both groups.[30] Benedict Anderson's expression "print-capitalism" aptly describes the close kinship books (and other types of printed matter) have long shared with the strategies of capitalist accumulation.[31] In the union of these elements one can glimpse the beginnings of what, in both our own century and the preceding one, have proven to be some of the signature features of the workaday world.

Consider the fact that books were among the very first commercial Christmas presents. Not only that, but they were integral to the development of a modern Christmas holiday primarily organized around familial gift exchange.[32] In the second quarter of the nineteenth century there emerged in the United States a new genre of books: gift books. These special anthologies, which publishers released on the cusp of the Christmas season, consisted of poetry, prose, illustrations, and, typically, a customizable bookplate.[33] The popularity of gift books as Christmas presents is attributable to many factors, chief among them their status as mass-produced merchandise. Indeed, industrial production not only facilitated their availability en masse at the appropriate moment but, even more important, provided for their reception as tokens of intimacy and affection in at least two ways. First, a gift giver had to select from among many editions the one that best suited the recipient. Making the correct choice wasn't easy since publishers produced a range of volumes, each targeted to individuals belonging to a particular social set.[34] Selecting a mass-produced consumer good, in other words, became a meaningful expression of one's consideration and goodwill in no small part through the popularity of gift books. Second, the bookplates allowed the gift giver the opportunity to further personalize his or her selection, for they generally included a small amount of blank space upon which to pen an inscription. These pages, however, were preprinted at the factory, again suggesting a blurring of boundaries between mass industrial production and personal sentiment.[35] In any case, these examples illustrate the crucial role that books played in turning Christmas into a consumerist holiday. "Publishers and booksellers were the shock troops in exploiting—and developing—a Christmas trade," writes Stephen Nissenbaum, "and books were on the cutting edge of a commercial Christmas."[36]

Books not only helped give rise to what's become the capitalist holiday par excellence but they also "were on the cutting edge" of a broader and more fundamental economic transformation that occurred as the nineteenth century flowed into the twentieth.[37] By this I mean the gradual transformation of capitalism from a form in which agriculture and intracapitalist exchange were primary engines of economic accumulation to one in which economic vitality increasingly hinged on working people's consumption of abundant, mass-produced goods. Books—along with sewing machines, pianos, and furniture—were among the very first items that people purchased with the aid of a resource newly extended to them toward the end of the nineteenth century, namely, consumer credit.[38] Although the practice of buying consumer goods on credit harbored negative connotations at the time of and even well after its introduction, an attractive set of books was considered by many to be a more or less acceptable credit purchase. Much like a sewing machine, it was assumed to be a productive investment rather than a frivolous purchase.[39] Clearly, the moral value many people attribute to books provided an alibi for their existence as mass-produced merchandise. Books consequently became a test case for debt-driven purchasing, an activity that's proven to be a lasting and even prosaic aspect of contemporary consumer culture.

Thus, *The Late Age of Print* explores not only how books have become ubiquitous social artifacts but also the cultural work involved in transforming them from industrially produced stuff into "sacred products" (and sometimes back again). One way to think about this process is to consider the tension surrounding the word "commodity." On the one hand, it can refer to generic wares or an undifferentiated product, typically in large quantities, where there's no attempt to distinguish one item from another of its kind on the basis of, say, who produced it. This understanding of commodities operates in places like the Chicago Board of Trade and the New York Mercantile Exchange, where traders buy and sell futures on soybeans, wheat, heating oil, steel, livestock, and other staples. On the other hand, there is the Marxist understanding of commodity, "a very strange thing, abounding in metaphysical subtleties and theological niceties."[40] According to this view, what may have started out as a more or less generic, useful thing assumes a unique and almost otherworldly quality. This occurs as goods multiply within the context of their mass manufacture, which tends to dissociate the value of specific items from the personalities of the workers who produced them. Marx writes: "Value, therefore, does not have its description branded on its forehead; it rather transforms every product of labour into a social hieroglyph".[41] By this he means that specific goods take on an identity or life of their own seemingly independent of human involvement, which then becomes an abstract index of their value. Instead of favoring either of these definitions of commodity, I wish to locate books in the tension between them. What interests me are those moments in which they're treated either as generic stuff or as hallowed objects, as well as the labor it takes to transform books from the one into the other. This is nothing other than the work of culture.

Edges

The everyday is a central organizing motif of this book. In its conventional sense the term generally denotes a matter of routine, or the way things simply are, as in the sentence "I take my coffee with cream and sugar every . . . single . . . day." This is a useful, first approximation of a definition. Here "everyday book culture" refers to a range of run-of-the-mill meanings, values, practices, artifacts, and ways of life associated with books. These characteristics are the "givens" of book culture, as it were. Their familiarity often makes them recede into the deep background of experience, so that at first glance—and maybe even after a second look—they're apt to seem boring or unremarkable. (Why do books have copyright pages? What allows me to pass along a book once I've purchased it? Why all those codes and symbols on the backs of most books?) Henri Lefebvre puts it nicely when he describes this facet of the everyday as "what is humble and solid, what is taken for granted and that of which all the parts follow each other in a regular, unvarying succession."[42] Or, as Paddy Scannell eloquently puts it: "It is essential for ordinary existence that the meaningful background remains *as* the background in order to preserve everyday life as an environment in which each and every one of us can operate effectively by virtue of its utterly normal, taken-for-granted, known-and-familiar, yet deeply meaningful character. This meaningfulness *must* appear, in effect, as its opposite. If we could grasp it in its fullness its roar would overwhelm us."[43] The everyday is what can be counted on, and as such its consequentiality can easily be overlooked or even forgotten. It's kind of like trusted friends, who are there for us day in and day out. It's as though they've always been a part of our lives, and the meaningfulness and stability they provide may not fully register until they're gone.

My use of "everyday" begins from this (forgive the redundancy) everyday understanding of the word, though ultimately my aim is to trouble the sense of givenness it evokes. Instead of taking the everyday for granted, I follow Rita Felski in wondering how we "conduct our daily lives on the basis of numerous unstated and unexamined assumptions about the way things are, about the continuity, identity and reliability of objects and individuals."[44] I not only investigate what people's specific habits of thought, conduct, and expression are with respect to books, but, in a more critical vein, I trace some of the key conditions under which those habits are produced, reproduced, and possibly transformed. This approach leads me to question how books and book culture become intelligible at the level of the everyday, as everyday, beyond people's immediate experiences with them.[45]

Although in this book I may appear to focus on contemporary book culture, in significant respects this is only nominal. What interests me are the legal codes, technical devices, institutional arrangements, social relations, and historical processes whose purpose is to help secure the everydayness of contemporary book culture. Their inner workings and, in some cases, even their existence may be unknown or irrelevant to all but a small minority of insiders. Nonetheless, they powerfully affect what a majority of people considers normal, mundane, or run-of-the-mill about books today. In his study of radio and television broadcasting routines Scannell offers a useful analog to what I'm getting at when he states that their everydayness "came to require . . . an immense institutional structure, the skills of thousands of people all geared towards the provision of programme services in such a way that they would appear as no more than what anyone would expect, as what anyone would regard as their due, as a natural, ordinary, unremarkable, everyday entitlement."[46] In a similar vein, a key question I want to ask is: How have books come to be perceived as "everyday entitlements," that is, objects that pretty much can be counted on to be wherever and whenever we expect them to be?

Like "everyday," the term "book" is also deceptively straightforward. It can obscure as much as—if not more than—it reveals. Most of us expect certain things from books, like covers; paper pages assembled neatly into versos and rectos; printed characters, illustrations, and other graphical signs; chapters; readerly amenities including title pages, tables of contents, and indexes; and more. John Updike has remarked that "books traditionally have edges."[47] In other words, there seems to be a certain solidity and a literal boundedness to the objects most of us call books. This explains why both scholars and nonscholars alike routinely use a generic term—"the book"—to refer to these objects. Yet that solidity belies the history of books, one whose only constant is the technology's relentless metamorphosis.

Books *conventionally* have edges, but they don't *necessarily* possess them. For all practical purposes people today tend to treat books—with the exception of anthologies—as if they were discrete, closed entities.[48] This hasn't always been the case. In the first century of printing in the West, it wasn't uncommon for a single bound volume to contain multiple works.[49] One could hardly consider these books to be closed, much less objective in the sense of being contained, given how the practice of their assembly—what, with some trepidation, we might call their form—provided for a range of textual juxtapositions. (The Bible is perhaps the most famous and enduring example of this mode of presentation.) Similarly, nearly all books that present-day consumers buy or borrow are finished works in the sense that they arrive without any need of additional manufacture. This characteristic is also a convention—and a somewhat recent one at that. To save on shipping costs, printers frequently sent unbound books to merchants, a practice that continued in earnest at least into the eighteenth century.[50] In fact, the practice of selling unbound books lingered into the first half of the twentieth century, though by then it had less to do with conducting business on the cheap. Custom-bound books had become marks of distinction in an age of ascendant mass manufacture, connoting the objects' rarity and their owners' prestige.[51] In any event, precisely when in the course of their printing, shipping, sale, and subsequent binding these objects definitively became books remains an open question. Maybe they were books all along. If so, then the word "book" denotes not so much a hard-edged product than a supple, diffuse, and ongoing process.

Reading is another aspect of books that is generally taken for granted. Though people undeniably engage in acts we call reading (you happen to be doing so right now), the verb "read" is about as vague as the term "book." Silently or out loud? Sight-reading or subvocalization? Alone or in a group? Linearly or in a hopscotch pattern? Closely or skimming? Where and for how long? What level of attention or comprehension? In conjunction with what other media, if any?[52] These questions suggest that reading is an intricate, multifarious activity, one that varies significantly across time and space. Little wonder, then, why Nicholas Howe has suggested that "read" and "reading" are among the most complex words in the English language—so complex and socially significant that they're worthy of Raymond Williams's list of cultural keywords.[53] In the present study reading denotes a range of techniques and activities whereby individuals and groups interact with the manifest content of books. Given the diverse skill sets and social relationships to which the word "reading" can refer, the more cumbersome construction "reading practices" might be more appropriate.

However it's defined, reading doesn't exhaust the range of possible uses of books. Though I tend to take good care of my books, two of them—which I've neither read nor intend to—currently prop up a bookcase, which was damaged during a move. For me these books serve a utilitarian function, nothing more; they will only ever be potentially semiotic. Some people even keep sizable libraries on hand, despite having read practically none of the volumes in their collection. They use their libraries to convey an air of bookishness or accomplishment, or simply to fill up what would otherwise be empty shelf space.[54] Still others use books to regulate and repel the incursions of others. For instance, Janice A. Radway has shown how the simple presence of a romance novel in a woman's hands can convey the impression to those around her that "this is my time, my space. Now leave me alone" regardless of whether she's actively engaged in reading it.[55] Books are more than just things people read. They're also props, part of the décor, psychological barriers, and more.

Ultimately, then, this book tends to decenter reading. My purpose in doing so is to provide a more detailed picture of the ways in which people use books beyond treating them as vessels for meaningful, imaginative, or communicative encounters. I particularly want to explore the "circulation" of books since too often they conjure little more than images of collectables or keepsakes. They can sit on shelves for years, decades, or even longer gathering dust—or worse. Similarly, the phrase "curl up with a good book" suggests that reading is a physically languid activity—one best carried out under a heap of comfy blankets.[56] Yet the fact of the matter is that books move, especially—but not exclusively—in the age of their mass reproduction.

From publisher to printer, binder, distributor, and bookseller; from library to borrower and back again; from family member to friend, colleague, and acquaintance; from hard copy to microfilm, photocopier, and scanner; from garage sale to second-hand store and beyond, books circulate widely. For some people their circulation's been a boon, providing relatively easy—and in some cases cheap and even free—access to what might be described as public resources. For others their circulation begets consternation. For example, those who have invested significant time, energy, and resources in bringing these intellectual properties to market often lobby insistently for measures to limit their circulation. With the globalization of the book trade, moreover, some people have come to resent the intrusion of books originating from foreign shores, especially when they seem to edge out locally produced works. Finally, for those knee deep in the trenches of distribution circulation poses countless logistical quandaries, not the least of which is how to keep tabs on millions of volumes each and every day. These brief examples suggest that the circulation of books correlates with specific values, practices, interests, and worldviews, which is just another way of saying that there's a politics to circulating books. In *The Late Age of Print* I am interested in the ways in which everyday practices of circulating books can both occasion and embody struggles over particular ways of life.

Sites

The approach of this book is strategically eclectic. Although it dwells where the history of media, technology, ideas, and mass culture all overlap, it isn't a work of history per se. It addresses the sociology of books and reading, yet it's not exactly a work of sociology. Although it ranges from literary theory and criticism to political economy and critical legal studies, it's a work proper to none of these fields. It's a book about communication, albeit one whose focus exceeds questions of communicative practice. What this book assuredly is *is* a work of cultural studies. Drawing on an interdisciplinary ensemble of theories and methods, it explores how, why, and for whose benefit books and book culture become politicized in specific contexts.[57]

The artifacts we call books naturally occupy an important place in this study. Given my approach, though, I am less interested in these artifacts in themselves than I am in what Elizabeth Long has called their "social infrastructure."[58] The latter is best imagined as a network composed of intersecting material, technical, interpersonal, institutional, and discursive relations. It provides for the production, distribution, exchange, and consumption of books, as well as for how people come to understand their uses and meanings at the level of the everyday. In more concrete terms, the social infrastructure of books determines—albeit never once and for all—the following: the physical and epistemological boundaries of books; the channels through which and the protocols by which producers, distributors, and consumers communicate about and convey books and the hierarchies by which individuals and groups come to value specific types of, and places associated with, books over others. My focus on the late age of print leads me to stress those infrastructural elements that have emerged roughly since the 1930s.

Each of the five main chapters of this book points to a topic rich enough for a book-length study in itself. I've opted to forgo a more intensive investigation of this kind, however, instead preferring to engage in a more extensive examination of everyday book culture. Intensive research lends itself well to exploring a particular object in greater depth, though it risks downplaying the extent to which that object connects to something and how. The difference between intensive and extensive research, in other words, is the difference between situating an object in context and treating the context—a multiplicity of elements—precisely as one's object of study.[59] Both types of research doubtless have their advantages, though the latter may lend itself better to representing complexity, contingency, contradiction, and change than the former. An extensive approach also lets me tell interrelated, although not entirely congruous, stories about the historical constitution of everyday book culture in the late age of print. Each chapter comprises a layer that partially overlaps with and conditions each of the others, so that the narrative of the book accumulates gradually, unevenly, and, like sediment in a river, shifts along the way.

In more concrete terms, each of the main chapters focuses on a particular facet of contemporary book culture, or what I prefer to call a "site." By this I don't mean a fixed object or a bounded geographical locale. Rather, sites are "pressure points of complex modern societies."[60] They're simultaneously singular and plural—singular in the sense that they have a definite character and value and plural in the sense that these attributes are determined only in relation to other sites, though never once and for all. Each chapter begins from a particularly charged site of contemporary book culture in which books and people's relationships with them become politicized. I then proceed to trace some of the key historical conditions leading to the emergence of each of the five sites, in addition to the ways in which they've collectively come to define everyday book culture's most numbingly repetitive and most splendidly transformative qualities. This diversity of foci allows me to move between spheres of book production, distribution, exchange, and consumption instead of privileging one of these aspects over any of the others. The end result is a dynamic investigation of the social and material circuitry not only through which books are constantly traveling but without which books as many people now know them probably wouldn't exist at all.[61]

Even more concretely, I try to discern recurrent patterns according to which books are discussed in professional, popular, and more quotidian discourse. I draw primary source materials on the status of book culture from book industry trade journals, in addition to the local and national news media. I examine recently published memoirs and related accounts that reflect on a century's worth of changes in the U.S. book industry. I engage the voices of people who have—and, in some cases, have not—decided to make books and reading an integral aspect of their daily lives. My research encompasses television shows and bric-à-brac from the popular media that say something about books, everyday life, and the late age of print. I also look at imposter editions of popular literary titles, in addition to exploring the ways in which legislation and court cases affect these and other patterns of book circulation and reception.[62]

Research into more than one medium has a tendency to devolve into hackneyed sloganeering (e.g., "TV kills books"), whereas medium-specific research at best can yield only a vague impression of the complexity of an increasingly crowded media landscape. Accordingly, I have been guided by the principle of "intermediation," a term I have borrowed from Charles R. Acland to describe the complex relations that media share in determinate historical conjunctures.[63] Intermedial relations exceed the "remedial," a term that Jay David Bolter and David Grusin use to describe the ways in which so-called new media borrow and adapt formal elements from older media.[64] Moreover, they differ from "intermedia," an idea developed by the noted Fluxus artist Dick Higgins to describe hybrid artistic "works which conceptually fall between media that are already known."[65] In a more affirmative vein, the principle of intermediation is grounded in three main propositions: first, media shouldn't be isolated analytically from one another; second, the relationships among media are socially produced and historically contingent rather than given and necessary; and, third, media rarely if ever share one-dimensional, causal relationships. Rather than resigning ourselves to writing insular histories of what some believe either explicitly or implicitly to be a medium in decline, intermediation pushes us to assume a less defensive posture. It compels those of us interested in the recent history of books to account for the technology's contemporaneity and to stress both its contrariety to and complementarity with an abundance of other—equally timely—media.

Chapter 1 presents a critical history of the conditions of possibility and broader effects of the artifacts some believe to be sounding a death knell for printed books, namely, their electronic counterparts, e-books. Though I focus on the relationship they share with printed books, on the whole I'm less concerned with the extent to which the former may be a worthy replacement for the latter. Instead, I examine the emergence of e-books in relation to public relations campaigns, litigation, legislative initiatives, and other technologies—all of which have helped call into question the circulation of printed books and, implicitly, that of other mass-produced consumer goods. Through the technology of e-books, cultural producers have problematized the notion that a majority of people ought to own these goods, not to mention the assumption that producers must relinquish in perpetuity their rights to the goods they sell. E-books thus portend a shift away from the widespread private ownership of salable consumer goods to the periodic licensing of intellectual properties—representing a significant shift to a foundational logic of consumer capitalism.

We're often told that independent booksellers are the guardians of good taste, cultural diversity, and grassroots community. Economics is a necessary, if unpleasant, aspect of their day-to-day affairs, but it's certainly not what drives them. Corporate booksellers, on the other hand, are predatory, profit-obsessed giants whose business practices threaten to transform the mindful art of bookselling into something akin to theme park management. This story is like a broken record, but what does it really tell us about the politics of bookselling in the United States? Chapter 2 considers the conflict between independent and corporate booksellers and dwells on the conditions leading to the enlargement of the scope and scale of bookselling in the twentieth century. It also focuses on a specific corporate bookstore located in Durham, North Carolina. I explore the store's embeddedness in a local dynamics of race and class and show how its history cuts against the grain of prevailing wisdom about the politics of retail bookselling in the United States.

The enormous growth in bookselling raises an important question: How has the book industry managed to keep up and at what cost? Chapter 3 presents a history of the technical processes and labor necessary to facilitate large-scale book distribution, or the back-office systems by which books have come to pervade everyday life. The heart of this chapter provides a history of the International Standard Book Number (ISBN), which the book industry implemented to regularize communications, rationalize distribution, and coordinate operations across the industry as a whole. The chapter ends with a critical look at online retailer Amazon.com's distribution apparatus, which weds ISBNs and other product codes to a massive physical and technical infrastructure. The company's fast-paced, ultraefficient workplace reveals how the everydayness of books depends not only on sophisticated digital technologies but also on intensive work processes for those employed in the area of book distribution.

Since the launch of her book club in 1996, television talk show host Oprah Winfrey has emerged as one of the key arbiters of bibliographic taste in the United States. Millions of people routinely swear by Winfrey's selections, much to the chagrin of established literary authorities. Chapter 4 explores why Oprah's Book Club has proven to be a source of inspiration and alarm. It dwells on the club's flair for connecting book reading with women's everyday lives, a talent that's yielded a distinct—and at times controversial—set of protocols by which to judge and read books. Hence Oprah's Book Club is a compelling site in which to scrutinize how the politics of reading, hierarchies of cultural value, structures of authority, and relations of gender all converge and work themselves out at the level of the everyday. It also provides an opportunity to reflect on an overlapping set of concerns, namely, the often vexed, intermedial relationship of books and TV.

Issues pertaining to the circulation of books and to the politics of intellectual property form the crux of chapter 5. It details how, where, when, and among whom the popular Harry Potter book series moves. Almost as captivating as the Potter stories themselves are the efforts of the rights holders to micromanage the release of each new installment and to police the appropriation of copyrighted and trademarked Potter material in a global context. The success of the Potter book series thus raises important questions about originality, propriety, reproducibility, and the global flow of commodities (in both senses of the term) in the late age of print. Who gets to define what counts as an acceptable or unacceptable appropriation of another's intellectual property? What happens to popular artifacts once they move across geographical boundaries and into new legal and political-economic contexts? I argue that Harry Potter has much to tell us about the ways in which the once arcane world of intellectual property has come to infiltrate and invest the practice of everyday life.

The conclusion to this book explores what these five sites can collectively teach us about politics in the late age of print. It begins by revisiting the role that books and book culture played in the rise and consolidation of consumer capitalism in the second and third quarters of the twentieth century. It next recapitulates how key aspects of consumer capitalism—particularly the notion of consumer sovereignty—have been problematized over the last thirty to fifty years by agents in the employ of capitalist accumulation. Lastly, I contend that in the late age of print emergent techniques of control increasingly impinge on the creative ways in which people have for decades made use of books and other mass-produced consumer goods. As such, it's a period in which a particular kind of politics—cultural politics—must confront new challenges and constraints.

1 E-Books and the Digital Future

AT EXACTLY 12:01 A.M. on March 14, 2000, Simon & Schuster began an experiment: the publisher released best-selling author Stephen King's first digital electronic book, or e-book, the sixty-seven-page novella *Riding the Bullet*, on the Internet. By 11:59 p.m. on the fifteenth, an estimated half million people had downloaded King's story, prompting Jack Romanos, Simon & Schuster's president, to declare the experiment a resounding success: "We believe the e-book revolution will have an impact on the book industry as great as the paperback revolution of the 60's."[1] Later that year, the soon-to-be notorious accounting firm of Arthur Anderson joined the celebration of e-books. In a dubious feat of actuarial prowess, Anderson's consultants predicted that by 2005 no less than 10 percent of all books sold in the United States would be in electronic form.[2] It appeared that the dusty old era of printed books was finally poised to give way to a sublime digital future.

Several years and a healthy dose of cynicism later, it seems clear that these heady claims about e-books were suffused with the same millennial hopes and dreams that had helped fuel the late 1990s dot-com boom and its accompanying faith in a resplendent technofuture. Despite the efforts of Stephen King, Simon & Schuster, and Arthur Andersen to locate themselves within the vanguard of an e-book revolution, the latter hasn't quite reached the fevered pitch that book industry insiders had anticipated. The turning point seems to have occurred around 2001 when, in the words of *Publishers Weekly*, the book industry trade magazine, e-book denizens faced a "reality check." Sluggish sales and the economic downturn following the 9/11 terrorist attacks in the United States led many hardware manufacturers and e-book publishers to divest themselves of their interest in e-books. Their doing so followed on the heels of Stephen King's decision, in December 2000, to discontinue writing his second e-book, *The Plant*, after the number of those who had downloaded installments from his Web site without paying had grown too high by his estimation.[3]

Still, interest in and sales of e-books have rebounded of late. A 2003 report by the Open E-book Forum found that close to a million e-books had been sold in 2002, generating nearly $8 million in revenue; the first half of 2003 saw healthy, double-digit increases in units of sale over the preceding year. A second report, compiled by the Association of American Publishers, showed more modest gains of nearly $3 million in e-book sales among the top eight trade publishers. Of course, these reports don't account for the innumerable e-books that people acquire for free from sites such as the University of Virginia Library's EText Center (now the Scholars' Lab). In 2001 alone the library recorded over three million e-book downloads of works that had passed into the public domain. Moreover, major academic textbook publishers such as McGraw-Hill and Thomson Learning continue to pursue e-books in earnest, with the former reporting per month revenue from e-publishing in 2002 in the hundreds of thousands of dollars.[4]

Two other higher-profile e-book ventures not only have helped to renew public interest in the technology but have also prompted some to begin imagining a world in which the content of books—perhaps of *all* books now in existence—would be little more than a click away. Since 2004, search engine giant Google has been busy digitizing part or all of the printed book collections of twenty-nine (and counting) major research libraries. The company's self-described "moon shot," also known as Book Search, promises to make content from millions of books freely available to those with Internet access, and perhaps one day even to realize the promise of a massively cross-referenced universal library accessible to all.[5] On November 19, 2007, online retailer Amazon.com released Kindle, a portable electronic reading device whose express purpose, according to CEO Jeff Bezos, would be to bring books—"the last bastion of analog"—into the digital realm.[6] Onboard mobile phone technology probably makes Kindle the first portable electronic reading device to provide for ubiquitous two-way communication between bookseller and consumer (available only in North America at the time of this writing). According to Bezos, "Our vision is that you should be able to read any book in any language that's ever been printed, whether it's in print or out of print, and you should be able to buy and get that book downloaded to your Kindle in less than 60 seconds."[7]

FIGURE 1 Printed books still seem to be the real thing.

SOURCE: CHRONICLE OF HIGHER EDUCATION, OCTOBER 31, 2005, B22. USED WITH PERMISSION OF CAROLE CABLE.

Despite all this think-big entrepreneurial optimism, many continue to doubt the worth of e-book technologies. Take a cartoon published in a 2005 edition of the *Chronicle of Higher Education*, whose caption reads: "The problem with e-books is that they are e-books" (fig. 1). If this tautological statement makes us laugh, we do so most likely because we share a highly specific, normative vision of books and book reading. This vision, which has been propounded for decades by journalists, literary humanists, educators, and academic theorists, places printed books and solitary, immersive acts of reading center stage in the bibliographic mise-en-scène. The joke works because for many people it's intuitive to see e-books as crude copies of vaunted originals—that is, of printed books—and, in turn, to imagine the reading of electronic content as intellectually or experientially impoverished.[8]

Amusing though they may be, jokes like these are anything but innocent. They're defensive assertions fueled by even more fundamental assumptions about the relationship between electronic and printed books. Just as "video killed the radio star," many partisans of print believe that e-books threaten to kill off their paper-based counterparts. Their fears may not be altogether unfounded. Some book-scanning projects have resulted in the destruction and discarding of countless printed books because of the method by which the codex volumes are prepared for flatbed scanning, namely, the "guillo-tining" of their spines.[9] (Google's method is the exception here.) However, it's not just the physical form of printed books that seems to be imperiled in the so-called digital age. Critics worry that their content could be jeop-ardized as well. The lack of standardization of e-books, combined with the penchant among hardware and software developers for "upgrading" file formats out of existence, would appear to render the digital existence of book content tenuous at best.[10] E-books thus appear to some as harbingers of loss—of knowledge, authority, history, artistry, and meaning.

How could it be that e-books seem to offer equal parts promise and peril? It's not enough simply to say they're complex and contradictory cultural artifacts. Most—perhaps all—such objects are. What's crucial to explore, rather, is the intricate web of social, economic, legal, technological, and philosophical determinations that collectively have produced them as such. The aim of this chapter is to map the conditions leading to the emergence of e-books in the late age of print and to investigate what's at stake politi-cally in current debates about their worth. Instead of trying to champion or condemn e-books, I'm more interested in considering their embeddedness within the broader history of consumer capitalism and property relations. Beyond their ability (or lack thereof) to store and retrieve information, what's most intriguing to me about e-books is their capacity to *manage* it and, by extension, the actions of those who purchase or otherwise consume e-book content. I argue that e-books are an emergent technological form by which problems pertaining to the ownership and circulation of printed books are simultaneously posed and resolved.

The first section of this chapter represents a ground clearing of sorts. Because so much of the debate surrounding e-books has tended to hinge on the degree to which they reproduce the form and function of their printed counterparts, I want to spend some time sifting through this particular line of argument. My aim is to challenge the assumptions about originality, presence, and authenticity by which the debate gets framed so as to open up a different line of conversation about the history and social function of e-books. The next two sections explore some of the key conditions of emergence of e-books. I begin by investigating how, in the second quarter of the twentieth century, a host of cultural intermediaries promoted printed book ownership as a means to consolidate the budding consumer capitalism. Next I trace how concerns about the ownership, circulation, and reproduction of printed books helped fuel a fear that the latter had become troublesome with respect to expanding capitalist relations of production in the final quarter of the twentieth century. The final section explores how some contemporary e-book technologies embody and attempt to resolve this perceived problem, especially through the implementation of digital rights management schemes.

I suppose this chapter is about the disappearance of information, though not exactly in the sense the partisans of print would take it. Though I may share their concerns about the well-being of the historical record in the late age of print, ultimately that is of lesser importance to me. More significant is the growing power of holders of intellectual property (IP) rights to make information appear and disappear whenever they see fit—often for a fee.

A Book by Any Other Name

With characteristic fanfare for all things technologically sublime, in July 1998 Steve Silberman of *Wired* magazine reported on the impending release of "Book 2.0"—a host of new, portable e-book readers set to be unveiled in American consumer markets. In referring to this generation of e-books as such, Silberman framed the devices as the latest iteration of an extant technology. Their purpose, therefore, was not only to repeat but also to improve upon the most familiar qualities of printed books. A certain sense of loss nevertheless pervades his account of reading Kakuzo Okakura's *Book of Tea* on a Rocket e-book. "I won't be returning this *Book of Tea* to its little slipcase on my shelf," he observed. "I miss the way the printed book's type, with its tiny irregularities, is a Western equivalent of the wayward bristles that make a brush stroke more living than a line. But through the text—the bits—alone, Okakura's mind speaks."[11]

Silberman could read *The Book of Tea* on screen, but he seemed to do so despite, not because of, the intervening technology. Boredom loomed, and the traces of what he took to be Okakura's presence are all that sustained his interest. Even they, purportedly, had been diminished, given how the e-book reader Silberman was using seemed to atomize the author's soulful prose into innumerable electronic impulses and then to reassemble them into lifeless, uniform digital text. Silberman claimed that e-books fail because, although they repeat, they don't repeat well enough. That is, they fail to duplicate the serendipitous flaws and minor variations that he believes imbue industrially manufactured printed books with warmth, difference, and depth—a personality akin to the aura Walter Benjamin said had *declined* because of mass reproduction.[12]

Essayist Sven Birkerts's popular *Gutenberg Elegies: The Fate of Reading in an Electronic Age* offers a similarly dour account of the relationship between printed and digital text. Birkerts recognizes that screens and digits increasingly complement both written and printed artifacts in patterning communication and social interaction, facilitating the circulation of people and things and, more abstractly, conditioning our relations to space-time. He goes further, however, in questioning the larger social and epistemological consequences that allegedly flow from what he describes as the "triumph of the screen and the digital program":[13]

> Nearly weightless though it is, the word printed on a page is a thing. The configuration of impulses on a screen is not—it is a manifestation, an indeterminate entity both particle and wave, an ectoplasmic arrival and departure. The former occupies a position in space—on a page, in a book, and is verifiably there. The latter, once dematerialized, digitized back into storage, into memory, cannot be said to exist in quite the same way. It has potential, not actual, locus. . . . The same word, when it appears on the screen, must be received with a sense of its weightlessness—the weightlessness of its presentation. The same sign, but not the same.[14]

The electronic word may repeat its printed counterpart as pure sign, but the word's transformation into abstract electronic impulses evidently leaves it listless, impalpable, diffuse—the same but different, deficient. Birkerts goes on to contend that this apparent dematerialization of the word results in the toppling of a whole tradition of textual authority. This coup d'état is epitomized by claims about the author's death, an insistence on readers' power, and a belief that writing occurs under conditions of erasure.[15]

Clearly Birkerts believes that our choices of reading and writing media are deeply consequential—even political—acts. Given his commitment to a quite traditional model of textual authority, it should come as no surprise that he eschews technologies that reduce the splendor of writing and reading to the vulgar processing of words. He writes: "I type these words on an IBM Selectric [typewriter] and feel positively antediluvian: My editors let me know that my quaint Luddite habits are gumming up the works, slowing things down for them."[16] Birkerts nevertheless delights in having opted to write with a typewriter rather than a computer. His editors' frustrations confirm for him that his choice constitutes more than a mere preference for one technology over another. He sees his decision as an act of defiance against a hostile insurgency, a social order in which speed, ephemerality, and relativism apparently rule the day.

Yet it is precisely here—in the confidence Birkerts feels in slowly, methodically, t-y-p-i-n-g o-u-t w-o-r-d-s on his IBM Selectric—that his claims about presence, social power, and media begin to get all jammed up. Langdon Winner once famously quipped that "technology is license to forget."[17] Indeed, only a profound act of forgetting could sustain Birkerts's claims about the transparency of typewriting. His typewriter, after all, is not only mechanical but electrical (hence, *Selectric*), and as such it's a technology engaged in an abstract process of rendering. The mechanical energy Birkerts exerts in his keystrokes doesn't directly result in the words he sees and reveres on the printed page. These words aren't signs that would index his "hand" in any straightforward way. Rather, they result from the machine's transduction of his keystrokes into electrical impulses, which then induce corresponding movements in the typewriter's mechanism. Like it or not, an electrical charge infuses all of Birkerts's writing, a charge produced by the very machine IBM touted in a 1962 advertising campaign as a device not for slowing you down but for making you "faster . . . more productive."[18]

Perhaps, then, the electricity flowing through the machine's intervening circuitry is the culprit. Would a purely mechanical typewriter more fully manifest Birkerts's presence in, and thus his authority over, the words he produces? We cannot know for sure because an answer by anything other than inference would require us to detect and quantify traces of latent "spirit" energy—a pursuit more in keeping with the field of parapsychology.[19] Nevertheless Martin Heidegger's lectures between 1942 and 1943 on the philosopher Parmenides offer a useful point of historical comparison. Here is what he says about the mechanical typewriter's prospects for conveying personality and authority: "Mechanical writing deprives the hand of its rank in the realm of the written word and degrades the word to a means of communication. In addition, mechanical writing provides this 'advantage,' that it conceals the handwriting and thereby the character. The typewriter makes everyone look the same."[20] It is, in other words, a technology of abstraction, one that seems to flatten the depths of difference into a bland uniformity.

How can a typescript evidence mechanism, homogeneity, and loss for Heidegger, while the very same document embodies personality, difference, and plenitude for Birkerts? Complicating matters even further, in the *Phaedrus* Plato (speaking through the figure of Socrates) impugned the hand for its apparent incapacity to manifest the authenticity of speech in writing—the same hand whose rank or authenticity Heidegger would exalt more than two millennia later.[21]

Given these conflicting accounts, the problem with e-books may have less to do with boredom, habit, or the authority of authors and their words than with their grounding in a logic of representation. The intellectual history of reading and writing technologies consists, as it were, of a recursive series of laments about the apparent incapacity of these technologies to represent or manifest fully—the word, presence, personality, meaning, intention, and beyond. It is, moreover, a history so densely laden with contradictions and role reversals that a time when something besides loss and alienation ruled the day seems almost unimaginable. Thus, we shouldn't presume to know that the point of e-books is to represent the formal or experiential qualities many people attribute to the reading of printed books, even if commentary, advertising, and common sense may be telling us otherwise. That's a historically produced and learned relation, not an inherent one.[22]

That said, it would be imprudent to suggest that printed and electronic books necessarily share no relation—or at best only an imaginary one. The latter are called e-*books,* after all, and the name should count for something. Yet if the history and politics of e-books cannot be reduced to the formal qualities they may or may not share with printed books, then we're confronted with two specific challenges: to explore a more diverse set of connections e-books share with both printed books and a host of other technologies; and to account for the embeddedness of e-books in a broader context of social, legal, and political-economic relations.

Shelf Life

At the start of the second quarter of the twentieth century, the U.S. book industry found itself at a critical crossroads. After a year of relatively sluggish sales in 1928, there emerged a general accord among industry insiders that the third and fourth quarters of 1929 would see a vigorous and sustained upturn. Their confidence was bolstered after initial reports showed modest sales gains in the first two quarters of 1929, but it was shattered in October, when the stock market crash propelled the country into an economic depression. Although some members of the book publishing industry persisted in believing that the downturn would be short-lived and pressed on accordingly, those who sensed the severity of the crisis scrambled to figure out how to avoid financial catastrophe.[23]

In 1930 Simon & Schuster, Harcourt Brace, and several other major New York book publishers contacted public relations doyen Edward L. Bernays, the "father of spin," to strategize how best to inject new life into the faltering U.S. book industry. In addition to attacking the industry's price structure, which at the time relied heavily on a volatile low price/high volume formula, Bernays proposed a novel idea for inspiring people to buy more books despite the economic downturn.[24] As Bernays's biographer Larry Tye has written: "'Where there are bookshelves,' [Bernays] reasoned, 'there will be books.' So he got respected public figures to endorse the importance of books to civilization, and then he persuaded architects, contractors, and decorators to put up shelves on which to store the precious volumes."[25]

Today accumulating printed books and shelving them in one's home may seem like mundane facts of life, at least among those economically enfranchised enough to do so. In the first decades of the twentieth century, however, those activities couldn't be assumed and needed to be learned. Much as Bernays and his biographers might have believed that the publicity industries were singularly responsible for persuading builders, homeowners, and others of the virtues of accumulating books and storing them at home, the emergence of these activities in the decades leading up to the Second World War cannot be explained by spin alone.

Already in March 1929 an article published in *American Home* magazine entitled "Housing Your Books" had suggested that "'books' and 'home' are indissolubly linked in the minds of most people." The article stressed that books "should be housed with loving care and one should find room to accommodate them at all costs."[26] Despite its call for books to be shelved in private homes "at all costs," the article was sensitive to the fact that its advice appealed to a class of not unlimited means. It reassured readers that they should take pride in shelving any and all books, even well-worn mass-produced editions. "If we can have our favorite [books] rebound when they look really disreputable, we are fortunate," the article observed, "but a moderately worn appearance lends flavor to a book. . . . If you want your books around you, you must have proper receptacles for them. While the covers of the books may be ever so worn, if they are attractively housed, the effect will be pleasing. Certainly you, yourself, will be far better satisfied when surrounded by your old favorites than if you had a most harmonious array chosen solely for good binding and designed to please the eye but quite devoid of anything within."[27] The article concluded by suggesting that bookcases, particularly the built-in variety, would allow homeowners "to introduce a little touch of modernism" into their surroundings.[28]

Likewise, in a November 1929 article in *Publishers Weekly* Joseph Wharton Lippincott, president of the National Association of Book Publishers, described built-in bookcases as a "growing fad" in the United States.[29] He even anticipated some of Bernays's later maneuverings when he exhorted his colleagues in the book industry to capitalize on the emerging trend: "We are profiting at the moment from the need for books in individual homes built during the past few years. . . . Now is the time to get behind it and keep going! . . . The problem is twofold: how to get all those who build new houses and who own old houses, to understand the value and ease of putting in as many as possible of these modern conveniences [bookshelves]; and how to bring the consequent business into the bookstore."[30]

Lippincott's remarks are striking not only for what he said but, equally important, for what he didn't say about private homes, built-in bookshelves, and the value of printed books. Rather than stressing the literariness of particular titles or the pleasures of reading them, Lippincott enjoined his colleagues to consider how built-in bookshelves could facilitate the mass accumulation of books largely on the basis of their formal characteristics and their capacity as a whole to add flare to modern home décor.

In certain respects the building of bookshelves was less about the content of books than about the appearance of respectability and plenitude the presence of books could confer on homeowners. A 1927 *New York Times* article on "mimic books" suggests as much. What's intriguing about the piece is that it posits built-in bookshelves not as solutions to the problem of too many books in the home but rather as problems in their own right. Some homeowners "build their bookshelves to the ceiling in the ambition some day to fill them up," wrote the article's author. The trouble, though, is that "they are sometimes book lovers with an eye for a bigger display than their purses can afford." To preempt any potential class anxiety empty bookshelves might cause, the article endorsed the use of bookbacks—"false" or "mimic" collections designed to reproduce "the semblance of books and not their substance." These typically consisted of lengths of cardboard or wood, upon which would be affixed imitation leather or similar material designed to look like a row of bound printed volumes. The article reported that department stores were enjoying a "prosperous trade" in mimic books, and that the bogus volumes were "having a considerable vogue in New York." Consequently, their class connotations started to change. So common were mimic books becoming that one "need no longer drop his voice to a whisper" in asking salespeople for them. Such a request might have seemed déclassé only a few years earlier, but now even "the best people are doing it," the article reassured its readers. Significantly, mimic books weren't sold as individual editions, nor were they available in sets. They were offered by the yard, as if to suggest that the quantity of books one could house (or the illusion thereof) mattered even more than their quality.[31]

Taken together, Bernays's PR strategy, the article in *American Home*, Lippincott's exhortations, and mimic books roughly trace the key discursive parameters within which home bookshelf construction became both thinkable and practicable in the United States between the two world wars. Put differently, the preceding examples all signal the political, economic, technical, and social relations embodied in these seemingly banal furniture fixtures. At the most basic level, built-in bookshelves represented the following: a particular orientation toward history, modernity, and its attendant ideologies of progress and convenience; the allure of propriety and abundance, which could be realized not only through the consumption but, equally important, through the accumulation and display of printed books or their stand-ins; and a growing (middle-)class consciousness.

In more abstract terms, the push for home bookshelf construction around 1930 emerged from a confluence of changes in the first decades of the twentieth century that redefined the private home from a space of moral and spiritual uplift to one increasingly focused on domestic leisure. As Lynn Spigel has noted, beginning around the turn of the twentieth century, builders, decorators, and a nascent group of middle-class homeowners began reconfiguring the architecture—especially the interior spaces—of private homes to accommodate all kinds of "secular pleasures" that just a few decades earlier had been barred from the homes of the Victorian elite.[32]

The campaign to install bookshelves in American homes in the 1930s was part and parcel of this shift in at least three ways. First, it represented the culmination of a critical passage in the sociology of books and reading. Around the turn of the twentieth century the Victorian custom of reading scripture aloud gradually gave way to the quite different domestic pastime of solitary reading, specifically of the novel, a literary genre about which Victorians had fretted incessantly for arousing sensational responses in readers.[33] The installation of bookshelves in private, middle-class homes thus signaled the home's passage from a site dedicated primarily to strengthening one's moral and spiritual fiber to one increasingly suffused with worldly pleasures. Second, the campaign squared nicely with a general reduction in the size of new homes built during this period. The costs of incorporating the latest modern conveniences (e.g., plumbing, electrical wiring, kitchen appliances) often compelled building contractors to cut costs elsewhere. Because superfluous square footage typically was among the first items to be excised, built-in bookshelves offered a means for utilizing the remaining space more efficiently.[34] Finally, home bookshelf construction might be interpreted as the bibliographic counterpart of efforts to domesticate electronic media. By housing gramophones, telephones, radios, and (later) television sets in fine cabinetry, the nascent home-electronics industry sought to render them consonant—functionally, aesthetically, and ideologically—with domestic space and existing furniture.[35] Built-in bookshelves offered a similar means for integrating a putatively older technology—printed books—more or less seamlessly into the home.

Not everyone, however, was encouraged to engage in home bookshelf construction and, consequently, the accumulation and display of mass-produced printed books. The periodicals that were instrumental in helping to publicize these practices—*American Home, House Beautiful, Popular Mechanics*, and *Woman's Home Companion*, among others—both appealed to and provided a key source of identification for a very specific group of people—a mostly white, increasingly suburban, professional middle class. As Richard Ohmann has shown, this burgeoning group had secured its place in American society in part by producing "useful knowledge."[36] Thanks to the development and implementation of advertising, public relations, and related forms of knowledge work, the middle class carved out a niche for itself by engaging in work practices designed to modulate the "growth of culture,"[37] or to regulate and rationalize the hitherto mysterious connections between capitalist production and consumption. In fact, the professional middle class frequently targeted members of its own class with its knowledge work, thereby instructing (and reproducing) itself, as it were, in a highly specific understanding of and practical relationship to an ever-expanding array of mass-produced goods.

In 1899 Thorstein Veblen coined the apt phrase "conspicuous consumption" to describe this emergent praxis, given how middle-class people, periodicals, and social institutions of the late nineteenth and early twentieth centuries constantly linked commodity ownership and display to possibilities for social advancement.[38] Insofar as "property . . . becomes the most easily recognised evidence of a reputable degree of success as distinguished from heroic or signal achievement" for middle-class people, Veblen wrote, "it becomes indispensable to accumulate, to acquire property, in order to retain one's good name."[39] Whereas an older, landed aristocracy's social and cultural capital was derived largely from patrimony and elite education, the nascent middle class saw the accumulation and display of private property—particularly mass-produced consumer goods—as necessary conditions for acquiring capital of its own.

I do not wish to suggest that printed books merely provided elaborate window dressing for middle-class people in the interwar years. Just as printed books were meant to be accumulated and displayed, they were also meant to be read—mimic books notwithstanding. The reading of books has never been an innocent activity, and the reading of mass-produced printed books in the interwar years was no exception. As Janice A. Radway has shown in her study of the Book-of-the-Month Club, reading became a privileged activity during this period. The burgeoning "consumer-oriented and information-dominated" economy of the early twentieth century required large numbers of workers proficient in the reading, sorting, processing, and distribution of information. Doubtless these skills could—and would—be acquired during one's formal education. Regular contact with mass-produced printed books at home made it possible for middle-class people, or those who aspired to middle-classness, to rehearse and refine these skills during their leisure time as well.[40] Bookshelves thus embodied a specific middle-class habitus expressed in and through knowledge work and the collapse of labor and leisure.

The built-in-bookshelves campaign could therefore be viewed as contributing to a complex social pedagogy whereby a growing middle class experienced the transition from a more producer-oriented to a more consumer-oriented economy. It also might be read as synecdochic for the ways in which this group simultaneously became subject and object of its own efforts to routinize consumption during the interwar years.[41] In this story the widespread private ownership of mass-produced printed books was crucial to the formation and professionalization of the middle class, its entrée into modernity. Significantly, this group's ability to carve out a distinctive, socially and economically relevant niche for itself depended on its ability to own (accumulate, display, read, use) mass-produced printed books—a practical relationship to capitalism that would eventually come to seen as hindering the task of expanding capitalist accumulation.

Book Sneaks

In addition to these political, economic, technical, and social determinations, a key enabling condition of this régime of privately owned, mass-produced printed editions was a relatively weak (or at least weakly applied) copyright doctrine. Antedating the built-in-bookshelves campaign by more than fifty years, this doctrine provided a legal framework within which such a campaign could become both thinkable and practicable.

In contrast to the present day, where intellectual property and intellectual property laws are among its leading exports, the United States refused to sign onto or abide by any international copyright treaties until March 1891. Its position thus diverged sharply from that of its European counterparts, virtually all of whom had acceded to various copyright unions in the preceding decades.[42] Between 1830 and 1890 legislators, jurists, publishers, printers, typesetters, booksellers, and other interested parties in the United States responded to European pressure to establish international copyright agreements by appealing ceaselessly to the language of civic republicanism. International copyright treaties, opponents claimed, would militate against the creation and flourishing of a vibrant reading public in the United States, thus confounding the American democratic project by restricting citizens' access to information.[43] Inasmuch as they offered an expedient way for the burgeoning U.S. book industry to protect its interests, these appeals doubtless reflected a genuine belief in the value of *civitas*.[44] Either way, despite the best efforts of mostly British diplomats and writers (including Charles Dickens and other highly influential figures) to persuade the United States to see the virtues of extending copyright protection to foreign works, in the second quarter of the nineteenth century Congress rejected no fewer than five copyright treaties.[45]

Until 1891, therefore, publishers, printers, and booksellers in the United States were relatively free to produce, distribute, and sell their own—some would say pirated—editions of foreign works to American readers. By refusing to extend copyright protection to foreign titles, the U.S. government de facto absolved the publishers of any responsibility for remunerating foreign copyright holders for the works they reproduced. Domestically produced editions of foreign books flourished, typically selling for a fraction of the price of imported European editions.[46] Coupled with the explosion of dime novels, inexpensive romances, and cheap reprint series, around the middle of the nineteenth century a truly mass book *industry* began to emerge in the United States. As Ohmann observes, it was "one of the few capitalist industries grounded in piracy" at the time.[47]

From a legal standpoint, weak international copyright protections, coupled with innumerable acts of publishing piracy, made possible the mass ownership of printed books in the United States. Inexpensive collections thrived, so that by 1877 American readers could select from among at least fourteen different book series.[48] Yet this praxis wouldn't achieve its fullest expression until the first half of the twentieth century, crystallizing in the built-in-bookshelves campaigns of the 1920s and 1930s. Indeed, the U.S. book industry's development in the second half of the nineteenth century, though intensive, remained uneven. According to Ohmann, "It achieved some of the methods of mass culture early but failed to consolidate them into a stable and controlled enterprise with enduring relations to the public" until the first decades of the twentieth century.[49]

Between 1850 and 1891, the hands-off approach of the United States to international copyright produced not only an explosion of printed books but also a bevy of book publishing houses. Among these publishers were the Harper Brothers as well as other firms that today constitute the center of the book industry, plus lesser-known firms that have been all but forgotten. The persistent refusal of the United States to endorse international copyright agreements empowered these upstarts to challenge the practical oligopoly, and thus the financial well-being, of already established firms like Henry Holt and others. The former did so mainly by underselling the latter. In addition to refusing to pay royalties to foreign authors and publishers, they typically ignored the informal agreements—the so-called courtesy principle—that had kept the price of books produced by more established firms artificially high. Older publishing houses responded in kind by slashing their prices, leading to the collapse of the courtesy system by the end of the 1870s.[50]

As far as the more established publishing firms were concerned, the ultracompetitive environment ushered in by this new crop of book publishers destabilized the book industry. As such, they found themselves forced to rethink their position on international copyright. If the success of this putatively reckless group of upstarts hinged on its ability to produce and sell large quantities of printed books, and if doing so depended on the refusal of the United States to recognize foreign copyrights, then it followed that tightening copyright laws would return stability to the book industry. Put differently, established book publishers like Henry Holt, book industry insiders like Richard Rogers Bowker, and other well-entrenched parties (e.g., authors like Mark Twain) reasoned that the accession of the United States to international copyright now represented a necessary condition rather than an impediment to maintaining their oligopoly.[51] Thus, the passage of the 1891 copyright agreement largely stemmed from a loosely coordinated—and no doubt highly expedient—effort on the part of already established book publishers to protect their interests from insurgent competition.[52] In 1891, the accession of the United States to international copyright didn't represent a Copernican revolution in its stance toward protecting foreign works inasmuch as it expressed the declining marginal utility of the discourse of civic republicanism relative to the development and consolidation of industrial capitalism.

Perhaps more important, international copyright allowed industrial capitalists, publishers, and authors to use the law to legitimize a growing obsession with how, where, when, and among whom printed books circulated and could be reproduced. This process depended on the ability of cultural producers and intermediaries to find creative ways to stimulate the widespread consumption of mass-produced consumer goods, printed books being chief among them. It also depended on their finding new ways to regulate the disposition of these goods, given their increased availability. Yet the events leading up to the passage of the 1891 copyright legislation suggest that, at least in the case of this particular measure, delimiting and regulating the activities of other cultural *producers* was of primary importance to those championing the legislation. Lawrence Lessig observes that "for much of the last century . . . copyright has worked fairly well as a compromise between publishers and authors. It is a law that has largely been applied to institutions. Individuals were essentially outside copyright's purview since individuals didn't really 'publish.'"[53] The movement to challenge and regulate how *consumers* disposed of mass-produced cultural goods—specifically printed books—would only crystallize around 1930, following another book industry price war, and come to a head a few decades later with the proliferation of photocopying technologies.

The book industry of the 1930s, while vaster and more highly differentiated than that of the late nineteenth century, in some respects still resembled its earlier incarnation. As before, a throng of upstart publishers, together with an emergent crop of book distributors and sellers, threatened the oligopoly that older and more established firms had secured around the turn of the twentieth century.[54] Among the former were publishing houses like Simon & Schuster (founded in 1924), Farrar & Rinehart (founded in 1929), and Doubleday, Doran, & Co. (founded in 1927 following the merger of George H. Doran & Co. and Doubleday). In May 1930 they jointly announced that they would reduce the price of their new hardcover fiction books to one dollar in order to compete with remainders and proliferating cheap reprint series. By doing so they hoped to respond to the growing perception among book buyers that printed books ought to be genuinely inexpensive and not merely affordable.[55]

It should come as no surprise that "old-line" publishers recoiled at the move.[56] Led by Alfred A. Knopf (also a relative upstart, though a bit older, having begun in 1915), a small group of senior representatives from Harcourt Brace; Harper & Brothers; Horace Liveright, Inc.; and other major publishing firms of the time again turned to Edward L. Bernays in the hopes of fighting the "dollar books" campaign with public relations. As Bernays later recalled, he proposed a two-pronged offensive: first, "to convince the public and the price-cutting publishers that dollar books were not in the public interest"; and, second, to "increas[e] the market for good books."[57] With regard to the first part of the strategy, in the summer of 1930 Bernays formed the Book Publishers Research Institute, a front from which he and his colleagues could carry out quasi-scientific research on, and issue professional-sounding reports about, the well-being of the U.S. book industry. The institute's first study was nothing short of a fait accompli, finding that dollar books would propel all segments of the industry into an economic tailspin, resulting in the "death of six thousand book retailers."[58]

Among Bernays's more intriguing strategies to "increase the market for good books" was to have his institute sponsor a contest in the spring of 1931 "to look for a pejorative word for the book borrower, the wretch who raised hell with book sales and deprived authors of earned royalties." Bernays drew his inspiration for the contest from another term that had been introduced into the American English lexicon in 1924, namely, "scofflaw," which originally referred to a "'lawless drinker' of illegally made or illegally obtained liquor."[59] To judge the contest Bernays convened a panel of three well-known New York City book critics: Harry Hansen (of the *New York World-Telegram*), Burton Rascoe (formerly of the *New York Herald-Tribune*), and J. C. Grey (of the *New York Sun*). Among the thousands of entries they considered were terms like "book weevil," "borrocole," "greader," "libracide," "booklooter," "bookbum," "bookkibitzer," "culture vulture," "greeper," "bookbummer," "bookaneer," "blifter," "biblioacquisiac," and "book buzzard." The winner? "Book sneak," entered by Paul W. Stoddard, a high school English teacher from Hartford, Connecticut.[60]

Despite his best efforts to popularize the new term, even Bernays eventually conceded that "book sneak" never garnered the lexical or cultural cachet of "scofflaw."[61] Nevertheless, both the contest and the term remain significant historically. They illustrate how, by the early 1930s, the proliferation/circulation of mass-produced printed books among *consumers* could be viewed as a problem by cultural producers and intermediaries—even, apparently, by schoolteachers! The contest was emblematic of the contradiction of mass culture, mentioned earlier, and, more specifically, of the folding of consumers into that network of relations and regulations. In this case Stoddard was rewarded with a collection of fifty books—a testament to the productive capacities that had facilitated the growth of culture for the better part of a century—precisely for coining a term meant to stigmatize one result of that process, namely, the custom of circulating printed books among friends, family, colleagues, and acquaintances.

The emergence and popularization of photocopying technologies further undermined the notion that ownership of printed books was fundamentally a positive thing for those living in the United States.[62] Although the earliest photocopying technologies were developed around the turn of the twentieth century, they were slow in catching on. Of course, there are myriad social, economic, and political determinations to explain the gradual uptake; another, more purely technical reason had to do with the nature of early photocopying processes. For those even aware of the technology, photocopying was generally perceived to be relatively slow, messy, and often unpredictable, far less useful or interesting than offset printing—except perhaps among a handful of curious engineers. Only after the Second World War, following experiments with photoconductivity by engineer Chester Carlson and others, would photocopying begin to be viewed as a socially useful technology. Carlson's process for duplicating images basically combined an electrical current and dry chemicals, which, in contrast to earlier wet processes, drastically shortened the time it took to reproduce high-contrast black-and-white images on plain paper.[63] Photocopiers became widespread and commercially successful in the late 1950s, following the introduction of the Copyflo and subsequent generations of fully automated copiers by the Haloid (now Xerox) Corporation.

Less than two decades later, concerns about the ease, speed, and quality with which copyrighted materials could be reproduced and circulated crystallized in the passage of the 1976 Copyright Act, the first major overhaul of federal copyright law since 1909. The 1976 act was especially careful in defining the scope of fair use, given the proliferation of photocopiers and other technologies capable of reproducing or retransmitting copyrighted materials (e.g., magnetic tapes, audio/video cassette recorders, cable television systems). The legislation was also instrumental in leading to the establishment in 1978 of the Copyright Clearance Center (CCC), a body representing a consortium of publishers. The CCC grants individuals and institutions permission to reproduce copyrighted printed materials on the condition that they agree to pay royalties to the copyright holder. Nationwide, some ninety billion pages were estimated to have been photocopied in 1979 alone.[64] This led many major corporations, libraries, and universities increasingly to turn to the CCC for duplication rights and prompted publishers to pursue alleged copyright violations more vigorously and extensively than they had in the past.[65]

The practice of photocopying the contents of printed books came under fire the following decade in a series of lawsuits testing the new federal copyright statute. They began with a 1980 suit brought by eight book publishers against the Gnomon Corporation, a photocopying outfit servicing major American colleges and universities. The publishers alleged having purchased from Gnomon shops some nine thousand copies of material culled from three hundred different copyrighted books—copies for which they received no royalties.[66] The Gnomon case was followed three years later by another, higher-profile suit brought by nine book publishers against New York University, ten of its faculty, and a local off-campus copy shop, the Unique Copy Center. The suit alleged impropriety on the part of these parties for "engaging in the unauthorized and unlawful reproduction, anthologizing, distribution and sale of the publisher's copyrighted work."[67] Finally, in 1989 a group of eight book publishers filed suit against Kinko's, specifically taking issue with its long-standing refusal to pay royalties for reproducing copyrighted materials and anthologizing them into academic course packs.[68]

Except in the case against NYU, in which the parties settled out of court on terms favorable to the publishers, the courts upheld the constitutionality of the 1976 copyright statute. In all cases, the photocopy outfits were barred from reproducing copyrighted material from books and other sources without first seeking clearance from the CCC or paying royalties directly to the copyright holders.[69] These decisions eroded the concept of fair use by restricting how consumers of printed books could dispose of the properties they had purchased.

These cases coincided with a renewed and intensified interest on the part of the book industry in the circulation of books among consumers. When, in July 1983, *Publishers Weekly* reported on the status of the pass-along book trade, it didn't need to hold a contest to establish the fact that the sharing of printed books posed a significant problem from the standpoint of capitalist production; fifty years after the coining of the term "book sneak" that much, apparently, could be assumed. Thus, the periodical reported on the results of a Gallup Poll in which respondents were asked to disclose what they did with printed books after they had finished reading them.[70] Although many of those surveyed indicated holding on to their books, more than half reported lending or giving them to friends and relatives, donating them to charity, or selling them. In light of these results, *Publishers Weekly* reaffirmed what Bernays had posited fifty years earlier as the economic consequence of the pass-along book trade: "The fate of a book after it is sold is an important one for the book industry, reflecting as it does the possibility of lost sales."[71]

The report coincided with the beginnings of a legislative initiative in the United States, at the behest of the Authors Guild, to convene a national commission to explore the feasibility of establishing a federal public lending right.[72] These rights vary from country to country, but in general they're designed to remunerate authors—and sometimes publishers—for the circulation of printed books and other intellectual properties to library patrons. The assumption is that books borrowed from libraries result in lost sales in the retail market and consequently to a decline in authors' royalties and fees. In countries where public lending rights exist, federal governments customarily compensate authors in the form of direct royalty payments, contributions to pension plans, and other financial schemes.[73] Nevertheless, the initiative to study and establish a public lending right barely got off the ground in the United States. It died in committee with the adjournment of the 98th Congress in 1984, owing in no small measure to poor timing. With the Reagan-era dismantling of the welfare state already well under way, the possibility of providing federal funds to authors seemed excessive and quixotic to many legislators. Despite its failure, the movement to establish a public lending right may be significant when considered alongside the book industry's response to the pass-along book trade. Both articulated a growing anxiety over the circulation of printed books following their initial sale.

Taken together, the litigation challenging the unrestricted photocopying of copyrighted books, publishers' fears about the pass-along book trade, and the movement to establish a public lending right in the United States signaled a shift in attitude toward the economic and cultural value of printed books and other mass-produced commodities. The reading of these books may have prepared members of the middle class to be productive in a consumer-based, information-oriented economy earlier in the century— and that very well may continue into this day. Toward the end of the twentieth century, however, those very same books seem to have grown increasingly problematic from the standpoint of capitalist production. In the case of the pass-along book trade, library loans, and professional photocopying, printed books continue to produce surplus value following their initial sale. By circulating among associates or through used-book shops, yard sales, photocopy shops, and the like, this additional surplus value circumvents publishers and authors. Moreover, the litigation surrounding the issue of photocopying begs the question of what it means to own printed books and other mass-produced commodities in the late age of print.

The larger issue at stake amid all of these considerations is the morphology of capitalism. Book sneaks, photocopying, copyright overhaul, the CCC, public lending rights, and a throng of costly lawsuits—what unites these is the selfsame obsession that both resulted in and was expressed by the affirmation of international copyright by the United States a century earlier, namely, the fear that, once purchased, books would circulate without restriction, leading to unrestrained copying and to who knows what. This suggests the beginnings of a shift away from consumer capitalism as it was understood for perhaps the first three quarters of the twentieth century. Then the widespread private ownership and accumulation of mass-produced goods were not only desirable but necessary conditions of capitalism's continued well-being. If the polarities are reversed, unrestricted commodity ownership in this emergent regime becomes something of an impediment to capitalist accumulation.

A 1983 essay on the book of the future evidences this shift. The piece begins with its author voicing his concern over rising paper and labor costs in the book publishing industry. He frets about how these factors seem to "jeopardize the long-term survival of the book as a major element of modern civilization."[74] He then goes on to ponder alternative book publishing and distribution systems. The so-called book of the future that emerges by the end of the piece resembles something akin to books produced by on-demand publishing systems, albeit with a significant twist:[75]

> Imagine . . . that in your living room beside the television set there is another black box with a rectangular slit in front of it. . . . On the shelf nearby is a row of books of different sizes and colors. Pull one off the shelf and observe with surprise and puzzlement that all the pages are blank. These volumes are, in effect, blank visual tapes of sorts, onto which it is possible to impress a text that can be read like a book and erased after use. . . . Even when they are not erased, it is probable that the printed contents of these books will not be permanent. There are many reasons for this, not the least of which is its commercial impact. After a period of time, perhaps one to three months, the text will have faded, and would have to be reprinted for another one- to three-month period.[76]

In this passage the author of the article anticipates a future that diverges from the dominant relations of commodity ownership I've previously described. Gone are the printed editions destined for long-term display on middle-class bookshelves. Gone, too, are the editions that could be passed along indefinitely among friends, family, colleagues, and acquaintances. These volumes, the author predicted, would be replaced by ephemeral editions in which the printing would eventually fade. At some indeterminate point in the future one would no longer own printed books in perpetuity. Instead one would lease their contents temporarily. Although his speculations appear to have missed the mark in many respects, less than a decade later the technological and economic possibilities of disappearing text would begin to be realized with respect to e-books.

Disappearing Digits

William Gibson is probably best known as the author of numerous cyberpunk novels, most notably *Neuromancer*. Gibson also authored a lesser-known, limited-edition work called *Agrippa (A Book of the Dead)* (fig. 2),

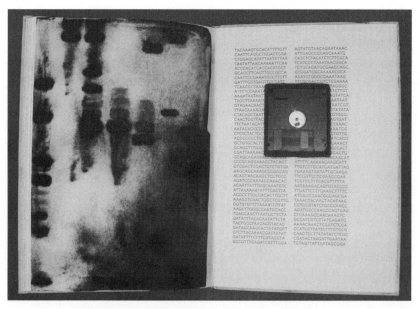

FIGURE 2 *Agrippa (A Book of the Dead)* (1992). A collaboration between Dennis Ashbaugh, William Gibson, and Kevin Begos Jr.

which bore an uncanny resemblance to the book of the future. Released in 1992, it was "an electronic book designed to disappear as soon as it [was] read."[77] More accurately, *Agrippa* was a hybrid work consisting of digital/ electronic text encoded on a three-and-a-half-inch computer disk and a collection of printed materials, all contained within a high-tech package designed to degenerate upon exposure to air and visible light. The disk contained not only the story of *Agrippa*, "a poetic effusion about [Gibson's] father, who died when he was very young,"[78] but encryption algorithms designed to ensure that the digital text would disappear as the text scrolled down the computer screen for the first and only time.[79]

Agrippa was a perfectly logical endeavor in light of the legislative initiatives, litigation, and technologies of reproduction that collectively challenged the cultural and economic values ascribed to mass-produced commodities in the first half of the twentieth century. Once accessed, it was improbable that *Agrippa* would circulate in the pass-along book trade. Like the book of the future, embedded technology undermined the possibility of the text's persistence and thus forestalled its circulation. Similarly, *Agrippa's* electronic text sidestepped the question of lending rights since it would vanish before libraries could catalog it, much less lend the book to more than one borrower.[80] Finally, *Agrippa* posed a novel solution to the related issue of reproducibility since its built-in encryption algorithms prevented duplication of the text.[81]

Agrippa admittedly is somewhat of an extreme case in that it's the only electronic book of which I'm aware that disappears after a single use. Yet in other ways it was prophetic, given the book industry's renewed concerns about the passing along of printed books and its high hopes about e-books and digital rights management schemes mitigating at least some aspects of the perceived problem. For instance, in a 2001 article on electronic publishing, e-book publisher Matt Moynahan commented on how the lending of library books "add[s] up to approximately 1.7 billion royalty-free reads each year." He went on to estimate that as many as a billion more "royalty-free reads" resulted yearly from the pass-along and used-book trades.[82] Little wonder, then, that algorithms akin to those the programmers used to encrypt *Agrippa* have become fairly common among commercial software and hardware developers anxious to regulate the dissemination of digital e-book content.

In July 2000 LockStream Corporation released a media delivery and rights management system intended for use with e-books and other forms of digital content. The company promised that copies of any files encrypted by their system would automatically degrade upon being made, thus rendering copied content inoperative or inaccessible.[83] Similarly, in 2001 e-book publisher RosettaBooks announced its release of a special edition of mystery novelist Agatha Christie's *And Then There Were None*. What distinguished this edition was a "time-limit license" that granted users a total of ten hours of access to the e-book for the meager sum of a dollar. Rights management software kicked in thereafter to render the text unreadable unless the user opted to renew the license for an additional dollar or purchase the title outright for five dollars.[84]

In 2004 textbook publishing giant McGraw-Hill began releasing e-books whose embedded rights management software locks them to the specific computers onto which they're downloaded, thereby forestalling any possibility of their duplication or circulation. The company's other main e-book format, which is online only, registers the total number of paying-customer page views and typically restricts them to four views per each edition's total number of pages. A company spokesperson provided this (depressing) rationale for limiting customers' page views to such a low number: "We arrived at that figure after talking with professors. . . . They said, read it once, study for the midterm, study for a final, and read it one more time. Four ought to be ample."[85] Collectively these e-books and their digital rights management schemes compel users to cede to e-book publishers, software developers, and other interested parties much of their ability to circulate, dispose of, and reproduce whatever titles they've purchased.

The problem of circulating and reproducing printed books is not only embedded in technological artifacts. Federal legislation also embodies this concern. In 1998 Congress unanimously approved the Digital Millennium Copyright Act (DMCA), a sweeping piece of legislation that, among numerous other provisions, prohibits end users of copyrighted material from bypassing encryption systems or distributing information that might permit others to do so. One of the first tests of the DMCA occurred in July 2001, when the Federal Bureau of Investigation (FBI) arrested Russian computer programmer Dmitry Sklyarov, who had come to the United States to attend a computer hackers' convention. The FBI alleged that he had written Advanced e-book Processor for his employer, ElcomSoft, a program that permits users of Adobe's e-book software to circumvent the program's safeguards against copying electronic books. Sklyarov was released five months later after agreeing to testify against his employer in exchange for immunity from prosecution.[86]

Sklyarov's arrest and ElcomSoft's subsequent prosecution underscore what a year earlier the *New York Times* had called the book industry's "ultimate nightmare." Peer-to-peer (P2P) music file sharing had recently entered the popular imagination thanks to the launch and immediate notoriety of Napster in 1999. The ease with which the service allowed music lovers to trade MP3 files directly with one another online, and thereby to circumvent the music industry, left many cultural producers fearing for the effects of P2P. The book industry was no exception, given its fascination at the time with the prospects of digital publishing. Hence the fear that "digital books will go the way of digital music: circulating for free over the Internet, at the mercy of pirates and hackers."[87] However, even after the court-ordered shutdown of Napster in 2001 and the company's subsequent reorganization into a paid service, the book industry still found itself in P2P's long shadow. In 2008 *Newsweek* reported on BookSnap, a new scanning device, or "book ripper," that would allow ordinary consumers to digitize their personal libraries. The story opened with the question, "Could the publishing industry get Napsterized?", which actually referred to the next generation of file-sharing and social networking sites that had grown up in Napster's wake.[88] Although *Newsweek* raised doubts about the user-friendliness of BookSnap, the implication behind the question it raised about home book scanning was clear enough: given the ease with which anyone with a few hundred dollars and an Internet connection can reproduce and redistribute book content, the long-term survival of the book industry was increasingly dependent on its ability to lock that content down.

As anyone knows who has scanned or photocopied a chapter from a printed book, the trouble with—or perhaps the best part about— intellectual property (IP) law is that while multiple parties maintain a controlling legal interest over the disposal of a specific intellectual property, that interest isn't always practical or enforceable.[89] While IP law unquestionably carries a significant degree of prohibitive force, it provides a legal remedy only after acts of duplication have occurred. It doesn't perforce forestall acts of duplication. Put another way, IP law doesn't so much protect against the *process* of duplicating copyrighted materials as redress the *result* of their duplication.[90] Digital encryption, on the other hand, prohibits the duplication and circulation of e-books before acts of duplication can occur—in extreme cases by erasing e-books after only a single use. Digital encryption thus allows authors, publishers, and others to monitor and regulate the disposition of e-books in ways that exceed the scope of existing intellectual property laws by circumventing such exceptions as fair use and the first-sale doctrine.[91] The technology does so by empowering interested parties to establish and maintain unprecedented levels of practical control over the social life of e-books and other forms of digital information even after the transfer of ownership (i.e., purchase) has occurred.

A Different Story to Tell

At the outset of this chapter I mentioned Google's book-scanning project, Book Search. By way of conclusion, I want to spend some time reflecting on it. Beyond the prospect of compiling a voluminous, cross-referenced digital library, what's striking about Google's initiative is the bizarre ambivalence surrounding it. Under the auspices of the Association of American Publishers, five presses—McGraw-Hill, Pearson Education, Penguin USA, Simon & Schuster, and John Wiley & Sons—filed a federal lawsuit against Google in October 2005 alleging copyright infringement. What makes the case so strange, however, is that the presses that brought the suit also happen to be partners in Google Book Search. How can one explain this apparent contradiction?

The simple answer is: the publishers who've partnered with and who are now suing Google object to the company's scanning of any books other than those they've specifically authorized. Their issue isn't with Book Search but rather with Google Library, the book-scanning operation whose aim is to digitize part or all of the printed book collections of major research libraries. Although Google Library is a facet of Book Search, it operates independently of the partnership agreements drawn up with a host of book publishers who want to promote their titles online. In the words of Pat Schroeder, former congresswoman and now president and CEO of the Association of American Publishers: "While authors and publishers know how useful Google's search engine can be and think the Print Library could be an excellent resource, the bottom line is that under its current plan Google is seeking to make millions of dollars by freeloading on the talent and property of authors and publishers."[92]

The answer may be more complex when considered in light of the preceding discussion of printed and electronic books. Because it's clear that the publishers who are suing Google want it both ways, one might be tempted to describe their actions as hypocritical. They're not. Instead, their actions are a function of the peculiar—even ambivalent—status of books-as-commodities in the late age of print. On the one hand, the publishers are trying to promote printed books (and, presumably, printed book ownership) by using one of the most salient publicity vehicles of our time, the

Internet, and, more specifically, Google, its most widely used search engine. In this way their actions are in keeping with the logic of consumer capitalism, whose influence has been felt in the book industry at least since the second quarter of the twentieth century, if not earlier. On the other hand, the lawsuit expresses a not altogether consonant impulse, a concern about how to control the reproduction and circulation of book content following a given volume's initial sale. Again, the issue here is ownership and its thorny status in the late age of print.

Both the controversy surrounding Book Search and the topics discussed in this chapter suggest that the social relations of commodity ownership characteristic of the first three quarters of the twentieth century continue to dominate today's market economy. By the same token, they also show that these relations have been troubled relentlessly since Bernays's book sneak campaign in the 1930s all the way up to *Agrippa*, the DMCA, and beyond. Given that many of today's most popular, commercially available e-book technologies allow cultural producers to micromanage the persistence, use, and circulation of content, these technologies are symptomatic of—indeed, further—the tense and uneven process of transforming three core principles of consumer capitalism: the belief that the widespread private ownership and accumulation of mass-produced consumer goods is desirable from the standpoint of capitalist production; the assumption that the sale of a certain item implies the more or less complete transfer of ownership rights to that item; and the principle that commodity ownership consists, in part, in the right to make use of the goods you've purchased with minimal—and, ideally no—outside interference by the party from whom you've purchased them.

E-books clearly have an important story to tell beyond their ability to reproduce the form and function of printed books. Theirs is a story about the logic of capitalist accumulation and how it has been shifting over the last century. Today's e-book technologies constitute the end result of more than fifty years' worth of effort to render problematic people's accumulation and circulation of printed books, as well as those of other mass-produced goods. As such, e-books both express and embody a practical critique of consumer capitalism. This is no cause for celebration, however. Whatever critique of capitalism they offer ultimately advances a more intensive mode of capitalist accumulation, one significantly premised on the management of commodities and hence the ways in which consumers interact with them. E-books don't suggest a waning of consumer capitalism. On the contrary, they point to its intensification or, rather, to the emergence of new practices of *controlled consumption*, a theme I will pursue in subsequent chapters.

Though I've examined the changing conditions whereby people have incorporated books into their everyday lives, on balance I've perhaps focused more on the efforts of cultural producers to reshape specific book technologies—and book culture more broadly—to suit their own ends. In the next chapter I demonstrate how specific social classes and communities have turned to large-scale retail bookstores as a means of challenging patterns of inequality at the level of the everyday.

2 The Big-Box Bookstore Blues

A RECENT TRIP to the Bay Area reminded me of just how much I enjoy trolling through well-stocked independent bookstores. Among my favorites is the cavernous Green Apple Books on Clement Street in San Francisco, where I almost always discover some rare or unusual gem to add to my already overstuffed library. Last time it was a copy of Meaghan Morris and Paul Patton's hard-to-find collection *Michel Foucault: Power, Truth, Strategy*, which had eluded me for years. Then there's my Berkeley duo: University Press Books, located on Bancroft Way, which is home to one of the finest collections of new scholarly titles west of the Mississippi; and Moe's, located just around the corner and down Telegraph Avenue, which offers an overwhelming assortment of new and used books. I could spend days thumbing through their stacks in search of selections that, I learn, ought to be in my library. Browsing through all three stores is always equal parts education and shopping for me.

My travels frequently involve side trips to local independent bookstores, often resulting in fortuitous discoveries. Though I've been there just once, the Seminary Co-op Bookstore in Chicago ranks among my favorites. Its inventory of scholarly titles surely rivals that of University Press Books, and I would venture to say its selection of titles is the most extensive in the Midwest. Also topping my list is the Prairie Lights Bookstore in Iowa City, Iowa, whose inventory is as impressive as the list of authors who have visited the shop to present readings. Trips to Amherst, Massachusetts, always involve stops at Raven Books. On multiple occasions I've benefited from the decision of University of Massachusetts students to cash in their books at the end of the term. Then there's the Strand. Located at the corner of 12th Street and Broadway in New York City, the Strand's floor-to-ceiling collection encompasses "miles of books"—eighteen at last count. Its stock may be exceeded only by that of Powell's Bookstore in Portland, Oregon. You could spend a week in either place and still not manage to touch every volume each store has on its shelves.

Would that I had been so mobile as a child. I grew up in Goshen, New York, a small, fairly rural community located about sixty miles northwest of New York City. The place has since transformed itself into something like a distant suburb. When I was young, though, Goshen might just as well have been six hundred miles from the Big Apple, given how rarely my family ventured there. The physical and psychological distance I felt from New York City and all that it had to offer was compounded by Goshen's relative lack of cultural resources. The town had no real bookstore to speak of—at least not when I was very young—though it did play home—as it still does today—to a horse racing hall of fame. The Goshen Public Library and Historical Society always seemed, well, more historical society than public library.

When a tiny bookshop (whose name escapes me) opened in the late 1980s, about a block from the town square and within walking distance of my home, I was intrigued. Would the place sell books that might actually interest me? Perhaps I had unreasonably high expectations—it couldn't have measured more than eight hundred square feet—but I recall being nonplussed by its stock each time that I entered. The gondolas and wall displays always seemed unusually spare. What kept me coming back was its supply of New York State Regents Examination review books and what was, admittedly, a noteworthy selection of Cliffs Notes. Despite my patronage, the bookshop soon folded and was replaced by a video store.

Nearby Middletown, New York, was a different story. Where Goshen's outskirts were still actively farmed, much of Middletown's outlying land had been sold off, rezoned, and subdivided in the 1950s and 1960s to make way for large tracts of mall space. One of those malls, Orange Plaza, measuring eight hundred thousand square feet, opened in the early 1970s and would, by the mid-1980s, house a substantial B. Dalton bookstore. I can't recall when I figured out that the place was a corporately owned chain. What was more important to me was the fact that it had an astonishing amount of books on hand that genuinely appealed to me. There I recall purchasing *First Flight*, a science fiction novel penned by one of my favorite comic book writers, Chris Claremont. I'm sure there were many others whose titles I no longer recall. As it happened, though, the sci-fi section stood adjacent to the customer service kiosk. Proximity taught me that I could obtain virtually any book in print, the whole catalog of which was stored on tiny microfiche slides. I remember placing my first special order, volume 1 of *The Art of Robotech*, and my exhilaration at its arrival within a week. (I still have the book.) Even though Middletown's B. Dalton was relatively small by today's superstore standards, its stock was nonetheless impressive. My twelfth grade summer reading list included the Grove Press edition of Eugène Ionesco's play *Rhinoceros*. Never, I believed, would I be able to find avant-garde literature of this kind—in translation, no less—anywhere in the Goshen area. I had resigned myself to ordering it when, sure enough, I discovered that B. Dalton had a copy on hand.

As a result of my own frustrations and more positive experiences with retail bookstores, I have come to appreciate the subtlety and pathos of Raymond Williams's essay "Culture Is Ordinary." Williams grew up in the harsh environs of the Welsh countryside in the early decades of the twentieth century. There he developed a keen sense of what real and perceived distance from major metropolitan centers—the centers of modernity—felt like and what that distance meant in terms of access to resources that could enrich one's quality of life:

> It was slow in coming to us, in all its effects, but steam power, the petrol engine, electricity, these and their host of products in commodities and services, we took as quickly as we could get them, and we were glad. . . . Moreover, in the new conditions, there was more real freedom to dispose of our lives, more real personal grasp where it mattered, more real say. Any account of our culture which explicitly or implicitly denies the value of an industrial society is really irrelevant; not in a million years would you make us give up this power.[1]

This sense of "personal grasp" captures my early relationship to B. Dalton. Here, finally, was my chance to share, more or less fully, in imaginative and informational worlds that had hitherto been denied to people like me, living in relatively rural places like Goshen, New York. Never would I give up that power—at least as long as there were no viable alternatives to speak of.[2]

The story has grown more complicated of late. The last decade and a half has witnessed the proliferation and supersizing of corporate retail bookselling chains, the results of which have been contentious, to say the least. Freestanding "big-box" book superstores have gradually, although not entirely, replaced smaller, mall-based chains like B. Dalton and Waldenbooks, to say nothing of independent bookstores. These behemoths typically boast between twenty-five and thirty thousand square feet of retail space, stock around a hundred thousand different titles, and feature cafés, upbeat music, sizable newsstands, ample public seating, and more. With over twelve hundred big-box bookstores between them, industry leaders Barnes & Noble (corporate parent of B. Dalton) and Borders (parent of Waldenbooks) now command extraordinary buying power and market share. As such, many people are apprehensive about the ways in which these large-scale booksellers seem to be reshaping the everyday landscape of books and bookselling—and of culture more broadly. Their growth, popularity, and considerable economic muscle thus raise important concerns about the well-being of local independent bookstores, the purported homogenizing effects of mass culture, and, ultimately, the future of books. Dismissing the value of an industrial society may be an exercise in futility. As Williams understood, however, embracing an industrial society's excesses may be an even more damaging exercise in servility.

The current tension existing between independents and superstores is the starting point of this chapter. In the first section I explore how their relationship has played out over the course of the last decade. Specifically, I try to make sense of the claim that big-box bookstores have forced independent bookstores to close en masse. My implicit purpose is to challenge how some people conceive of big-box bookstores and other mass cultural institutions as ideal types, that is, as placeless and without history, and hence as agents of cultural homogenization. The next section consists of a history of Barnes & Noble, the oldest extant large-scale bookselling chain in the United States. There I describe the structural conditions leading up to the emergence of large-scale retail bookselling in the United States. The chapter then focuses on a *particular* Barnes & Noble branch located in a *particular* place: Durham, North Carolina. I go on to explore the role this one superstore has played in a central North Carolina community's struggle to redress persistent racial and economic inequalities.

The point of all this storytelling is to enrich debates about the moral, economic, and cultural value of corporate big-box bookstores, although not merely for the sake of being contrarian. The goal is for those of us who have a stake in book culture to engage in a more historically and geographically grounded discussion about the social uses and effects of these stores and, more broadly, about the politics of mass culture. As such, I try to strike a delicate balance. Though I deeply respect people's practical, psychological, and affective investments in specific kinds of bookstores, the stories I tell may at times cut against the grain of received wisdom about the well-being of bookselling in the United States. I will argue that mass culture possesses a deep, rich history, one that shows how seemingly repetitive artifacts and institutions can serve to open new pathways for repeating everyday life differently.

Chain Reactions?

To begin, consider the oft-repeated claim that corporate big-box bookstore chains drive independent booksellers out of business. Certainly there's ample evidence to support it. I suspect many of you reading this book know of at least one independent bookseller who went out of business in the last decade or so after a big-box bookstore chain opened nearby. I can think of at least two: the Chapel Hill, North Carolina, branches of the Intimate Bookstore; and the Bloomington, Indiana, bookstore Between the Lines. The pattern is straightforward enough: where the one opens, the other is likely to close. Could it be any less complicated than that?

An abundance of fragments of everyday book culture reinforce these observations. The most salient probably is the 1998 feature film *You've Got Mail*, in which a profit-obsessed corporate CEO named Joe Fox (played by Tom Hanks) plops one of his big-box bookstores down on New York's Upper West Side and forces the owner of a quaint children's bookstore, Kathleen Kelly (Meg Ryan), out of business. (Inexplicably the two still manage to fall in love.) Their confrontation comes to a head in this bit of dialogue, where Joe and Kathleen debate whether Fox Books is a bona fide bookseller or a boorish imposter:

JOE: You probably sell, what, $350,000 worth of books in a year?
KATHLEEN: How did you know that?
JOE: I'm in the book business.
KATHLEEN: *I* am in the book business.
JOE: I see. And we are the price clubs. Only instead of a ten-gallon vat of olive oil for $3.99 that won't fit under your kitchen cabinet, *we* sell cheap books.

The implication here is clear enough: "real" bookstores care about economics only as a means to an end, namely, staying in business, so that they can deliver worthwhile books to intelligent, community-minded people. Large-scale corporate booksellers, on the other hand, see economics as an end in itself. Fast, cheap, and en masse are their guiding principles; they care about the cultural value of books about as much as Costco cares about the moral and intellectual value of cooking oil.

Though I don't mean to contradict these claims and characterizations outright, I do want to scrutinize them a bit. The familiar refrain "corporate big-box bookstores drive local independents out of business" has calcified into a kind of commonsense mantra, so that imagining more complicated relations of causality has become somewhat difficult of late. Is there really a straight line leading from the one to the other? And what about the inventories of corporate big-box bookstores? Are they really comparable to "commodities" in the sense of homogeneous, bulk merchandise? Are these even the right questions to be asking of bookstores today?

Oddly, the American Booksellers Association (ABA) keeps no formal, long-term records that would indicate exactly how many independent bookstores have gone under since Barnes & Noble opened its first superstore outside Minneapolis, Minnesota, in 1989. According to the *New York Times*, the ABA estimates that between 200 and 260 independent booksellers closed in the four years between 1993 and 1996.[3] A report on *The NewsHour with Jim Lehrer* in 1997 stated that 200 independent bookstores closed in the United States between 1995 and 1996.[4] In a memoir describing her time as owner of New York City's Books & Co. (now defunct), author Lynne Tillman mentions an "informal tally" by the ABA showing that 221 independent bookstores shut their doors in the United States between 1993 and 1998.[5] Along these same lines, the press routinely reports on fluctuations in ABA membership, which it presumes reflects the number of independent bookstores opening and closing in the United States. Numerous stories convey how the organization's growth in the early 1990s was undercut by a significant downturn in membership by decade's end. The ABA swelled from 5,100 to 5,400 members between the early and mid-1990s, but membership fell to 3,300 by the close of the decade.[6]

Often the press juxtaposes these figures with statistics tracking the growth of corporate superstore bookselling outlets. For instance, in 1996 the *New York Times* reported that approximately 450 superstores opened nationwide in the same period that saw the estimated closing of 200 or more independents.[7] In a story about Buffalo's independent booksellers and their struggle to survive economically, the *Buffalo News* similarly wrote that Barnes & Noble and Borders Group "opened more than 250 new stores" between 1996 and 1998.[8] Coverage of changes in the retail bookselling market in the United States tend to paint a similar picture. It's widely reported that independent bookstores accounted for about 32 percent of all new books purchased in the United States when the construction of superstores began to take off in the early 1990s.[9] The year 1994 appears to be a pivotal one in which corporate bookselling chains overtook independents. According to *Publishers Weekly*, the market share of the former rose from 23 to 27 percent between 1993 and 1994, while that of the latter slipped from 24 to 19 percent.[10] By 1999 the national bookselling chains accounted for just over half of all new books sold in the United States, while independent booksellers accounted for between 14 and 17 percent.[11]

Beyond the statistical evidence, the press routinely turns to narratives in which, like *You've Got Mail*, national superstore bookselling chains encroach on and force nearby independent booksellers to close. In 1993 a story in the *Los Angeles Times* relied on this narrative, beginning with its very title: "Chain Reaction: As Mega-Bookstores Move into Their Neighborhoods, Independents Worry About the Future."[12] The piece opens with the story of Earthling Books, a Santa Barbara, California, bookstore struggling to remain financially solvent after a superstore has opened down the block:

> She survived a recession, painful rent increases and the wrecker's ball. For years, Penny Davies has scrambled to keep her bookstore operating in downtown Santa Barbara. But now, she may have met her match. Last month, a new neighbor moved in down the block. A competitor with plenty of cash flow and influential friends in the publishing world. Someone who might crush Davies' business and laugh all the way to the bank. It was a super-store—the latest trend in mass-market bookselling and either a blessing or a curse, depending on whom you talk to.[13]

In 1995 the *New York Times* filed a similar report on the closing of Endicott Booksellers, a fixture on Manhattan's Upper West Side for fourteen years:

> With the arrival of Barnes & Noble superstores, places like Endicott's are finding themselves up against the wall. For independents, the success of the superstore formula means adapt or die. After Barnes & Noble opened a superstore on 86th Street and Lexington Avenue in January 1990, the Burlington Book Shop went out of business. So did Eeyore's and Storyland, children's bookstores that could not compete with the superstore's large children's annex. Eeyore's second store, on the Upper West Side, also closed.[14]

Likewise, in a story in 1997, PBS recounted the closing of Odegard Books in Minneapolis, Minnesota: "In 1989, a New York–based bookstore company called Barnes and Noble decided to expand its operations nationwide. It started in the Minneapolis area with a store . . . which covered thousands of square feet and stocked nearly 200,000 titles. It had a coffee bar that sold food and latte—and it discounted prices. Within three years, Odegard was out of business."[15]

The superstore threat seems to run even deeper. In 1997 the *New York Times* covered the closing of a Brooklyn-based bookseller called Booklink Too. What's unique about Booklink's closing is that it apparently was preemptive. "Three months before it is scheduled to open," the *New York Times* reported, "the first Barnes & Noble superstore in Brooklyn has claimed a victim. In anticipation of stiff competition from the retail juggernaut, the owners of Booklink Too in Park Slope have decided to consolidate their operations and close one of their two small bookstores."[16] It should thus come as no surprise that the *Buffalo News* concluded: "The small, neighborhood bookstore is an endangered species, threatened by the same national chain domination that all but wiped out neighborhood pharmacies."[17]

Clearly there are instances nationwide in which superstore bookselling chains cut into the sales of local independent booksellers so deeply that it became economically unfeasible for them to remain in business. Unlike the national bookselling chains, many independent booksellers lack the financial resources to allow them to remain solvent during even brief economic downturns. Smaller stores are particularly vulnerable to competition, and no doubt Barnes & Noble, Borders, and other big-box booksellers have claimed their share of independent booksellers in this way.

The newspaper articles and various other reports mentioned earlier suggest that national superstore chains are the principal—and possibly the sole—cause behind the recent decline of independent bookstores. But to what extent is that the case? Does the opening of corporate superstores necessarily cause a "chain reaction," forcing nearby independents to close? While there are some reports circulating in the popular media that address these kinds of questions, on the whole they are few and far between. It doesn't follow, however, that their relative scarcity substantiates the chain reaction narrative. Quite the opposite, I believe the narrative consistency evident in the reporting is symptomatic of an unwillingness to question conventional wisdom.

As I previously noted, a PBS report in 1997 attributes the closing of Minneapolis-based Odegard Books solely to the opening of a nearby Barnes & Noble superstore. In contrast, *Publishers Weekly* indicates that "by the end of '94 [Odegard] had recovered from the superstores." According to both the owner and the store manager, Odegard felt pinched by competition from the superstores, but its closing was attributable to far more banal circumstances: many customers refused to continue shopping there after the owner of its two main parking lots began charging patrons a fee to park their cars.[18]

It's important, then, not to permit the steady repetition of offhanded political-economic analysis to obscure the myriad local factors that contribute to the failure of independent bookstores. For example, Huntington's Book Store of Hartford, Connecticut, closed in 1993. *Publishers Weekly* explained that the opening of several superstores nearby contributed to the decision to suspend operations. Significantly, the decision was also the result of a severe economic downturn brought about by the flight of insurance, banking, and defense industries from the greater Hartford area.[19] Similarly, Weiser's, New York City's oldest New Age bookstore, closed in 1995 after a Barnes & Noble superstore opened about four blocks away. So far so good. But another key reason for its closing was the departure of Metropolitan Life Insurance, one of the neighborhood's largest companies, whose employees often visited the store. Weiser's owner also noted the lack of other businesses in the area, sporadic problems created by nearby drug sales and prostitution, and the steep rise in rents across Manhattan as factors contributing to the closing.[20]

Following a highly publicized three-year battle with a Barnes & Noble superstore that had opened about a block away, in 1996 Shakespeare & Company closed its store on Manhattan's Upper West Side. However, as the *New York Times* rightly observed, "Shakespeare & Company . . . developed something of a reputation for surly service, with some customers expressing the feeling that the store clerks looked down on anyone whose tastes might run to, say, John Grisham."[21] In other words, some customers refused to continue shopping at Shakespeare & Company because its salespeople intimidated them with their narrow views of "worthwhile" culture. Another Manhattan bookseller, Books & Co., closed its doors in 1997 after a dispute with its landlord, the Whitney Museum of American Art, which refused to renew the store's lease without a sizable rent increase.[22] Bookland of Maine, an independent bookselling chain in New England, closed four stores in early 2000. Although *Publishers Weekly* began its story by attributing the closing "to the triple whammy of Borders, Barnes & Noble and Amazon. com," it added that additional factors contributed to the shutdowns, among which was "the collapse of a downtown redevelopment project in Portland" in which Bookland was to have played a part.[23]

Likewise, consider how membership fluctuations in the ABA get taken up. In his 2001 memoir entitled *The Business of Books*, publisher André

Schiffrin observed that chain bookstores, price clubs, and Internet booksellers "have brought about a dramatic decline in the number of independent bookstores, from 5,400 stores in the early 1990s to 3,200 today."[24] Similarly, in 1999 the *Columbus Dispatch* reported: "The number of [independent] booksellers nationally declined, from some 5,000 in 1990 to 3,500 by decade's end."[25] On the basis of the ABA's decreasing membership, *Boardwatch* magazine wrote: "Competition has led to the closing of more than 1,000 independent book stores in the last three years [1996–99]."[26]

Collectively these accounts err in at least two ways. First, they conflate the total number of ABA members with the total number of independent booksellers operating in the United States. In 1997 the ABA estimated that some twelve thousand independent retail bookstores were in business nationwide.[27] Less than a third, in other words, actually belonged to the ABA. Second, because these accounts fail to differentiate between the number of ABA members and the number of independent booksellers, they obscure the fact that falloff in the ABA's ranks doesn't necessarily correlate directly with the closing of independents. A canceled or lapsed membership doesn't guarantee that a specific independent bookstore has gone out of business, only that, for whatever reason, it no longer belongs to the ABA. The bottom line is that independent bookselling may be better—or worse— off in the United States than these stories and statistics suggest.

Thoroughly Modern Bookselling

One of the problems with public discourse about bookselling in the United States is that tends to pay short shrift to what Meaghan Morris has called the everyday "sense of place" within which corporate superstores emerge.[28] Without a clear sense of history and of the ways in which these big-box bookstores affect daily life in concrete contexts, it becomes easy for critics to dismiss them as soulless, homogeneous institutions—the Costcos of bookselling, or mass culture at its worst. What other stories, I wonder, might present themselves were we to imagine big-box bookstores not as an abstract concept but as particular institutions embedded in both time and space?

Corporate superstore bookselling chains such as Barnes & Noble emerged from a constellation of economic and sociological changes that began over a century ago in the United States. As the preceding discussion has shown, the final quarter of the nineteenth century and the first quarter of the twentieth marked a turning point in the cultural history of the nation. This was the period that saw the nation's economy shift from agriculture to industry. The change helped stimulate the production of consumer goods, which in turn altered the country's opportunity structure. Janice A. Radway and others have shown how during this time a society that had been founded and run by a quasi-aristocratic elite began giving way to a more flexible and inclusive configuration—to something approaching (though never quite achieving) a meritocracy. Instead of continuing to pin social mobility on existing systems of wealth and privilege, the nascent consumer capitalism helped to mitigate sociological differences and class distinctions by linking social mobility, however imperfectly, to the consumption of books and other mass-produced goods.[29]

As both cause and effect of these changes, the first decades of the twentieth century saw the initial rise of so-called middlebrow cultural goods and institutions. These included the Book-of-the-Month Club, John Erskine's "great books" curriculum, and numerous book publishers, some of which would go on to become premier publishing houses in the United States (e.g., Random House and Simon & Schuster). What distinguished middlebrow goods from other cultural goods was their unique blend of commerce and culture, their linking of mass-produced consumer goods to possibilities for learning and social advancement—hitherto the provenance of high cultural forms and institutions.[30]

The middlebrow may have emerged during the first half of the twentieth century, but its effects remained relatively limited during the Great Depression and throughout the lean years of the Second World War. As war output gradually gave way to the production of consumer goods, and as real wages again started to climb, the middlebrow underwent a second, more intensive period of growth. In terms of books, this process took a number of forms: the proliferation of "quality" paperbacks, originally published under the imprimatur of Anchor Books, Knopf, and Random House beginning in the early 1950s; the growth of book clubs; and the launch of the *New York Review of Books* in 1963, among numerous other literary periodicals, radio programs, and television shows devoted to providing the book-buying public with up-to-date information.[31] With these the middlebrow was institutionalized, infusing the realm of cultural production—indeed, the realm of culture writ large—with its tastes and sensibilities. The process was given a further boost with the passage of the G.I Bill in 1944, which significantly enlarged higher education in the United States. In the years immediately following the Second World War, only about 5 percent of the population had earned a bachelor's degree. That figure doubled within a generation and quadrupled within two generations. The result was a better-educated population, with the added bonus of a significantly expanded market for middlebrow cultural goods.[32]

The boom in higher education in the postwar period posed a number of practical problems since many colleges and universities lacked sufficient physical space to provide for their rapidly growing student populations.[33] Campus bookstores in particular faced the serious crisis of how best to accommodate the increasingly high volume of textbooks and course materials required of students without a corresponding increase in store space. According to Ken White, one of the leading figures in bookstore design, many campus bookstores in the immediate postwar years adopted merchandising strategies privileging sales volume over aesthetic concerns.[34] "A lot of customers weren't buying with cash, but with G.I vouchers," he recalled. "To get books out fast, the stores sold them out of cartons. It was a matter of case-cutting, as supermarkets do with soup cans."[35]

The analogy White draws to supermarkets points directly to what Rachel Bowlby has called "the peculiar history of the relations between book-selling and food-selling."[36] White has suggested that following the Second World War campus bookstores began looking to supermarkets for a new, more efficient merchandising model. As Bowlby has shown, modeling bookstores on supermarkets is a case of history come full circle:

> In the history of shop design, it is bookstores, strangely enough, that were the precursors of supermarkets. They, alone of all types of shop, made use of shelves that were not behind counters, with the goods arranged for casual browsing and for what was not yet called self-service. Also, when brand-name goods and their accompanying packages were non-existent or rare in the sale of food, books had covers that were designed at once to protect the contents and to entice the purchaser; they were proprietary products with identifiable authors and new titles—not just any novel, but the latest by such-and-such a writer.[37]

Critics have tended to disparage those who compare bookselling to large-scale food selling. As You've Got Mail demonstrated, books are supposed to be treated as sacred artifacts, not as bulk merchandise. To treat them otherwise is to fall prey to the crass trifecta of volume, efficiency, and commercialism. What Bowlby suggests, however, is a much closer kinship between these two seemingly antithetical domains. Bookselling helped set the stage for the modern supermarket—the very form of merchandise delivery to which it now seems opposed.

In any event, as enrollments continued to grow, an influx of tuition dollars and government funding in the 1950s helped many campuses expand significantly by the early 1960s. In addition to building more student housing, another frequent capital improvement project included the enlargement of student service facilities, particularly union buildings and campus bookstores. Many leading college and university bookstores grew substantially. For example, the Harvard Coop in Cambridge, Massachusetts, mushroomed from a comparatively paltry eight thousand square feet to around twenty-five thousand square feet—roughly the size of one of today's typical book superstores.[38]

These expansions led to the gradual phasing out of case-cutting in campus bookstores and its replacement by more sophisticated bookselling techniques.[39] Case-cutting offered a pragmatic solution to the problem of distributing large quantities of books quickly and efficiently to passels of students who had little choice but to purchase them. It didn't encourage browsing and impulse buying, nor was it meant to. Given the relatively tight quarters many campus bookstores occupied in the 1950s, it seems reasonable to assume that most simply wanted to supply students with their required textbooks and hurry them out the door. Yet the expansions of the early 1960s led to a reconsideration of the purpose of some stores. Although they still needed to engage in fast-paced, high-volume textbook selling at strategic times of year, their increased size meant that people could—indeed, might actually want to—spend some time browsing. As White observed, many college and university administrators subsequently began viewing campus bookstores not only in terms of their primary function, namely, furnishing students with required books and supplies at the start of each term, but for their potential to generate revenue on a more steady basis.[40] This recognition led to a greater emphasis on merchandising: the use of specific techniques of store planning, layout, design, and display to organize the store space so as to capture shoppers' attention and encourage them to buy.[41]

The combination of industrial production, middlebrow cultural dispositions, and the move toward mass higher education helped give rise to the idea of large-scale retail bookselling in the United States. A pivotal, historically earlier element should be factored in here as well, namely, the invention of retail shopping. Given the latter's ubiquity today, it may be hard to imagine that it was an exchange form that many people once distrusted—even scorned. Yet, as E. P. Thompson has shown, this attitude prevailed (at least in Britain) into the early nineteenth century owing to the significance of the public marketplace and the nature of the exchange occurring therein. Public marketplaces typically brought together producer/sellers and a crowd of potential buyers, who, if all went well, negotiated the prices of goods in a manner more or less sensitive to local needs, conditions, and customs. (Today's farmers' markets are a vestige of these marketplaces.) As Thompson notes, the immediacy of these interactions provided for the possibility of "moral" rather than purely economic pricing.[42] In times of widespread economic downturn, an intimidating throng of buyers might demand that producer/sellers reduce prices lest they face the wrath of those who had fallen on hard times.[43]

Toward the end of the eighteenth century new faces began appearing both inside and outside the marketplace. Retailers sold goods others had produced at a markup and jobbers (wholesalers) circumvented the marketplace by purchasing goods directly from local producers and reselling them elsewhere at a profit. It's important to recognize that neither group was especially welcome—at least initially. Because retailers confounded the intimacy of the producer-buyer relationship, it wasn't uncommon for local authorities to refer to them in the same breath as "hucksters" and to exclude them from marketplaces during the busiest hours.[44] Jobbers didn't fare much better. Critics disparaged them as "interlopers" who disrupted local supplies and thus undercut local pricing and product availability.[45] Thompson points out that jobbers flourished in times of shortage, which were frequent in the eighteenth and nineteenth centuries, thanks to their ability to move large quantities of goods "from areas of surplus to areas of scarcity."[46] Jobbers thus became an increasingly lucrative resource for farmers and other producers of goods since they tended to buy regularly and in bulk, unlike the ordinary folk to whom producers otherwise might have sold their goods.

This gradual shift to a less geographically specific economy of scale had dramatic consequences for the sociology of buying and selling. Local marketplaces waned as the nineteenth century progressed, and those that remained began excluding the general public. They ultimately served as a meeting place for producers and jobbers. "Hence the labourer was driven to the petty retail shop," Thompson writes, "at which prices were enhanced."[47] However, these were no longer the prices of old, that is, prices negotiated face to face by producer/sellers and a sometimes morally charged buying public. As goods increasingly emanated from a generalized elsewhere, and as retailers shouldered added responsibility for selling these products—produced by others—prices became more uniform and abstractly determined. Increasingly impersonal conditions, in other words, contributed to the eclipse of moral pricing by its more purely economic counterpart, so much so that by the mid-nineteenth century the latter had become the norm rather than the exception.[48]

It is from these as well as other conditions that Barnes & Noble emerged. In 1873 Charles Montgomery Barnes founded a wholesaling outfit in Wheaton, a burgeoning although still quite rural Chicago suburb whose settlement had begun in the late 1830s. Barnes launched his upstart company based on an unexpected decision: he opted out of the new book trade and decided instead to specialize in secondhand texts. For this reason his wholesaling operation has been described as possibly "the first business of its kind in this country."[49] Indeed, Barnes's timing couldn't have been better. The railroad, which arrived in Wheaton in 1849, had established the town as a viable hub from which to ship and receive used books. Equally important was the opening in 1874 of a new public school in Wheaton, which taught grades 1–12 and drew students from across DuPage County, and the presence of Wheaton College. Both institutions would require a steady supply of affordable books, and Barnes was more than happy to oblige.[50] Barnes eventually added new books and stationery to his product lines. His fledgling book business, which began in his home on the corner of Lincoln and Cross Streets, slowly began to gather momentum.

The business quickly outgrew these cramped quarters. In 1876 Barnes relocated to 23 LaSalle Street in Chicago under the name C. M. Barnes & Company. The firm reorganized in 1894, whereupon Barnes began dealing solely in the school textbook trade—a growth industry, to be sure, given the widespread passage of compulsory schooling acts beginning in the 1870s. Meanwhile Barnes's son, William, joined the company in 1884. John W. Wilcox, William's father-in-law, partnered with the company shortly thereafter. William succeeded his father as president upon the latter's retirement in 1902. With the death of C. M. Barnes in 1907, the company changed its name to C. M. Barnes–Wilcox Co.[51]

In 1896 G. Clifford Noble formed a partnership with a fellow New Yorker, Arthur Hinds, resulting in two companies: the publishing outfit of Hinds, Noble, & Eldridge; and the bookstore Hinds & Noble, which specialized in educational texts.[52] After a little more than two decades, the partnership was dissolved, with Hinds selling his shares in the bookstore to Noble, who agreed to relinquish his interests in the publishing firm. Noble appears to have intended to make his eldest son, Lloyd Adams Noble, his partner. Having gained exclusive control of the bookselling operation, he was successful. In 1917 the bookstore's name was briefly changed to Noble & Noble, though the outbreak of the First World War forced Lloyd into active military service and left his father searching for a new partner. Meanwhile,

William Barnes had sold his stake in C. M. Barnes–Wilcox Co. and moved from Chicago to New York in 1917, whereupon he became partners with Noble in the educational book trade. Together they established Barnes & Noble.[53]

Throughout the 1920s Barnes & Noble dealt almost exclusively in the wholesale end of the educational book business, becoming a key supplier of textbooks to New York City schools, colleges, libraries, and other book dealers.[54] In its early years the company generally ignored the retail side of the book trade except to sell single copies to the occasional passerby who happened into the company's offices. As such visits increased, the firm realized that retail bookselling might very well prove profitable. Barnes & Noble relocated to a larger office space occupying the second floor of 76 Fifth Avenue in Manhattan. The new location provided sufficient room to continue the wholesale operation while also adding a small retail store specializing in textbooks. The retail side of the business soon flourished, prompting Barnes & Noble to relocate in 1932 to accommodate the increase in customer traffic. The company leased a generous ground-floor space at 105 Fifth Avenue (at the corner of Eighteenth Street), where the company's flagship store remains to this day (fig. 3).[55]

Noble left the partnership in 1929 to start a publishing company with his sons. Under the tutelage of William Barnes and his son, John, who had purchased Noble's interest in the company, Barnes & Noble continued to expand its operations throughout the 1930s.[56] In addition to wholesaling, the firm added a publishing division in 1931, beginning with a series of glosses covering "practically every major subject taught in college."[57] The retail operation enjoyed the most rapid growth during this period, with Barnes & Noble becoming a major bookseller to students, particularly those attending the many colleges, universities, and private schools in and around Manhattan.

To better accommodate the influx—particularly during the twice-yearly rush at the beginning of each college term—the store and offices underwent major renovations in the fall of 1941. The company began by securing a lease for the second floor of 105 Fifth Avenue. All of the Barnes & Noble administrative offices were moved upstairs, thus freeing up the entire main floor and mezzanine levels for retail sales and storage space. The store incorporated a unique, modular-display system into its design scheme to better manage fluctuations in store traffic. During periods of high volume, the company would set up a 125-foot-long textbook counter, occupying the entire length of two sides of the store, dedicated to servicing students enrolled in area schools and colleges. Specially designed built-in panels could be pulled

FIGURE 3 The Barnes & Noble Bookstore as it looked in 1941. The company's flagship store still occupies the same location at 105 Fifth Avenue in New York City, at the corner of Eighteenth Street.

SOURCE: *PUBLISHERS WEEKLY*, DECEMBER 6, 1941, 2091. USED WITH PERMISSION OF BARNES & NOBLE.

out during a crush and inserted into the side of the counter facing outward toward the customer, thereby concealing the books contained therein. This system helped ease overcrowding in the store by cutting down on browsing during the busiest periods. Customers simply submitted requests for the textbooks they needed to the store clerks, who were stationed behind the counter, whereupon the customers were expected to pay for their merchandise and exit the store. Seven years after its introduction, *Publishers Weekly* reported on the successful implementation of this bookselling system: "In view of the size of New York City and the enormous enrollments in the hundreds of schools, one can readily imagine what a madhouse the store must be at the beginning of a semester, and what a difference these new methods have made to the sales people. (By far, the largest part of the store's business is the student trade.)"[58] Once business slowed, the long textbook counter could be disassembled into individual tables, with the front panels stashed to open up the units for display and browsing.[59]

Barnes & Noble's effort to streamline customer service was inspired by the burgeoning fields of industrial psychology and scientific management, which sought to rationalize product purchasing and to render it more efficient. These architectural and organizational features were complemented by a sonic component. In the early 1920s the Wired Radio Company of Cleveland, Ohio, introduced a special, closed-circuit radio-programming system. It pitched its soothing, "scientifically" timed and sequenced background music as a kind of ambient instrument with which to steady the cadence of workers' and consumers' otherwise unpredictable routines. The service quickly attracted a loyal clientele consisting of restaurants, hotels, and other commercial establishments, as well as a limited number of private homes in and around the Cleveland area. Its success eventually prompted Wired Radio to relocate to New York City in 1936 and to change its name to Muzak.[60] On the heels of these developments, in 1940 Barnes & Noble installed a storewide loudspeaker system and was among the first retailers in the city to feature "Music by Muzak" during business hours. Three minutes of advertisements, store announcements, and news updates—from baseball scores to war bulletins—were interspersed between music programming every twelve minutes.[61]

Barnes & Noble's unique audio system appears to have served three related functions. First, in keeping with Muzak's marketing claims, it was meant to stimulate employees to work more efficiently by counteracting boredom and fatigue with strategically timed up-tempo music. In this sense it applied the values and techniques of industrial production to retail bookselling. Second, at least in theory it motivated customers to make purchases by providing them with a stimulating atmosphere within which to shop. Finally, it brought the activity of bookselling into better synergy with everyday life; the periodic, ambient news bulletins transformed the otherwise leisurely activity of browsing into an opportunity for patrons to encounter and process timely information. Little wonder, then, that *College Store* magazine called the Barnes & Noble of this period, "as progressive and modernly equipped a firm as one could wish."[62]

Perhaps the most unique innovation Barnes & Noble introduced during this period was "book-a-teria," a bookselling system whose name explicitly acknowledged the "peculiar history" of books and food.[63] As it had done in the 1941 store expansion and addition of modular fixtures, the company implemented book-a-teria as a practical solution to the problem of selling large quantities of books to an expanding book-buying public. Unlike the textbook counter, which remained in service only during the rush preceding each school term, book-a-teria functioned year-round to accommodate both students and nonstudents alike. It was modeled on the principles of a cafeteria (hence its name), a Taylorized method of food service predicated on the division of labor, high volume, and efficient—if not personalized—service. An article in *Publishers Weekly* in 1941 described the system in detail:

> As one goes into the modernized entrance to the store, one is handed a charge slip, somewhat like a price ticket in a cafeteria. When purchases are made, the clerk who gets the books for the customer will simply mark the titles and prices on the charge slip, and then go on to the next customer. The customer, when he leaves the shop, has to pass a cash register and wrapping desk, where one clerk ties up the package and another clerk takes in the charge slip and the payment for the books. . . . This system speeds up service enormously during the rush periods, since the book clerks can give their entire time to selling books. During the in-between seasons, the system is continued, with apparently no deterrent effect on browsers.[64]

By the end of the decade, *Publishers Weekly* reported, several college bookstores in and around Manhattan had implemented similar systems in an effort to service their expanding student populations with comparable efficiency.[65]

It's not altogether apparent precisely when or why Barnes & Noble discontinued its book-a-teria component. What is clear is that the company significantly expanded its operations in the 1950s and 1960s. It added an additional retail store on Twenty-third Street in Manhattan, along with several shops located near the City University of New York, Harvard University, and other college campuses in the Northeast. Moreover, the company became the chief used textbook supplier to approximately fifty colleges.[66] Throughout this period it remained under the principal control of the Barnes family. After John Barnes's death, in 1969, Amtel—a corporate conglomerate trading in toys, tools, and fashion, among other goods—purchased Barnes & Noble's retail and wholesale divisions.[67] Despite Amtel's diversified holdings, the company appears to have been ill-suited to the bookselling business. Amtel began closing unprofitable Barnes & Noble stores within a year of purchasing the company.[68] Within just two years it abandoned bookselling altogether, selling its interests to a young New York bookseller named Leonard Riggio.[69]

By 1971 Barnes & Noble consisted of a significantly reduced wholesale operation and a single retail location—the store at 105 Fifth Avenue. That year Riggio purchased the company from Amtel for $1.2 million—a bargain, to be sure, given the store's existing inventory of over two million books, not to mention the forty-two thousand square feet of prime retail space on lower Fifth Avenue.[70] Born in 1941, Riggio grew up in Bensonhurst, a predominantly working-class Italian neighborhood in Brooklyn, New York.[71] Because he lacked sufficient financial resources to attend college on a full-time basis, in 1958 he supported himself by taking a job at the New York University bookstore in Greenwich Village. He worked there by day while pursuing studies in engineering by night, though he never earned a Bachelor's degree. In 1965 Riggio borrowed five thousand dollars and opened the Student Book Exchange (SBX) on Waverly Place, across the street from the NYU bookstore. Over the next six years SBX contracted to run six college bookstores in New York and New England. SBX changed its name to Barnes & Noble after Riggio purchased the company from Amtel in 1971.[72]

Like the Barneses and the Nobles, Riggio entered retail bookselling at the educational end of the business, selling books primarily to college students. His biography reflects the extent to which large-scale retail bookselling—and, later, superstores—was to a certain degree made possible as a result of the postwar expansion of higher education in the United States, the rise of middlebrow reading and consumer culture, and the related sociological and economic transformations previously discussed. Indeed, Riggio has claimed that campus bookselling "basically created the culture that dominates [Barnes & Noble] until today," including its present emphasis on retail superstores.[73]

Until the early 1970s there remained a tacit disconnect within Barnes & Noble with respect to how it approached its clientele. While the company no doubt serviced nonstudent customers in increasing numbers, it nevertheless saw students as its principal audience and formulated its bookselling strategies accordingly. It thus conceived of and implemented its retail business in a manner cognizant of yet somewhat out of sync with the many nonstudents who patronized the store. Even though large-scale retail bookselling may have served as a model for educational bookselling, it wasn't exactly viewed as a model for bookselling in general.

That changed in 1975, when Barnes & Noble opened its first sale annex. Occupying three floors and covering forty thousand square feet, the outlet was located directly across the street from its main store on Fifth Avenue. It specialized mainly in closeouts (e.g., damaged and remaindered books), review copies, books acquired at auction (typically a bookseller's overstock or the inventory of stores that had gone out of business), and buybacks from college students and other customers.[74] The distressed conditions under which Barnes & Noble acquired these texts meant that it could sell them in the annex at tremendous discounts, typically between 40 and 90 percent of the original retail prices. Texts considered final closeouts, located in the basement "bookends" section, sold for as little as twenty-nine cents. Others located throughout the store cost just a few dollars, and still others apparently sold by weight.[75] In addition to the closeouts, the store featured multiple stacks of current *New York Times* best sellers along a wall on the second floor. The annex sold these books at dealer's cost as a loss leader, that is, as a strategy for generating store traffic and sales that would, with any luck, more than compensate for discounting the best sellers so steeply.[76]

While book retailers in the United States had long traded in remainders, damaged books, and used texts, rarely had a single store dealt in quantities on the order of the Barnes & Noble Sale Annex. If, in the immediate postwar years, some college bookstores attempted to emulate the look, feel, and merchandising tactics of supermarkets (which themselves had been adapted from bookstores), then the annex helped to propel that trend into the broader domain of retail bookselling.

Three aspects of its approach stand out. First, the practice of pricing books by the pound, while limited to a select portion of the store's total inventory, nevertheless underscored the extent to which the "ideology of the singularity of the book" had been disturbed by the mid-1970s.[77] Books sold by weight weren't necessarily set apart as individual works of creative genius deserving of contemplative study and careful handling. Rather, they were viewed as fully fungible or interchangeable staples meant to be purchased in bulk, much like flour, salt, cooking oil, or even toilet paper.[78] They were also functional in the sense that their comparatively low price meant that customers could put them—and, indeed, all books priced under a dollar—to good use. As *Publishers Weekly* reported in 1976, a "heavy proportion of customers in the annex . . . have no intention of reading the books they buy. They buy them as shelf fillers . . . in order to project images of themselves through their collections."[79] These volumes thus fulfilled essentially the same function as the bookbacks, or "mimic" books, mentioned in the preceding chapter. They were stock whose purpose was to occupy what would otherwise be empty bookshelf space.

Since printed books generally tend to be fairly heavy, buying books in bulk could prove to be a rather cumbersome activity. The second unique aspect of the annex represented a practical solution to this dilemma. By supplying supermarket-style shopping carts to its patrons, Barnes & Noble encouraged them to purchase more books than they otherwise could carry comfortably around the store (fig. 4). The carts helped to further the image of an inventory consisting mainly of fungible, bulk merchandise and quite possibly encouraged shoppers to approach it as such.

Finally, although the annex dedicated most of its floor space to books and bookselling, its unusually large size meant that it also could reserve room for customer amenities, such as park benches, tables, chairs, and public restrooms. These facilities encouraged customers to linger, and in doing so they helped distinguish the store from other, more transitory retail environments.[80] The annex consequently became a destination, or hangout. It was a place not only to browse but to pause and maybe even conduct research in the midst of an array of consumer goods—"an endless 'perhaps.'"[81] Significantly, all this occurred without any immediate expectation to buy (fig. 5).

FIGURE 4 New York City's Barnes & Noble Sale Annex on Fifth Avenue. Note the patrons in the foreground and the supermarket-style shopping carts they're using.

SOURCE: PUBLISHERS WEEKLY, JANUARY 19, 1976, 71. IMAGE © NANCY CRAMPTON. USED WITH PERMISSION.

FIGURE 5 Store patrons relaxing and reading books at public tables at the Barnes & Noble Sale Annex. Note how they're practically surrounded by books for sale.

SOURCE: PUBLISHERS WEEKLY, JANUARY 19, 1976, 72. IMAGE © NANCY CRAMPTON. USED WITH PERMISSION.

The Barnes & Noble Sale Annex thus sold not only books but, through its layout and operational policies, a particular vision of bookselling. It didn't aspire to cultivate its patrons' literary sensibilities, much less their ability to distinguish among a vast array of books. According to Leonard Riggio, the annex purposefully avoided addressing store patrons "as potential scholars."[82] What it did actively cultivate, however, was an "unintimidating atmosphere."[83] It catered to people who, for a variety of reasons, desired to incorporate large quantities of books into their daily lives and everyday surroundings. It reached out to them not by promoting any given title but by stressing the sheer volume of books the store unfailingly had on hand.

In the mid-1970s Barnes & Noble opened several smaller (2,500–3,000 square feet) sale annexes throughout the Northeast, along with a handful of retail stores in malls within the New York/New Jersey area.[84] Nevertheless the company's growth remained somewhat uneven. Initially it began branching out nationwide in the early 1980s by aggressively pursuing leasing arrangements with college bookstores. In 1983 it ran about forty of these stores; just three years later it managed a hundred additional stores.[85] With respect to its retail division, however, Barnes & Noble remained a comparatively small, regional bookselling operation until the mid-1980s. In 1986 it operated thirty-three Barnes & Noble trade stores and thirty-seven mini-annexes, located mostly in the Northeast. By comparison, Waldenbooks, the leading bookselling chain at the time, operated about a thousand stores nationwide.[86]

The year 1986 marked a turning point for Barnes & Noble. In partnership with Vendex International, a Dutch retail conglomerate, and with the financial backing of junk bonds brokered by Drexel Burnham Lambert, it purchased the national bookselling chain B. Dalton, chief competitor of Waldenbooks, from Dayton Hudson Corporation for three hundred million dollars.[87] Barnes & Noble subsequently became the largest bookselling chain in the United States, a position it retains to this day.

Things to Do with Big-Box Bookstores

Thus far I've focused primarily on two Barnes & Noble bookstores in Manhattan in an attempt to show how local and macrohistorical conditions intersected, giving rise to these particular stores. The moment in which a company becomes a national chain presents a challenge in terms of how best to represent it, given the apparent increase in the scale of the institution. One way is to view this moment as a consolidation upward, which would seem to demand a more sustained macrolevel, political-economic analysis. Alternatively, one could demonstrate how those who visit chain stores are attempting to resist the latter's operative logic of power and dominance, which have been superimposed from without. Neither path, I believe, is adequate to the task at hand. Instead of trying to write a history of Barnes & Noble superstores as abstract, ideal types, I want to continue writing from a more grounded perspective. What follows is a brief history of a Barnes & Noble superstore located in central North Carolina. My purpose is to explore how a "local instance of a general model" inhabits and is inflected by the "sense of place" in which it's located—beyond the corporation's deliberate efforts to "localize" particular stores.[88]

Durham, North Carolina, has a Barnes & Noble superstore that's deeply enmeshed in local and regional history. Although it's situated along a heavily trafficked automobile corridor, like most of the company's superstores its location is anything but incidental.[89] The store is housed in a freestanding, 25,000-square-foot structure detached from the main section of New Hope Commons, a 458,000-square-foot strip mall that opened in 1995. The mall lies just off of U.S. 15–501, a major thoroughfare connecting the city of

Durham and the nearby town of Chapel Hill, and about a quarter mile from I-40, which forms the county line. Besides the bookstore, New Hope Commons contains major national retailing chains, including Best Buy, Dick's Sporting Goods, Linens 'n Things, Marshall's, Michael's Arts and Crafts, OfficeMax, Old Navy, and Wal-Mart, in addition to smaller, regional chains such as the Chesapeake Bagel Bakery.

The history of the Barnes & Noble superstore at New Hope Commons is directly related to the rise of the so-called New South or Sunbelt, and the uneasy relations between the city of Durham and the town of Chapel Hill.[90] Its history is rooted even more deeply in Durham's own need to reinvent itself in the wake of two wars, each of which helped transform the municipality's patterns of racial and economic organization.

The story begins in the years leading up to and immediately following the Civil War. Although agriculture had been the chief source of Durham's economic well-being since the first European settlers arrived in the area in the 1740s, it hardly fit the stereotype many now associate with the antebellum South. The small farms that dotted Durham were a far cry from Tara and the other colossal plantations epitomized in Margaret Mitchell's 1936 novel *Gone With the Wind*. Slavery certainly wasn't unknown in Durham. The 1860 census indicated more than five thousand slaves living in Orange County, North Carolina, of which Durham, then a small village, was a part.[91] Farming in and around the village tended to be more subsistence oriented, and only the wealthiest of farmers were slave owners. Even then, most could be counted on to own one or maybe two slaves. The scale and organization of slavery in Durham thus paled in comparison to other parts of the South, where a single aristocratic plantation owner might profit from the bondage of hundreds upon hundreds of men and women cultivating his vast acreage.[92] Nevertheless, its existence still produced deep rifts whose impact would be felt in and beyond the Durham community for generations to come.

The economy and character of Durham were already beginning to change in the decade leading up to the Civil War. At the heart of the transformation was the cash crop of tobacco, whose popularity enjoyed a remarkable upswing following the introduction of cigarettes in the mid-nineteenth century.[93] Between 1850 and 1860 tobacco production increased fivefold in Orange County, and after the war its long, steady rise continued. This was due in no small measure to Union soldiers having made a habit of plundering Southern tobacco stores during the fighting, which in turn led many soldiers to develop another type of habit—smoking—that their former adversaries were only too happy to encourage.[94] By 1870 large tobacco-processing facilities such as those owned by Washington Duke and Julian Carr had grown up in the vicinity of Durham's railroad stop, which had been built in the 1850s. Their output was staggering even by today's standards. Duke's facilities produced the better part of a billion cigarettes in 1889 alone, a result of its having replaced its contingent of hand rollers with machinery earlier in the decade.[95] All told, the new infrastructure was instrumental in helping to transform Durham tobacco from a locally peddled product into a national—and even international—export.

Thus, within a matter of two or three decades Durham had entered the burgeoning industrial economy of the United States. This was due in no small measure to former slaves, many of whom had found employment in the community's thriving tobacco plants. Within this two-tiered system, however, principles of white supremacy inherited from the slave system persisted and prevailed. Black men, women, and children were generally relegated to the most labor-intensive tasks, such as hauling, stemming, pressing, and heating tobacco leaf. Their white counterparts were more likely to serve in supervisory positions, or in less physically demanding jobs, such as cigarette rolling and tending to machinery.[96] Those who didn't find employment in tobacco processing might find work in Durham's textile, hosiery, milling, or bag-making industries, which had prospered since the latter half of the nineteenth century.

The entrenched nature of the color line kept Durham's emerging working class from forging cross-race solidarity. According to Dolores E. Janiewski, "Although blacks and whites were being forced into similar economic classes by the rapid changes, few individuals saw themselves as linked by such a novel and abstract notion as class. Distinctions of sex and color were much more obvious and time-honored."[97] This was also true, by and large, higher up in the economic hierarchy. In the early twentieth century black entrepreneurs such as John Merrick, Richard Fitzgerald, and William G. Pearson established key insurance and financial institutions in Durham, whose purpose was to provide a safety net for the town's black working class. With the founding of the North Carolina Mutual and Provident Association (1899), Mechanics and Farmers Bank (1907), and other black-owned businesses, Durham came to be seen by some as the "capital of the black middle class."[98] Yet the economic self-determination these entrepreneurs enjoyed didn't translate into a comparable degree of social self-determination. Durham's white elite counted on them to keep the town's black working class in line. According to Jean Bradley Anderson, "this small group of men understood that their own liberty and success were hostage to the whites."[99]

Despite—or perhaps because of—these enduring racial inequalities, Durham's industries thrived for the better part of a century. However, the city experienced a dramatic reversal of fortune in the decades following the Second World War when the product that had long sustained its economic vitality—tobacco—came under attack. Though tobacco use had long been linked to negative health effects, the first definitive studies of its impact on the human body only appeared in the 1950s. They culminated in Surgeon General Luther L. Terry's infamous report of 1964, which connected cigarette smoking to increased incidence of lung cancer and other life-threatening ailments. This led to mandatory cigarette labeling in the United States, which boldly declared the product to be "hazardous to your health," and eventually helped bring an end to cigarette advertising on American television in 1971. Durham's industrial infrastructure more or less deteriorated in lockstep with tobacco's declining public image, as evidenced by the city's loss of nearly 20 percent of its manufacturing jobs between 1947 and 1959. Pressure from without only compounded pressure from within. As the twentieth century wore on, most of Durham's textile mills closed down, a result of strong unions at home competing with cheaper foreign labor abroad. The city bottomed out economically in the late 1980s and early 1990s, after three of its largest remaining industrial employers—American Tobacco, Liggett and Myers, and Erwin Mills—relocated in the same gray year of 1986, leaving hundreds of Durham's citizens jobless.[100]

The collapse of Durham's industrial base helped set the stage for the construction of the New Hope Commons shopping center and, by extension, its Barnes & Noble bookstore. Together with the state capital of Raleigh, the city of Durham and town of Chapel Hill comprise central North Carolina's Triangle area. Situated almost equidistant between the three municipalities is Research Triangle Park (RTP), the largest office park in the nation, which opened in 1958. Like Atlanta, Georgia, and other areas in the southeastern United States, the Triangle area as a whole has undergone intensive growth since the early 1990s. An economic slowdown in the Northeast in the late 1980s helped fuel a population boom in North Carolina, as many high-tech, biomedical, and telecommunications firms relocated to RTP and the surrounding area. In the mid-1990s the combined population of Durham and Chapel Hill grew at a rate of 5 percent, or roughly five times the national average. In 2000 the Triangle area was home to about 1.2 million inhabitants, roughly 10 percent of whom lived within a five-mile radius of the New Hope Commons Barnes & Noble superstore.[101] Real and perceived growth in the Triangle area have attracted national developers, who traditionally had little interest in the South but now see it as an "underserved retail market."[102]

Chapel Hill is perhaps best known as the home of the University of North Carolina, the flagship educational institution of the state's public university system. Bolstered by a relatively high median family income and somewhat idiosyncratic zoning regulations,[103] Chapel Hill can afford to maintain a certain "image-conscious[ness]."[104] In the face of the recent population explosion and accompanying building boom, it's tried to preserve a "small town character" by resisting an influx of national chains.[105] Durham, on the other hand, seems to be caught between two competing senses of self. Though renowned for Duke, its elite private university (named for tobacco titan James B. Duke, who endowed it in 1924), Durham also maintains a solid community/technical college infrastructure, which caters to a mostly adult working-class population. Despite a palpable professional presence, the city has a considerably lower median family income than its neighbor Chapel Hill.[106] Durham may tout itself as an internationally recognized "City of Medicine" by capitalizing on the presence of the Duke University Medical Center and other health-care facilities. However, it can't quite seem to shed its identity as a working-class tobacco town—the minor league "Bull City," where many struggle just to make ends meet.

The Barnes & Noble superstore at New Hope Commons is technically located in Durham, but it's actually situated closer to Chapel Hill's town center than it is to Durham's downtown. The location has been a bone of contention for the two municipalities, given their contrasting attitudes toward development. Chapel Hill's town council urged the city of Durham to block the mall's construction at the proposal stage, citing concerns over its potential environmental impact on nearby New Hope Creek (in Durham) and worries about an upsurge in traffic along U.S. 15–501, where the number of vehicles already exceeded the aging highway's design specifications. So adamant was the resistance that Ken Broun, the former mayor of Chapel Hill, personally attended a 1993 demonstration at the proposed New Hope Commons site in the hope that direct action might sway Durham city officials.[107] But many citizens of Durham and a good portion of the city council saw things differently. For them New Hope Commons offered an opportunity to expand the city's tax base and, more important, a chance to draw wealthier Chapel Hill residents into Durham to shop. It also gave the city a chance to redress some of its persistent racial inequities. The city council pinned approval of New Hope Commons on commitments by Homart, the center's Chicago-based developer, to meet specific minority hiring goals with respect to the construction and staffing of the new mall, in addition to agreeing to use minority-owned banks to finance the project.[108] In 1994 the city council approved construction of the New Hope Commons shopping center by a vote of eight to five.

This wasn't a new strategy for the city. Durham had been building shopping malls along its outlying areas since the 1950s, often annexing large tracts of land in the process. This may have helped augment its tax revenue and thereby mitigate some of the immediate economic impact of deindustrialization, but the creeping sprawl, aided and abetted by new highway construction, only worsened the situation in downtown Durham. Not only was industry leaving, but now local businesses were relocating to the malls popping up on the city's outskirts. For a time Durham's once bustling downtown became an eerie landscape consisting of empty buildings, vacant lots, and hardly any people.[109] The concentration of businesses in the new malls also created unique political opportunities for Durham's African American population. For instance, in 1968–69 it staged a successful boycott of Durham's Northgate Mall as well as other area businesses. The protest shined a light on the merchants' discriminatory hiring practices and helped pressure city officials into addressing the uneven racial impact of Durham's housing and redevelopment policies.[110] While the Barnes & Noble at New Hope Commons may outwardly appear to be just another corporate bookstore located in just another shopping center, it reflects Durham's history of leveraging mass cultural institutions for the sake of improving social justice.

The Barnes & Noble store's relationship to area bookstores is also more complicated than simply causing all those nearby to close. Before the superstore arrived in the autumn of 1995, the Durham–Chapel Hill area already had a vibrant bookselling community in place. Prominent independent booksellers included The Regulator in Durham and the Intimate Bookshop in Chapel Hill, in addition to those affiliated with UNC (the Bull's Head Bookstore) and Duke University (the Gothic Bookstore). Barnes & Noble's relationship to these and other area booksellers has been uneven. The Regulator opened in 1976 and underwent a major renovation in 1998, three years after Barnes & Noble opened its doors at New Hope Commons. Thanks to its customers, it doubled its square footage and added a coffee shop/lounge area. Tom Campbell, a co-owner of The Regulator, suggested that its distance from Barnes & Noble has helped to insulate it somewhat from competition with the superstore. The store also happens to be located near Duke University's East Campus and within walking distance of both

Watts-Hillandale and Trinity Park, which the *Raleigh News & Observer* describes as two of Durham's most "well-read" neighborhoods.[111] The Regulator has since become a member of IndieBound (formerly Booksense), a consortium of independent book dealers who engage in online bookselling.

By contrast, the Intimate Bookshop fared poorly. Ab Abernathy opened the store in 1931 above Sutton's, a pharmacy/luncheonette that still operates on Franklin Street, Chapel Hill's main drag. Wallace Kuralt, brother of the late Charles Kuralt (former host of CBS's *On the Road* TV series), began working in the store as an undergraduate at the University of North Carolina. Following a stint in the military, in the mid-1960s he purchased it from then owners Paul and Bunny Smith. By the early 1990s the Intimate Bookshop had expanded to become a formidable regional bookselling chain in its own right, with nine branches in North Carolina and another four throughout the Southeast, stretching from Georgia to Washington, D.C.[112] However, mounting debt forced Kuralt to close all but one of its locations, including, in August 1998, its flagship Franklin Street store. On March 31, 1999, the Intimate Bookshop closed its only remaining store in Chapel Hill's Eastgate Shopping Center, which was located less than five miles from New Hope Commons.

There are conflicting explanations for the Intimate Bookshop's demise. In 1998 Kuralt filed a thirty-eight-million-dollar federal lawsuit against Barnes & Noble, Inc., and Borders Group, alleging that both companies had brokered secret deals with book publishers and distributors that unfairly undercut the competition. In September 2003 U.S. District Court judge William H. Pauley III issued a summary judgment in favor of the defendants and dismissed Kuralt's complaint based on insufficient evidence, writing: "Intimate has provided no evidence, in any form, that defendants' alleged violation of the [Clayton Anti-Trust] Act, as opposed to other intervening market factors, was a material cause of its lost sales and profits. In fact, Wallace Kuralt . . . acknowledged at his deposition that some of Intimate's business loss may be attributable to factors other than discriminatory activity." These included: competition with bookstores like Books-A-Million and with other retail outlets that sell books, such as Wal-Mart and Home Depot, none of whom Kuralt had named in the lawsuit; questionable business decisions, including a too rapid expansion of the chain in the late 1980s and early 1990s; and a September 1992 arson fire that destroyed the store's main branch in downtown Chapel Hill (it reopened a year later). The judge, however, added that the "Court suspects that another plaintiff may be able to bring causally related evidence supporting a damages claim against the defendants."[113]

Sadly, less than three months after the court had handed down its decision Kuralt died from complications due to skin cancer.

This brief history is intended to show some of the ways in which so-called big-box bookstores emerge within, respond to, and partially transform the specific local and regional contexts—the senses of place—of which they are a part. It would be easy to read Barnes & Noble's opening at New Hope Commons as symptomatic of the "malling" of America and thus of the growing dominance of national chains. At some level it probably is. Yet the store's presence there also needs to be recognized as an important engine of economic development for the city of Durham and, more specifically, as a strategy for redistributing the area's wealth. It is but one facet of a much larger struggle to redress socioeconomic and racial disparities, whose origins extend back to well before the Civil War. Efforts to resist the building of the shopping center were equally complex. Protesters certainly responded to real concerns—especially environmental ones—about the mall's location and construction. By the same token, the desire to resist the spread of national chains in the area, particularly among some Chapel Hill residents, could also be construed as an indirect way of preserving the area's existing distribution of wealth and racial privilege.[114] This isn't to say that building more malls is the correct path to development, nor the best way to combat economic and racial inequality. The protests, however, do raise two interrelated questions: Why do certain communities have the privilege of *not* opening big-box bookstores? Under what historical conditions do communities choose to accept or reject those stores?

History's Folds

Popular institutions don't arrive out of nowhere to transform local communities. For example, superstores are not the only cause of independent bookstores being forced to close, though that may be one indirect consequence among many of their opening in specific communities. Rather, it's more accurate to say that they're folded into the intricately woven historical fabric of specific regions and locales—often before they even open for business. As such, their effects tend to be more complicated and broad-ranging than conventional wisdom suggests. Superstores may be bound up with the repetitive routines that structure everyday life, yet they also offer the possibility of repeating everyday life differently.

Corporate big-box bookstores also clearly transcend the local. In this sense they're folded a second time into an even denser, more expansive historical fabric. As was mentioned earlier, throughout the last century books have been instrumental in furthering the growth of mass-produced culture in the United States. They were and continue to be important social artifacts through which groups of people—especially a burgeoning middle class—have accrued educational and cultural capital and, in the process, have come to enjoy some positive measure of social mobility. Getting those books into the hands of increasingly large numbers of people, however, has required the conception and implementation of an appropriately sized apparatus for selling them. The large-scale educational booksellers of the second and third quarters of the twentieth century—and the retail book superstores that followed in their wake—clearly helped meet that need. The success of corporate big-box bookstores isn't reducible to profit-obsessed corporations figuring out how to sell massive quantities of dreck to unwitting consumers. These stores also are part and parcel of a larger historical project to democratize American education and culture—despite how imperfectly and inconsistently that process has worked itself out and the fact that this project may now be coming apart at the seams.

Large-scale retail bookselling chains are part of the struggle to determine the purpose, value, and various ways of operating in relationship to mass culture. Their history ought to be explored, not rejected or explained away by repeating clichés like "manipulation," "homogenization," and "debasement"—though, indeed, sometimes people do get fooled and our choices are narrowed. What makes mass culture in general and big-box bookstores in particular so attractive and popular? One answer may be infrastructural, as in the case of Barnes & Noble at New Hope Commons. Despite offhand claims about the corporate big-box bookstore chains trading only in "dumbest titles in fantastic quantities," best sellers reportedly account for only about 3 percent of Barnes & Noble's total sales—which is consistent with the rest of the retail book trade.[115] This figure suggests that large-scale corporate retail booksellers—or Barnes & Noble, at any rate—aren't dumbing down the world of letters to attract ever greater numbers of book buyers. Rather, they are developing effective strategies for communicating the relevance of, and generating interest in, books to both the actual and potential book buying public. They're not selling different books, inasmuch as they're selling a different image of bookselling.

Ultimately, these destination bookstores throw into relief the extent to which the book industry has tended to undersell itself and its wares. Many publishes and booksellers have persisted in the belief that books ought to sell primarily on the basis of the qualities particular to individual titles, and that relying on exogenous factors to move them somehow diminishes the worth of these goods. Yet the rapid growth and extraordinary success of superstores reveal just how much built environments and other factors related yet extrinsic to specific titles can make or break the selling of books and bookselling, a theme I explore at greater length in the next chapter.

3 Bringing Bookland Online

THE HEADLINE FOR the origin of online bookselling probably would read something like this: "Restless High-Tech Genius Starts Bookselling Revolution from Garage!" By most accounts, the "genius" is Amazon.com founder, president, and CEO Jeffrey Preston Bezos. Legend has it that Bezos's eureka moment occurred in May 1994, while working as an analyst for D. E. Shaw & Co., a Manhattan-based hedge fund.[1] There he learned that Internet usage was projected to grow by 2,300 percent annually. Delirious with excitement over the prospect of getting in on the ground floor of an impending boom, Bezos promptly quit his job and set out for Washington State, home of software giant Microsoft and other high-tech industry leaders. While his wife, Mackenzie, chauffeured the two across the country, Bezos drafted what would become Amazon.com's business plan on his laptop computer.

The Web site for the "Earth's biggest bookstore" went live in July 1995—ironically from the cramped quarters of Bezos's garage in the Seattle suburbs. A meager four years later *Time* magazine named the upstart CEO its person of the year. Bezos's selection was deeply symbolic, marking what many at the time believed to be a series of epochal passages: from the long twentieth century to a new millennium; from the bulky old bricks-and-mortar economy to an ultra-slick "dot-economy"; and (for some) from the possibility of a more equitable society to the total victory of corporate capitalism. As *Time* half-jokingly noted in its profile: "It's like the Cultural Revolution meets [Wal-Mart founder] Sam Walton. It's dotcommunism!"[2]

The washout in the dot-economy and the cynicism that now pervades many of those left jobless, underemployed, and/or financially compromised has tempered some of this triumphalism. Nevertheless, a kind of common sense persists in stories about the history and politics of online bookselling. The *Time* magazine article, like numerous other headline histories published before and after—especially in the popular, business, and trade press—implies that Jeff Bezos and his brilliant ideas serve as the most sensible starting point for the story.[3]

Without denying that he's a consequential figure, I want to craft an alternative fable about the origins and effects of online bookselling. Critical-technology scholars have rightly questioned the propensity among professional and lay historians to champion "great men" and "big ideas." I won't belabor their concerns here except to say that such a narrow focus tends to obscure the contingent array of social, economic, and material forces leading to the emergence (rather than the invention) of particular technical devices. More to the point, in the specific case of Amazon.com, privileging the work of only one public figure deflects attention from the work of those laboring behind the scenes of a modern, connected book business—not to mention the conditions that created the business in the first place.

In the preceding chapters I chronicled the history and politics of books as an everyday commodity in the United States. However, at least one question was never asked, which is directly relevant to the matter at hand: Through whose effort, and by what means, do all those books get to where they need to go? Janice A. Radway once remarked that printed books "do not appear miraculously" in people's hands. "They are, rather, the end product of a much-mediated, highly complex, material and social process."[4] Integral to this process, I feel, is distribution. Developments in this perhaps more arcane aspect of the circuit of culture have paralleled transformations in the more closely scrutinized domains of book production and consumption. These developments include intensive and scrupulous sorting, coding, and inventory-control schemes and their union with computer/database technologies, without which the mass production of printed books, the modern book industry, and large-scale bookselling would have been neither thinkable nor practicable.

Just as Karl Marx once asked readers of *Das Kapital* to take leave of "the noisy sphere" of market exchange, "where everything takes place on the surface and in full view of everyone," and to descend into "the hidden abode of production," we would now benefit from undertaking a similar passage.[5] In the company of cultural intermediaries and other owners of labor power, let us venture into the back office of book distribution, on whose door there hangs the innocuous-looking sign "Staff Only." Once inside we'll see not only how books are disseminated but how their constitution as everyday objects is a function of both the coming online of new technologies and of a growing set of demands on the subjects whose labor sustains book culture.[6] Significantly, stepping across this threshold constitutes an enactment of what Michael Denning calls "a labor theory of culture" intent on "reminding us that the apparent confrontation between cultural commodities and cultural consumers obscures the laborers in the culture industry."[7]

My contention here is that the seemingly contemporary phenomenon of online book*selling* is best appreciated within the broader and more historically dense problematic of book *distribution*. A distributional perspective illuminates how online bookselling encompasses a far greater range of activities, technologies, and communicative processes than many headline-grabbing historians would care to assume. In fact, Amazon.com and other large-scale corporate Internet booksellers emerged as a result of changes in the norms and protocols for inventorying, warehousing, and communicating about books, which both anticipated and resulted from the arrival of large-scale retail bookselling in the latter half of the twentieth century. This chapter thus presents a history sensitive to the depth, character, and range of activities that justifiably could be called, "online bookselling." It does so by continuing to sift through the sedimentary history, specifically by stressing the back-office apparatuses, processes, and labor practices through which books have become everyday commodities.

The first part of this chapter investigates the so-called Cheney Report, a notorious study released in 1932 that blasted the U.S. book industry's lack of coordination. I explore how the Cheney Report perceptively anticipated the growing demand for printed books in the period following the Second World War and stressed the need for more systematic processes for distributing them. The second part looks at indirect outgrowths of the Cheney Report, the International Standard Book Number (ISBN) and machine-readable bar codes, which are two of the most important yet rarely considered technologies through which the book industry coordinates its operations as a whole. I argue that their emergence in the postwar period was integral to speeding book distribution and standardizing communication across the book industry. The chapter ends with a critical analysis of the book distribution apparatuses of Amazon.com and other online retailers. I look at how living labor, the ISBN, and machine-readable bar codes combine in colossal warehouse/distribution facilities—arguably the nerve centers of the book industry's operations—as a way of drawing out some aspects of the labor politics of everyday book culture in the late age of print.

"The Tragedy of the Book Industry"

To say that the book industry of the early 1930s was volatile would be an understatement. In the first chapter I explored some of the repercussions of the October 1929 stock market crash and the desperate, albeit creative, measures publishers and other book industry professionals engaged in to remain solvent. Among these were the campaigns concocted by public relations counsel Edward L. Bernays. He championed the cause of building bookshelves in private homes, lambasted upstart publishers for selling books for a buck, and poked fun at people for passing on books to friends and family. His efforts corresponded to a more general fear among book industry insiders about a looming crisis involving overproduction. Their fear was so palpable that some even recommend the pulping of any unbound books that publishers had on hand, given that prospects for the market drying up seemed both real and imminent.[8] A "spectacular rise" in the practice of remaindering in the first years of the decade only confirmed their fears.[9] The book industry had, in a sense, become a victim of its own success. Its capacity to produce books had grown so rapidly and to such a degree in the early twentieth century that it had lost touch with supply and demand—if it ever had it to begin with.

The book industry's struggle to remain solvent was thus symptomatic not only of the stock market crash and the resulting economic depression but also of a broader crisis brought on by a perhaps too rapid expansion of mass-production processes in and beyond book publishing. According to James R. Beniger, "By far the greatest effect of industrialization . . . was to speed up a society's entire material processing system, thereby precipitating what I call a crisis of control, a period in which innovations in information processing and communication technologies lagged behind those of energy and its application to manufacturing and transportation."[10] It's doubtful whether many in the book industry perceived this crisis of control as such. Most seemed to be preoccupied with the immediate realities of profit margins and bottom lines rather than the more abstract concerns of logistics and communications. Although they knew something was wrong, publishers and booksellers seemed content to point fingers at one another.[11]

Desperate for answers, in August 1930 the National Association of Book Publishers (NABP) commissioned the first industry-wide study to investigate "the economic structure of the industry and to suggest practical means for improving it."[12] NABP president Edward S. Mills tapped Orion Howard (O. H.) Cheney, a retired New York City banker, to direct the landmark project (fig. 6). Cheney was a practical and pedantic man whose sideline career as a consultant to some of the leading industries of his day (e.g., dry goods, furniture, groceries, steel, wholesaling) suited him only too well.

In some respects Cheney was a paradoxical figure. His actions and attitudes were consistent with those of his peers, yet he was slightly out of

FIGURE 6 Orion Howard (O. H.) Cheney, author of the *Economic Survey of the Book Industry, 1930–1931.*

SOURCE: *PHI GAMMA DELTA MAGAZINE*, 37, NO. 1 (OCTOBER 1914): 8.

step with them in important ways. Like Bernays, he belonged to the upper echelons of the professional managerial class, the budding group of knowledge workers implicitly charged with the task of harmonizing capitalist production and consumption.[13] Unlike Bernays, however, Cheney was not a "captain of consciousness" per se.[14] Both men were seemingly infused with the same combination of leadership and optimism—a pragmatic commitment to "making it work"—and both carried out their labors principally behind the scenes of commercial exchange. Whereas advertisers and press agents mainly engaged in ideological work—swaying the masses, to put it crudely—Cheney's concerns lay elsewhere. He seemed to intuit that all this ideological effort was futile unless the concrete conditions for distributing consumer goods were as efficient and reliable as those sustaining mass industrial output.

Cheney first articulated these thoughts publicly in a 1926 essay for *Nation's Business* entitled "The New Competition." He dwelled on how current conditions of overproduction resulted in new levels of "distributive pressure," which, he argued, the economic infrastructure of the United States was ill equipped to handle.[15] Advertising, discounts, and clever public relations schemes might mitigate the crisis, but they wouldn't fix it once and for all. For industry to thrive without significantly scaling back output a broad-ranging effort was required to modernize its sluggish distributional apparatus. Cheney felt that the scale and scope of such a fundamental overhaul would require business competitors to work together as partners for the sake of mutual advantage in the marketplace. "Those of us who are thinking in terms of yesterday's competition are asleep," Cheney stated bluntly.[16]

As rousing as Cheney's thesis may have been, it lacked specifics regarding how to improve the country's capacity to distribute massive quantities of consumer goods. One particularly frustrated reader of the essay complained that Cheney "offers no solution of existing conditions, no remedy for existing abuses, no hope for future evolution and development".[17] Never one to shrink from the chance to offer advice, Cheney quickly set to work concretizing his vision. He did so twice, first in an October 1927 piece for *Nation's Business* called "The Answer to the New Competition"[18] and later in an April 1929 *New York Times* interview: "The secret of the present high degree of efficiency of American production is not size but the use of modern methods of control and management. In them is the only hope of meeting competition and putting distribution on the same basis as production."[19]

Though provocative, Cheney's insights went against the grain of the prevailing wisdom. To be sure, his catchphrase "the new competition" enjoyed a healthy uptake in both the trade and mainstream press,[20] so much so that *Nation's Business* even suggested that Cheney's piece was "perhaps the most widely discussed business article of the last few years."[21] Nevertheless, few industry leaders seemed willing to deliver on the sweeping infrastructural and logistical changes Cheney was calling for. Among those responding publicly to Cheney's writings, most embraced the notion of a new competitive environment. Many even conceded that their industries faced challenges with respect to distributing consumer goods on a national scale. For the most part, though, they held fast to the publicity industry's not disinterested line, which touted more advertising and better marketing as the keys to squaring commodity production and consumption.[22] The minutiae of modern accounting and the tedium of inventory control couldn't compete with more captivating concerns, like the mass psychology of commodity consumption—at least for a time.

The fallout from the October 1929 stock market crash left most industries scrambling for explanations and direction. Doubtless it had also negatively impacted Cheney, at least in his capacity as a banker. He blamed the crash on his colleagues' having "lost touch with the real economic needs of the people."[23] For Cheney the consultant, however, the crash proved to be something of a windfall. Desperate economic times meant that industry leaders could no longer afford to let any advice go unheard, which may partially explain why the book industry came knocking at his door late the following summer. A punchy and well-timed contribution to *Publishers Weekly* in June 1930 undoubtedly helped. In that piece he criticized the book industry's plans for stimulating demand in the face of dismal economic conditions. He argued that its main strategy of price-cutting would need to be counterbalanced not only by a significantly higher sales volume but, more important, by large-scale infrastructural changes and greater attention to "the minor art of economics" in the book industry as a whole.[24] The NABP was clearly intrigued and selected Cheney to administer the book industry study because of his "special interest in publishing facts and figures."[25]

After fifteen months of exhaustive research on Cheney's part—and a comparable degree of nervous anticipation on the part of the NABP—the 150,000-word *Economic Survey of the Book Industry, 1930–1931* (Cheney Report) was published in early January 1932. The eminent sociologist Robert Lynd assayed it in the *Saturday Review of Literature*, concluding that "it blows the lid off the book industry."[26] Indeed, the report was incisive and unrelenting in its criticisms of every aspect of the book industry and beyond. Cheney blasted publishers and booksellers for relying on intuition to guide important business, editorial, and purchasing decisions rather than operating on a scientifically sound, statistically driven "fact basis."[27] He disparaged editors and publishers for their lack of creativity in developing the talents of first-time authors[28] and scolded them for "murdering" potentially successful titles by releasing them into a field already so overcrowded that they simply "cannibalized" one another.[29] Cheney was troubled by the lack of uniformity in the size and materials of printed books, which, he believed, drove up manufacturing costs unnecessarily.[30] He chided advertisers and book critics for generating insufficient interest in books and consequently for failing to help readers make informed decisions about which to buy.[31] He condemned librarians for overstocking popular fiction and (like the booksellers) for making practically no effort at systematically studying the interests and reading habits of their clientele.[32] Cheney even lambasted "uninspiring teachers" for their "unsound teaching methods," which, he believed, resulted in their failure to stimulate adequate interest in reading among students ranging from preschool to college.[33]

As important as publishing houses, bookstores, factories, libraries, schools, and institutions of book marketing and criticism were to Cheney, he saw book distribution as the linchpin holding the entire book industry together. Given the tenor of the report, it should come as no surprise that he reserved his most damning criticism for that particular segment of the industry: "At this point . . . the publisher has books; at that point is the book buyer. Between these two points is *the tragedy of the book industry*. Between these two points are so many gaps, so many confusions, so much utter ignorance of what is being done that unless these gaps are filled and unless every branch of the industry learns to know exactly what it is doing, the industry, as it is today, is threatened with destruction."[34] In other words, miscommunication, conflicting information, and a lack of coordination among authors, agents, publishers, editors, advertisers, critics, librarians, booksellers, and readers coalesced at the point of book distribution. There, Cheney reasoned, what may have started out as relatively insignificant discrepancies, missteps, or errors was amplified, whereupon inefficiency reverberated back out into the system.

Cheney's prescriptions for the book industry were as pointed and broad-ranging as his criticisms. Among his many recommendations were the following: he called on the NABP and other organizations involved in books to work directly with educators to promote book reading among students; he implored book publishers to market their titles more strategically and, failing this, called upon booksellers to refuse to stock them; he proposed that more bookstores be opened in the United States; and he pleaded for increased standardization in the sizes of books and the materials used in their manufacture.[35] Above all, Cheney insisted that the book industry be more tightly and systematically organized, particularly at the point where the whole operation came together, namely, distribution. "The time is long past," he wrote, "for demands and vague discussions of 'cooperation between publishers and booksellers'—what is urgently needed is *absolute coordination and integration*."[36] He thus urged all parties of the book industry to engage in intensive and ongoing data collection with respect to sales and readers' interests, which, he believed, would eliminate the guesswork that had earlier guided virtually all aspects of decision making in the book industry.[37] He also called upon the industry to implement standardized communication systems. In fact, Cheney may have been the first to advocate a machine-based book-coding system, which, he believed, would help publishers better manage their inventories and permit all segments of the book industry to coordinate their activities and interactions.[38]

Despite Cheney's claim to have produced the report "in a spirit of objective sympathy,"[39] his pedantry, harsh criticism, and acerbic tone seem to have gotten the better of him. The document generated what's best described as a mixed yet largely defensive response from book industry insiders. "The first impulse of most publishers has been to welcome the report with one hand and to resent it with the other," wrote the *New York Times*.[40] Elsewhere the article described industry reaction as "caustic," and quoted an anonymous "leading book publisher" as saying, "I could have had a better report prepared in a week in my office without the cost of a penny."[41] Even a fairly complimentary piece published in the *Retail Bookseller* described some of Cheney's prescriptions as "bad tasting."[42] *Publishers Weekly* likewise marveled at Cheney's conception of "frictionless" book flow while simultaneously bristling at his sarcasm.[43] He had, to put it mildly, upset an already disquieted audience.

Cheney's survey didn't result in a collective "aha," much less an immediate, industry-wide transformation. Instead there was even more self-study and entrenchment. In February 1932 the NABP appointed a special blue-ribbon task force that included the publisher W. W. Norton and other industry luminaries. The group's report, released in June 1932, almost completely ignored what Cheney had said about logistics and the everyday demands of book distribution. Instead, Norton and his colleagues toed the line for advertising, albeit with the caveat that it needed to be deployed more deliberately, pointedly, and economically. They also urged publishers to produce fewer and better books each year and to work cooperatively to stabilize prices.[44]

Given the book industry's fixation on immediate economic exigencies and on advertising's seemingly unlimited potential to sway consumers, the panel's rather unimaginative conclusion was only to be expected. In fact, six months earlier Robert Lynd had suggested that Cheney's controversial findings might provoke just such a response: "If the Report means anything, it means that the book industry must be *more* business-like and cooperative than any other industry. . . . The Report will have to fight for its life in the trade if these inescapable next steps are not simply to be 'received and filed' by the industry."[45] Indeed, the Cheney Report had fought for its life and lost—at least in the short term. Rather than addressing the problem of overproduction creatively and affirmatively—fighting through rather than recoiling from dismal economic conditions—book industry leaders balked. They were content to maintain the status quo, albeit on a somewhat leaner scale, using already familiar methods.

It's difficult to determine what effect, if any, the Cheney Report may have had on the book industry in the years since it was first published. Most evidence points to its having had only minimal direct influence on the attitudes of industry insiders and on the structure and functioning of the industry as a whole.[46] Historian John Tebbel claims that once the initial controversy had subsided, most book industry leaders returned to business as usual.[47] However, a 1992 *Publishers Weekly* article that appeared on the occasion of the Cheney Report's sixtieth anniversary contended that its long-term effects proved more uneven.[48] What is known is that the Cheney Report was reprinted in 1960 and became a lively topic of conversation when *Publishers Weekly* revisited the document in 1992. It has also been referenced a few times, mostly by book historians.[49] To the best of my knowledge, there's been little effort to explore the report's enduring historical significance.

My contentions as to why are twofold. First, although the Cheney Report may not have instantly transformed the book industry, it seems to have had indirect and gradual—though no less significant—effects. Among the relatively few documents that even mention the report, it's telling that most focus on the controversy it stirred up in 1932 rather than speculate on its afterlife. Certainly the report wasn't a magic bullet, but the fact that it failed to transform the book industry radically in the short term doesn't mean that it was inconsequential in the long term. Second, the Cheney Report's full significance has been underappreciated owing to its untimeliness, as well as to that of its author. According to Tebbel, "These were the observations of a banker and a businessman, attempting to find a way to make the publishing industry conform to the norms and standards of other businesses. As such, it made good sense to like-minded people who read about the report in the newspapers. To those in the industry, much of what the report had to say seemed unrelated to the realities they knew."[50] Universal product coding, statistically based marketing, standardized book production, and the dream of "frictionless" commerce may be completely obvious aspects of the book industry today. However, they were quite farfetched ideas at the time. Beyond that, Cheney's thinking was somewhat out of sync with that of other leaders of the professional managerial class, who staked their reputations on their ability to move the masses to purchase consumer goods rather than to move consumer goods to the masses.

In hindsight, Cheney's outsider status meant that he understood only too well what needed to be done during conditions of overproduction—and this is why the Cheney Report still haunts the book industry. The document appeared amid the growing everydayness of printed books and the corresponding growth of the middle class. Its publication roughly dovetailed with the emergence of large-scale retail bookselling and new processes for commodifying printed books. Over the next fifty years, the gradual increase in both the reading public and the size and number of outlets servicing them would pose a series of challenges that Cheney perceptively anticipated in his report. Among the questions raised in the latter were the following: How can the book industry distribute books efficiently and in sufficient quantities to satisfy the growing demand? By what means can it keep track of all those books as they move through the supply chain and after they arrive at an ever-increasing number of stores? On what basis can the industry monitor customers' preferences and match books to their interests?

Encoding/Decoding—Sort of

Like Cheney, critics both inside and outside the book industry have long complained about its atavistic business practices and lack of coordination. As almost any person in the industry will tell you, there's at least a modicum of truth to these characterizations. Since the early 1970s, however, critics and supporters alike have exaggerated the industry's lack of commercial and organizational savvy. Those who persist in spotlighting the book industry's backwardness or resistance to commercialization overlook the fact that it pioneered the development of highly sophisticated back-office systems, whose aim was to speed distribution and improve inventory tracking and control. Regardless of how some might wish to romanticize books today, they're products. While the book industry might be faulted for the awkward missteps it still occasionally makes with respect to marketing and sales, like the auto parts industry it was among the very first to have agreed on and made use of a universal merchandise-coding system—the International Standard Book Number (ISBN). ISBNs allow each part of the book industry to speak the same language, as it were. In conjunction with the development of computer/database technologies, they've enabled all parts to better coordinate their activities in a manner consistent with Cheney's call for "absolute coordination and integration."

Far from being a recent invention, publishing firms have engaged in the numerical coding of books at least since the third quarter of the nineteenth century. Most of these early coding systems, however, were unique to individual publishers, who used them mainly to facilitate in-house record keeping rather than industry-wide communications. Consequently coding remained haphazard, idiosyncratic, and was only narrowly applied until the third quarter of the twentieth century.[51]

The need for more standardized methods of coding books gained in importance when W. H. Smith & Son, Britain's largest bookselling chain, decided to computerize its new warehouse in 1965.[52] The publisher's management team had determined that, given the exceedingly specific criteria according to which books were—and continue to be—classified (e.g., author, title, edition, publisher, binding, publication date, language, etc.), keeping track of books by hand was too costly, time-consuming, and prone to error. Even a small mistake or omission could result in an erroneous order, leading to inefficiency, increased costs, and the possibility of lost sales. Transferring inventory data and oversight to Smith & Son's new computers, however, posed its own set of challenges. The relatively limited processing power (by today's standards) of computers in the 1960s made long lists of identifying characteristics untenable, a shortcoming compounded by the fact that the company's computers could only handle numerical data.[53] It thus needed to devise a concise, numerically based coding system to identify each and every edition that passed through its high-tech warehouse.

The costs and logistics associated with the design and implementation of such a system exceeded Smith & Son's capabilities. The company subsequently contacted the British Publishers Association (BPA) in early 1966 to pitch its idea for a numerically based coding system that would serve the British book industry as a whole. Smith & Son's representatives argued that assigning a unique, standardized numerical code to all books published in

Britain would facilitate better communication industry wide. If the BPA assumed leadership of the project, moreover, no single company would be forced to shoulder all the risks and up-front costs associated with such a cutting-edge distribution system. The BPA concurred and approached F. Gordon Foster, a professor at the London School of Economics, who conducted a pilot study. In May 1966 Professor Foster concluded that "there is a clear need for the introduction of standard numbering, and . . . substantial benefits will accrue to all parties therefrom."[54] Within a year sixteen hundred British publishers agreed to the new coding system, dubbed the Standard Book Number (SBN).[55] Thoroughly impressed by its simplicity and effectiveness, the International Standards Organization (ISO) adopted the International Standard Book Number in 1970, which relied on the British SBN scheme in most respects.[56]

Across the Atlantic the implementation of the British SBN generated significant excitement among publishers, wholesalers, booksellers, and librarians. Given the ever-increasing number and volume of printed books in which they trafficked, many in the United States similarly longed for a precise, universally recognized coding system. The Library of Congress Catalog Card Number had served as the industry's informal inventory standard for some time, but it didn't really meet the needs of the book trade as a whole, much less compel adoption among everyone involved. For these reasons, major trade organizations of the U.S. book industry moved to adopt the British SBN in 1967. That September *Publishers Weekly* optimistically predicted the SBN's "widespread acceptance" in all branches of the book trade.[57] However, because its use remained voluntary it took at least a decade—by some estimates as long as fifteen years—before the ISBN achieved truly widespread acceptance in the United States.[58]

It should be emphasized that the ISBN isn't merely a glorified stock number. Rather, it's a carefully conceived, highly significant, and mathematically exact *code* that contains detailed information about the identity of each book. It also contains something like a built-in fail-safe mechanism to guard against the transmission of erroneous information. All ISBNs consisted (until December 31, 2006) of ten digits broken down into three clusters, or identifiers, and a final check digit (e.g., 0-674-21277-0). The first cluster, the group identifier, refers to the language, nation, or region in which a given book is published. Here 0 designates the English language. The second cluster identifies the publisher. In this example 674 refers to Harvard University Press; all books produced under its imprimatur will bear that number. The third cluster, or title identifier, designates not only the book's name but also its edition and binding. Here 21277 refers to the paperbound edition of Pierre Bourdieu's *Distinction*. The final check digit, which is derived from a mathematical formula called modulus 11, guards against inaccurately recorded and/or transposed digits. It's computed by multiplying each of the ISBN's first nine digits by a corresponding weight, as illustrated in the accompanying chart. These products are then totaled. The check digit is the number required to bring this sum to the next whole-number multiple of eleven.

ISBN	0	6	7	4	2	1	2	7	7	
Weight	10	9	8	7	6	5	4	3	2	
Product	0+	54+	56+	28+	12+	5+	8+	21+	14	= 198

Because the sum (198) is divisible by 11, nothing more needs to be added. Thus the check digit is 0. The letter X is used in cases where the check digit works out to be 10.[59] Computers programmed to track ISBNs basically run this algorithm in reverse when verifying an ISBN's validity. It's an elegant and rather ingenious system since it guards not only against inaccurately recorded digits but also against the apparently more common error of transpositions.

In chapter 2 I looked at some of the marketing, display, and pricing techniques by means of which large-scale retail booksellers like Barnes & Noble have rendered mass-produced printed books fungible or commensurable with one another, rather than treating them as inherently distinct cultural goods (a theme I will revisit in the next chapter). The book industry's adoption of the ISBN was a crucial back-office counterpart to these processes. As Janice A. Radway explains, the primary challenge involved in marketing printed books is "how to create an abstraction that would allow the endless repetition of individual instances . . . without particularizing those objects too much."[60] This explanation perfectly describes the logic underlying the book industry's decision to devise and implement the ISBN—except that it had little to do with book marketing. The ISBN is an abstract coding system by means of which the fine distinctions and minute particularities of printed books can be resolved into a general—in this case numerical—set of equivalences that permit publishers, wholesalers, and booksellers to communicate about and coordinate the distribution of large quantities of myriad titles rapidly and reliably "without particularizing those objects too much." Marketing and packaging are among the more publicly apparent processes through which printed books are sorted, classified, and organized—which is to say commodified in the Marxian sense of the term. Those processes would undoubtedly be undercut without an efficient and sophisticated back-office system for managing the distribution of books to the appropriate buying public.

In October 1979 *Publishers Weekly* reported that all books currently in print carried an ISBN for the first time since the system's introduction in the United States: "After years of being simply an aid to efficient book-ordering control, the ISBN is now becoming the essential central data link for automated handling and communication systems in the book indus-try."[61] However, a dozen years into its implementation both the idea and practice of universal book coding continued to meet with resistance, much as they had in Cheney's time. Part of the reason was pragmatic. As efficient a system as the ISBN was in theory, every number still needed to be input manually at one or more points in the supply chain. Though it was a lingua franca, to be sure, it wasn't much of a great leap forward compared to how in-house stock codes had been recorded more than a century earlier.

Thus, in the late 1970s the book industry began looking for alternative ways to tap the ISBN's potential. Just as some campus booksellers in the 1950s had turned to the grocery industry for merchandising techniques, so members of the book trade now turned to the grocery industry for ideas about how to make the ISBN system more serviceable. In the preceding chapter I explored the perhaps unexpected kinship both industries share— unexpected because the book trade often touts itself as a culture indus-try, while grocers tend to present their trade as more basic and utilitarian. These value associations notwithstanding, both deal in large quantities of highly differentiated goods. As such, they often face similar quandaries with respect to inventory, logistics, and the task of coordinating processes across the industry as a whole. The manual inputting of product codes and pricing information was no exception.

In an effort to make inventory control more reliable and to ensure a pleasant experience for customers plodding through the checkout, in the late 1960s the Grocery Manufacturers of America and the Supermarket Institute examined the feasibility of machine-readable bar codes and scan-ning systems. Among the first of these was a system introduced in 1972 by RCA (fig. 7) modeled on an earlier bull's-eye-shaped bar code developed in the late 1940s. The system's impressive record of reliability and perfect accuracy after seven million scans proved compelling enough for the gro-cery industry's Ad Hoc Committee on a Uniform Grocery Product Code to determine that an industry bar-coding standard would indeed be desirable. Still, the bull's-eye system had at least two purported drawbacks: its size

1234567890

FIGURE 7 Model for RCA's bull's-eye
bar code, ca. 1972.

relative to that of the products upon which it would be imprinted was prohibitively large; and its ten-digit encoding scheme was prohibitively small.
Thus, in 1973 the Ad Hoc Committee rejected RCA's bull's-eye bar code.[62]

On March 30, 1973, the group's Symbol Selection Subcommittee
announced that it had chosen IBM's entry—a rectangular symbol dubbed
the Universal Product Code (UPC)—to become the industry standard
after IBM privately agreed to modify its original entry to accommodate an
eleven-digit coding scheme.[63] Within a year a small but growing contingent
of grocers started using the UPC and attendant technology to track sales,
returns, and inventory and to eliminate the repetitive, time-consuming, and
often error-prone work involved in pricing and ringing up merchandise.[64]
Following the grocery industry's lead, in 1978 the U.S. book industry began
exploring the possibility of bar coding as a means to improve distribution.

With equal interest the book industry investigated a second coding
scheme—an optical character-recognition system called OCR-A. Bar coding, though alluring, had two main drawbacks from the book industry's
standpoint. First, because the bars themselves had been designed to be
read principally by machines, they were less friendly to the naked eye.
More important, the book industry's adoption of the eleven-digit UPC
would require it to abandon the ten-digit ISBN and/or to adopt a second
product-numbering scheme in addition to it.[65] Given the ISBN's relatively
slow adoption and the infrastructure that had grown up around it, the
prospect of getting the industry to agree to a different numbering standard seemed off-putting indeed. Besides, having two industry standards
defeated the purpose of having *an* industry standard. Optical character recognition had four advantages: it was both machine- and eye-readable and
thus potentially more user-friendly; the code was more discreet and aesthetically pleasing than glaring black and white bars and would affect book
cover designs only minimally; it would allow the book industry to preserve
not only the ISBN structure but also its significant financial investment in
the technology; and it had already been adopted in the mid-1970s as the

industry standard by the National Retail Merchants Association, which portended further communicability concerning products beyond the book industry.[66]

As it turned out, neither the UPC nor OCR precisely matched the book industry's needs. The fickle OCR readers worked best when presented with black characters set against a smooth, lightly colored, and highly reflective background.[67] Since the book industry refused to standardize the colors, shapes, sizes, and materials it used in book design and manufacturing as an accommodation to OCR-A, the system was virtually abandoned. The UPC symbol posed its own set of dilemmas as well. By the time the book industry began exploring UPC bar coding seriously in the late 1970s and early 1980s, it had already invested substantial resources in implementing the ISBN. The two systems weren't exactly incompatible, but they weren't ideally suited to one another either. Whereas the UPC was designed primarily to facilitate information gathering and to speed transactions at the point of sale, the ISBN was initially conceived in terms of easing distribution. Their respective coding structures reflected this fundamental difference.[68]

Undeterred, the International ISBN Agency began exploring the possibility of another machine-readable bar-coding system, this one based on the European Article Number (EAN). Introduced publicly in 1976, the EAN bar-coding scheme closely resembled that of—indeed, was derived from—the UPC yet differed from it in important respects. For one thing, EANs were longer, having been designed primarily to facilitate international commerce. Thus, they could be encoded with a given item's country of origin, price, and the currency in which the price was rendered, whereas the shorter UPCs could not.[69] The EAN bar-coding scheme thereby promised to resolve language and pricing issues that had confounded earlier efforts to translate ISBNs into a machine-readable form.

The International ISBN Agency clearly recognized this potential. In 1980 the agency contacted its counterpart, EAN International, and asked the governing body to devise an ISBN-based bar-coding system for books. Their efforts resulted in what came to be known as the "Bookland EAN" bar-coding standard, which derives its name from what may appear to be an unusual reason. "Since the book industry produces so many products," a trade source explains, "it has been designated as a country unto itself and has been assigned its own EAN prefix. That prefix is 978 and it signifies Bookland, that wonderful, fictitious country where all books come from."[70] As capricious as that may sound, EAN International's decision to designate the book industry a country was calculated and practical, allowing it to preserve the integrity of the ISBN structure within the EAN coding scheme.

Having observed Bookland EAN's successful implementation in Europe, in 1985 the Book Industry Systems Advisory Council endorsed the bar-coding system. Less than a year later it started testing it in the United States.[71] Implementing Bookland EAN presented its own set of challenges, however, given the growing entrenchment of the UPC. Indeed, only in the late 1980s did the U.S. book industry finally arrive at a compromise solution on the intractable matter of machine-readable book codes. All books intended for sale in bookstores would be imprinted exclusively with the Bookland EAN bar code. Mass-market and other books intended for sale at nonbook outlets (e.g., supermarkets, pharmacies, warehouse/price clubs) would be the exception. They would be imprinted with both symbols since in most cases the retailers who sold these books could only decode UPC bar codes, if any (fig. 8).[72]

Nevertheless, even this compromise solution has proven untenable in the long run. Though the International ISBN Agency had designed the ten-digit code for longevity, more books and book-related items bearing ISBNs have been produced in the past two decades than nearly anyone had anticipated. By the turn of the millennium the book industry had to confront the daunting prospect of running out of ISBNs sooner rather than later. After careful study and deliberation, it decided to move to a thirteen-digit code effective January 2007. The new ISBN numbers formally include the 978 Bookland prefix instead of treating it as an add-on, resulting in the ISBN's absorption into the EAN coding scheme. Once all the 978 ISBNs are exhausted, the book industry will begin using the new prefix 979, which should accommodate its item-numbering needs for the foreseeable future. An upsurge in global commerce has led the Uniform Code Council to phase out the UPC in favor of the EAN (renamed the International Article

FIGURE 8 UPC and EAN product codes for a book intended for sale in nonbook outlets, printed on the outside back and inside front covers, respectively.

Number), which means the book industry's coding system is now the same one used for national and global product exchange.[73]

All this encoding, decoding, recording, and cross-referencing is clearly tedious business. It's precisely the kind of tedium that, decades earlier, Cheney had insisted would be integral to the long-term survival of the book industry in a growing capitalist economy. The successful implementation of the ISBN, bar coding, and other measures bear witness to the book trade's unusually high level of integration, this despite both proponents and critics' persistent criticisms of its organizational savvy. Yet these systems don't exist merely to coordinate the ebb and flow of books between publishers, wholesalers, dealers, and others, important as that function may be. They're part and parcel of the process of commodifying books, no more and no less than advertising, book jackets, and other—more manifestly ideological—forms of marketing. The main difference is that for the most part the purpose, significance, and material infrastructure of these distribution systems remain hidden from the public eye.

Without these deceptively understated transformations in the book industry's back office, the emergence of large-scale retail bookselling following the Second World War—especially since the mid-1960s—would have been impractical. Indeed, quantities of books haven't miraculously appeared on bookstore shelves and elsewhere. They've arrived there because the strategies and techniques for distributing and communicating about printed books finally caught up with the extraordinary number of books being produced.

A Political Economy of Commodity Codes

ISBNs and bar codes are technologies of abstraction. Examine the back cover of this book. Before reading the foregoing pages—before cracking the code, as it were—had you ever stopped to consider what those symbols and numbers stood for or the processes they helped to facilitate? It's worth pointing out that product codes involve abstraction in another sense. Bar codes and ISBNs stand in, albeit indirectly, for the people and labor power necessary to deliver this as well as other books to you. Thus, it's time to peer further into the back office of book distribution, to see how the process of connecting the book biz and bringing it online manifests itself in the form of everyday labor practices.

When the Bookland EAN bar-coding system first came online in 1987, an anonymous "top-ten New York publisher" had such high expectations that it would greatly expedite order and returns processing that it reportedly planned to lay off 75 percent of its warehouse staff.[74] Random House anticipated that bar-code scanning would allow the company to reduce "payroll"—clearly a euphemism for laying off employees—by 35 percent in its returns warehouse. Following the initial investment in the technology, Random House further projected that bar-code scanning would generate an annual cost savings in the hundreds of thousands of dollars.[75] Bookland EAN's implementation not only created new efficiency standards in the book industry but also provided incentives to downsize the labor force working behind the scenes in distribution.

The negative effects of bar codes and ISBNs on those working in distribution initially remained isolated to just a handful of book publishers. That began to change in the mid-1980s when the bookselling chain Waldenbooks noticed the bar-code scanning system that Warner Books had just installed in its warehouse facilities. The management team of Waldenbooks was excited to discover that one fifth the number of employees at Warner could process the same quantity of books in a given period of time compared to its own, unwired warehouse staff. This discovery helps to explain the motivation behind the aggressive campaign by Waldenbooks in the late 1980s to bring its warehouses and 1,000-plus retail stores online, as well as to compel the book industry at large to make fuller use of the Bookland EAN coding scheme.[76]

Cheney's untimely dreams concerning distribution were finally coming to fruition. The book industry was: demonstrating an unprecedented degree of commitment to what was hitherto perceived to be the tiresome business of logistics and control; beginning to unite in an ultraefficient lockstep, albeit sometimes begrudgingly; tending toward calculable, profit-intensive bookselling; and investing the resources necessary to sustain operations on a national and even international scale. For many people, myself included, these behind-the-scenes changes resulted in access to books and bookstores whose existence we were previously unaware of (see the previous chapter). That surely came as a benefit, living as many of us do in "scriptocentric" societies. Yet these changes depended on a restructuring of the book industry's labor force and, more specifically, on the downsizing and speeding up of those working in the area of book distribution. The pleasure and opportunity I derived from visiting my local B. Dalton bookstore as a youngster was a function of new techniques the book industry had devised for exploiting people's labor. These techniques would be expanded and intensified with the coming online of large-scale corporate Internet bookselling in the mid-1990s.

I wish to conclude this chapter by returning to the story with which it opened, namely, that of Amazon.com, the current leader in Internet bookselling. In addition to the heroic stories of founder Jeff Bezos circulating in the popular and business press, most people have learned what they know about the company through its sophisticated Web site, a trendsetter in the world of electronic commerce and the company's public face. It not only provides an array of consumer goods but also detailed product information, sales rankings, suggestions for related items of interest, and interactive features, such as customer reviews. All of these elements are intended to keep you browsing at the Web site—and, hopefully, buying—for as long as possible.

As interesting as those features may be, I do not wish to dwell on them at great length. Stopping at the level of the interface obscures what Andrew Ross has called, following Karl Marx, "'the material conditions of production' of cyberspace." Ross writes: "Masses of people work in cyberspace or work to make cyberspace possible. It is not simply a medium for free expression and wealth accumulation; it is a labor-intensive workplace."[77] Just as bar codes and ISBNs obscure a panoply of material and socioeconomic relations, so, too, do Web sites. In the case of electronic commerce, pages and links constantly refer back to themselves and rarely point elsewhere. Yet it's precisely this elsewhere that's so vital not only to the Internet's continued functioning but also to the success of electronic commerce.

Rather than referring to Amazon.com as an online or Internet bookseller, perhaps it would be more apt to call it a large-scale, direct-to-customer warehouse bookseller whose interface happens to be the World Wide Web. That's admittedly a mouthful, but the cumbersome phrasing is necessary in order to place the company's warehouses or order-fulfillment facilities center stage, where they belong. Inside these structures Amazon.com has deployed the ISBN and Bookland EAN coding schemes (along with other technologies) in the service of distributing large quantities of printed books to millions of customers. Although in its 2004 annual report to shareholders the company claimed that "we consider our employee relations to be good,"[78] what's clear is that getting books and other products out to such a vast client base quickly and efficiently demands highly intensive—and intensifying—work environments.

After generating a list of some twenty possible retail goods that he determined could be marketed easily on the Internet, Jeff Bezos decided to begin with printed books. Despite the ethos of bookishness the company subsequently cultivated through stylized magnets, coffee cups, bookmarks, and other paraphernalia touting the wonder of books and reading, Bezos's decision to start an online bookstore was largely driven by a pragmatic appraisal of the book industry's level of standardization. Books, he reasoned, were more "meticulously organized" than almost any other type of consumer good owing to the book industry's decision to adopt the ISBN twenty-five years earlier.[79] That the book industry already had taken the unusual step of assiduously inventorying, coding, and maintaining a detailed database of its wares convinced Bezos that books would be relatively easy to integrate with his company's burgeoning distribution and inventory-control systems. Standardized product coding also meant that Amazon.com could more readily establish dependable communications with book publishers and wholesalers, which would be critical to meeting the company's promises of speedy delivery, not to mention its ability to compete with local bookstores.

Given a sizable but still relatively limited startup budget, Amazon.com initially could only afford to lease a small, four-hundred-square-foot warehouse facility when its Web site went live in July 1995.[80] Knowing that the company could stock only a small number of the most popular titles at any given time led Bezos to locate the company's headquarters close to a major book distributor. Its Seattle, Washington, offices and warehouse placed it in reasonably close proximity to Ingram Book Company's colossal regional distribution center in Roseburg, Oregon, which for a time became the company's de facto other warehouse.[81] Because of Amazon.com's limited warehouse space, it could neither maintain a large inventory of books "just in case" nor could it procure books "just in time," given the short but inevitable lag between ordering books from Ingram and shipping them off to customers. Thus, Amazon.com's first eighteen months of bookselling have been described as a kind of compromise period in which it specialized in delivery that was "almost in time."[82]

Freshly infused with venture capital, in November 1996 Amazon.com leased a ninety-three thousand-square-foot warehouse/distribution center in Seattle. The new facility helped move the company closer to a more rapid, just-in-time distribution structure,[83] although its increasingly streamlined operations still remained somewhat "primitive" from the standpoint of production/distribution.[84] Most significantly, it lacked the ability to scan EAN bar codes. That, coupled with its inventory, which consisted of an estimated two hundred thousand volumes, resulted in copious amounts of data entry, with employees painstakingly logging the receipt and shipment of each and every book into the company database by hand. Keeping up must have been a feat, given the frequency with which the company's stock turned over.[85] Further impediments to efficiency included the manual packaging of completed orders and the warehouse's interior layout, which, management later determined, required merchandise pickers to engage in excessive amounts of walking.[86]

Beginning in January 1997, Amazon.com tapped a series of efficiency-minded executives to serve as its vice presidents of operations. The first among these was Fernando Duenas. For many years he had overseen logistics at FedEx, the hyperkinetic "when it absolutely, positively has to be there overnight" parcel delivery service. Duenas insisted that Amazon.com should organize its fulfillment operations more systematically by introducing computer-controlled bar-code scanning systems that would be integrated with additional machinery throughout the warehouse.[87] Duenas was succeeded by Wal-Mart executive Jimmy Wright, who brought sophisticated sorting machines to the warehouses. He, in turn, was replaced by Jeff Wilke, a plant manager for chemical giant Allied Signal, who wedded these systems to surveillance technologies aimed at monitoring—and thus increasing—employee productivity.[88]

In November 1997 Amazon.com opened its second warehouse/distribution center, a two-hundred-thousand-square-foot structure in New Castle, Delaware.[89] Because of its location, size, and bar code–based inventory-processing systems, the new facility enabled the company to speed distribution to customers living in the eastern portion of the United States, expand its on-hand inventory, and handle a substantially higher sales volume than before. The timing couldn't have been better, given how the company expanded its base from 1.5 million customer accounts in 1997 to 6.2 million just a year later.[90] By mid-2000 that figure reportedly reached a staggering 20 million.[91] Between the Delaware facility and the newly enlarged Seattle distribution center, Amazon.com could now stock multiple copies of between two and three hundred thousand different titles—representing roughly a fifth of all titles in print.[92]

The company's decision to begin trading in music, videos, toys, electronics, and other consumer goods starting in 1997 quickly erased whatever gains it might have made in terms of space. Amazon.com consequently added five new warehouse/distribution centers in 1999 alone, all of which were strategically located to service the interior and southern regions of the United States: McDonough, Georgia (800,000 sq. ft.); Campbellsville, Kentucky (770,000 sq. ft.); Grand Forks, North Dakota (130,000 sq. ft.); Coffeyville, Kansas (750,000 sq. ft.); and Fernley, Nevada (332,650 sq. ft.). A sixth facility, in Lexington, Kentucky (600,000 sq. ft.), opened in October 2000.[93] All told, Amazon.com's operations encompassed about 3.6 million square feet of space, or roughly the equivalent of 140 book superstores. Given its extraordinary fixed capital investments, one would be hard pressed to argue that Amazon.com exists solely, or even primarily, on the Internet. Rather, it's very much a bricks-and-mortar business anchored in the material world.

Inside, Amazon.com's warehouse/distribution centers resemble something out of *Modern Times*, Charlie Chaplin's 1936 tragicomic film about the demands of industrial labor, in which workers, overseen by an efficiency-obsessed boss, scurry about the factory and literally get sucked into its imposing machinery. Indeed, Amazon.com's computer-controlled fulfillment facilities are complex, highly organized operations designed to engender and sustain increasingly intensive levels of worker productivity.

The ISBN and Bookland EAN bar codes imprinted on nearly all books are particularly crucial with respect to coordinating and executing all phases of its order-fulfillment operations with the utmost efficiency. Workers at each of Amazon.com's facilities scan the EANs on all printed books upon receipt from suppliers, thus allowing the company to maintain up-to-the-minute inventory records. A second scan upon shelving each volume records its precise bin number/location in the fulfillment center's main computer. Because Amazon.com adheres to a random stow shelving system in these facilities, this scan is absolutely crucial for the computer to keep tabs on the quantity and whereabouts of every item in stock. From the time a book enters one of Amazon.com's warehouses to the time it leaves, its EAN will have been scanned and its ISBN recorded and checked as many as fifteen different times.[94]

Once a shopper places a book order at Amazon.com's Web site, its main computer system determines the appropriate distribution center to which to assign it. Typically it makes the selection on the basis of geographical proximity to the customer and whether or not a particular warehouse has the requested title(s) in stock. Within the next couple of hours, the chosen distribution center's in-house computer breaks down the order into its component items, matching each requested book to the unique address of the bin containing it. The computer subsequently radios the merchandise picker located nearest to each bin, each of whom carries a hand-held scanning gun that receives the transmission. The gun's LCD readout directs the picker to the designated bin number to retrieve the appropriate number of copies of the title. In the case of best sellers, Amazon.com employs a more rapid "pick to light" system. A small red light located on the shelf below each bin is illuminated when the computer receives a request for the item contained therein. Upon retrieving the volume, the picker turns off the light by pressing a small button located nearby.

In either case pickers must once again scan each specific volume's EAN upon removing it from the shelf. The scanning gun then radios this information back to the warehouse's main computer, indicating that the item has been located and that the computer should update its inventory records accordingly. The scan also registers that the book is now in the system, waiting to be joined with whatever remaining items were included in the order. Thereafter pickers distribute their items randomly into plastic tubs on a nearby conveyor belt, which moves along at a precisely calculated 2.9 feet per second.[95] The whole system reportedly is configured to "minimize the number of steps the pickers must take to gather all of the items needed,"[96] thus remedying one of the inefficiencies endemic to its earlier fulfillment operations.

Eventually the tubs containing the books wind their way to a receiving area, at which point they've moved to the induction phase. There, orders are reassembled with the help of a twenty-five-million-dollar sorting machine, which can process up to two thousand discrete orders simultaneously. Employees remove books from the tubs upon their arrival at induction, scan their EANs to confirm their arrival, and feed them onto another conveyor system leading to the sorter. The latter then scans each book's EAN and determines to which of the machine's order chutes to route it; the sorter will then route all remaining items in the order to the same chute. Once the order is complete, a flashing light cues personnel waiting nearby to remove the items and box them up. The packed boxes are subsequently invoiced and sealed by another machine and sent, via conveyor belt, to a loading dock, from which they are shipped.[97]

Together with Amazon.com's complex order-fulfillment apparatus, the ISBN and Bookland EAN coding schemes have helped the company move toward a "spectacularly capital-efficient" just-in-time operation.[98] Any given volume reportedly remains in one of Amazon.com's warehouses for an average of just eighteen days, in contrast to the typical 161 days the same volume would spend on the shelf of a more traditional retail bookstore.[99] This arrangement provides for incredibly fast-paced turnover in its inventory of printed books—as high as 150 times per year in the case of some products. By comparison, most booksellers generally turn theirs over less than four times in a given year.[100] Amazon.com's systems also have enabled the company to minimize the percentage of unsold books it returns to publishers. Estimates vary, but typically this figure fluctuates between 30 and 40 percent industry-wide. Amazon.com, on the other hand, has one of the lowest return rates among all retail booksellers in the United States, purportedly around 4 percent, which the company attributes both to its streamlined warehouse operations and the fact that it acquires many titles (those that say "usually ships in 2–3 days" on its Web site) only after a shopper has ordered them.[101]

Still, there's a potentially more pernicious side to Amazon.com's use of the ISBN and Bookland EAN coding schemes. Not only do they allow the company to coordinate complex operations inside its order-fulfillment centers but they empower management to monitor worker productivity to an astonishing degree. Its implementation of these everyday—often unnoticed—commodity codes has resulted in a workplace increasingly suspicious of and hostile to living labor.[102]

In 2001 Amazon.com "upgraded" employee bar-code scanners with new software, allowing management to track the number of times employees shelved or retrieved items erroneously. (In the case of shelving, the device records an error when a scan of a book's EAN doesn't match that of the bin into which it is placed; in the case of retrieval, it records an error when the item scanned doesn't match up with the item requested.) The new software also enables management to monitor and compare each worker's level of productivity on the basis of the number of scans made during a given period of time. To its credit, the company offers remedial programs to retrain underperforming employees, though repeated errors or a consistently low level of productivity will result in an employee's dismissal.

These bar code–based tracking capabilities have resulted in both a practical and psychological speedup in Amazon.com's warehouses, given the ever-present threat that management *will* know if a worker has slowed down. Indeed, the company boasts that its new monitoring systems have doubled the average productivity of temporary workers,[103] and it seems reasonable to assume that they've also increased that of its permanent staff as well.

Amazon.com's management also predicts that other "incremental improvements" in the coming years will double productivity in its distribution centers.[104] One recent "improvement" is the addition of a "flowmeister," who, despite the cheeky-sounding name, acts as a master overseer, monitoring and maintaining the rhythm of operations within each fulfillment center. For this reason the *New York Times* likened this person to an orchestra conductor.[105] Using a computer linked to the fulfillment center's critical systems—picking, induction, and packaging—the flowmeister measures and compares productivity in each area and anticipates where backlogs are likely to occur. Employees are then reassigned to areas where the tempo has slowed, thus theoretically ensuring that worker productivity never dips below prescribed levels. The result is not only a more intensive but also a denser workday. To use Marx's terminology, the flowmeister concentrates "a greater mass of labour into a given period."[106] In this regard, the image of the flowmeister as conductor could just as easily have been plucked from the pages of *Das Kapital*, or even Jacques Attali's *Noise*, as it could from a mainstream news source such as the *New York Times*. As Attali observes, "The orchestra leader appears as the image of the legitimate and rational organizer of a production whose size necessitates a coordinator. . . . He is thus the representation of economic power, presumed capable of setting in motion, without conflict, harmoniously, the program of history traced by the composer"—or capitalist.[107]

Amazon.com's efforts at systematizing operations have occurred against the backdrop of its having successfully staved off unionization. In November 2000 the Washington Alliance of Technology Workers initiated a campaign to organize the company's four hundred Seattle-based customer-service employees. Three rather serious concerns had prompted the unionizing effort: low wages; poor working conditions (e.g., unreasonable mandatory overtime); and the substantial devaluation of company stock options, resulting in undercompensation. Despite—or perhaps because of—this agitation, Amazon.com closed its Seattle customer-service facility in January 2001. This action coincided with the shutdown of its McDonough, Georgia, distribution center, resulting in the elimination of an additional 450 jobs. Indeed, in early 2001 Amazon.com seemed to be hemorrhaging employees, dismissing a total of 15 percent of its workforce—about 1,300 jobs company-wide—in an intense effort to "streamline" operations and achieve profitability.[108] Though the company has since rebounded, the layoffs surely resulted in an increased pace for those Amazon.com employees trying to keep up at its remaining warehouse and customer-service facilities.

The Remarkable Unremarkable

Hidden in plain sight, product codes have emerged alongside a more familiar cast of characters (e.g., advertising, book clubs, large-scale retail bookstores, paperbacks) to become a vital element in the growth and consolidation of the modern book industry and, more broadly, of everyday book culture in the late age of print. Without these codes, the book industry and book culture would still exist. However, neither would exist as we now know them, and certain actions many people now take for granted, such as ordering books online, might very well become impracticable and perhaps even inconceivable. Indeed, at first glance ISBNs and EAN bar codes may seem innocuous. After all, they're just a bunch of tiny digits and dashes. "Don't pay us much mind," they seem to say. However, as they've been implemented in capitalist production, distribution, exchange, and consumption, these seemingly unremarkable symbols have played a remarkable role in the processes whereby books have been transformed into ubiquitous commodities. They've not only helped Amazon.com and myriad other enterprises in the book trade to better coordinate activities with one another, but they've also helped them to cultivate more rigorous and exploitative work environments—this despite the air of gentility that continues to pervade large swaths of the industry.

As I discussed in the preceding two chapters, the gradual enfranchisement of the American middle class hinged, in part, on the public's purchasing, interacting with, and displaying books and other mass-produced goods. Certainly such a radical shift in the nation's political economy demanded substantial ideological labor to ensure its success. In the specific case of the U.S. book industry, that shift also demanded the development of a highly complex yet streamlined commodity-distribution apparatus capable of keeping pace with a surfeit of printed books. Although it's doubtful whether the book trade has managed to achieve the level of "absolute coordination and integration" that Cheney envisioned in 1932[109]—would he ever have been satisfied?—ISBNs, bar codes, and related back-office systems have gone a substantial way toward achieving that goal. The experiences, practices, technologies, and values that many now associate with online bookselling represent more than fifty years of radical infrastructural changes whose end result, as it were, was Bookland.

Nevertheless, the very same material, social, economic, technological, and communicative processes that both provided for these changes and opened paths to middle class social mobility have resulted in more intensive labor patterns for working people. Keeping track of hundreds of millions of books and getting them into the hands of middle class people quickly, efficiently, and in a profitable manner is hard work. It is through living labor's hard work that the growth of culture sustains itself. Ultimately the history of books, ISBNs, and bar codes reveals that the more hopeful narratives touting culture's democratizing potential must nevertheless be tempered with a deeper appreciation for the ways in which the enfranchisement of the many might result in more rigorous processes for exploiting many more. As Laura J. Miller pointedly states, "Books, as . . . objects being sold, act as a kind of cover for unfavorable labor conditions."[110]

For all his talk about efficiency, profitability, and business-mindedness, even Cheney recognized the importance of compensating workers fairly for the role they played in furthering economic relations. In 1931, in the throes of the Great Depression, he wrote: "As rehabilitation improves conditions and tends to stabilize and increase profits, the personnel of the industry should be properly rewarded for its share of the work."[111] Although book industry leaders initially cringed at Cheney's harsh criticisms and biting tone, today's book industry looks remarkably like the one the aging banker long ago envisaged—with one significant exception. On the matter of redistributing its wealth more equitably, Cheney's advice seems to have fallen on deaf ears.

I've spoken at length in this and the preceding chapter about economics, technology, distribution, and selling as they pertain to the making of everyday book culture. I haven't said much, however, about one of the principal activities for which books are known, namely, reading. The next chapter will attempt to remedy this situation by looking at one of the most iconic—and tumultuous—book-related institutions of the late twentieth and early twenty-first centuries: Oprah's Book Club. Improving distribution might have helped make books more readily available at the level of the everyday, but that hasn't guaranteed their incorporation into people's daily routines. Rather, they've had to learn how to do that as with any skill. In this regard, Oprah's Book Club has proven to be an important source of information about how to connect literature and life.

4 Literature as Life on Oprah's Book Club

"I WANT TO get the whole country reading again."[1] These nine little words represent an enormously ambitious project. Who could have predicted back in 1996 how Oprah Winfrey's announcement would affect people's everyday habits of book consumption? This was, after all, an odd gambit: a TV talk show personality forming a book club rather than, say, the American Library Association or some other respected agency organizing a national literacy campaign. In any case, the ensuing days and weeks offered a glimpse into just how much clout the newly formed Oprah's Book Club might wield. Jacquelyn Mitchard's *Deep End of the Ocean* proceeded to sell more than seven hundred thousand copies and shot to number one on the *New York Times* best-seller list after Winfrey had declared it her inaugural selection. The public's sudden, intense interest in this hitherto well-regarded but unassuming novel stunned the book trade, so much so that the *Washington Post* decided to profile the book club as a page-one story.[2] The piece's significance wasn't lost on Winfrey. She quipped that Oprah's Book Club enjoyed "an even bigger start than Watergate"—a scandal that first broke in this muckraking newspaper's pages—and surely a more favorable one.[3]

The success of *The Deep End of the Ocean* might have surprised some, but it was hardly a fluke. Three picks and a scant four months into the life of the book club and the trade journal *Publishers Weekly* had already coined the phrase "the Oprah effect" to describe the club's apparent knack for creating instant best sellers.[4] Without fail each Oprah's Book Club selection has sold between half a million and a million copies—sometimes more—

beyond those it had sold prior to receiving Winfrey's endorsement.[5] The average time on the *New York Times* best-seller list—four months—further substantiates this consistent pattern of success.[6]

Of course, the book club's success hasn't insulated it from controversy. Its unusually high profile likely has attracted and intensified debates over the cultural value of certain kinds of books and reading practices. Nobel Prize–winning author Toni Morrison, four of whose books grace Winfrey's list, applauded the club for fomenting a long-overdue "upheaval" in the culture of books and reading.[7] Others have disapproved. One particularly frustrated *Newsweek* reader, responding to the magazine's coverage of the book club, wrote: "Come on, people; Oprah isn't a literary critic, or a family therapist, or a priest. She's a talk-show host. Some perspective here, please".[8] Indeed, critics have seemed troubled by the prospect of book industry insiders and consumers valuing the judgments of a popular TV icon over those of seasoned literary professionals.

Despite differences of opinion, the debate attests to the club's having become a significant feature of everyday book culture in the late age of print. At stake here is nothing less than who reads what, where, when, how, why, and with whom—and, just as important, who's empowered to make those decisions. Also at stake, clearly, is the relationship between printed books and television, not to mention a series of normative assumptions underlying each medium's presumed moral worth. Finally, in addition to these considerations is the thorny issue of culture's involvement with commerce, a theme that weaves in and out of the preceding chapters, one whose complexity is here compounded by the political economy of celebrity. These issues are embodied in the two main questions raised in this chapter: Why has Oprah Winfrey's book club been so popular? What have been the end results of its popularity?

All the news reports trumpeting how Winfrey's selections have skyrocketed to the top of best-seller lists—the so-called Oprah effect—shouldn't eclipse the fact that media influence alone cannot account for the success of any mass cultural phenomenon—Oprah's Book Club included. The latter owes its genesis and success to myriad factors, two of which are of primary importance. First, the club has managed to articulate a sophisticated, albeit practicable, vision for books and book reading that's both grounded in and directly confronts everyday life's multitudinous demands, especially those traditionally associated with women. It's worth mentioning, in this regard, that the target audience for *The Oprah Winfrey Show*—women between the ages of eighteen and fifty-four—roughly corresponds to the largest aggregate book-buying public in the United States. Second (and closely related to the first point) is the book club's educative function, not merely regarding the content of books but also their broader uses. I don't mean to attribute a romantic vision of teachers and teaching to Oprah's Book Club. Although Winfrey may be the book club's figurehead, and although her presence and celebrity are difficult to ignore, the club's didacticism exceeds her role as coach, teacher, mentor, leader, role model, counselor, or friend. Consequently, in this chapter I part company with much of the existing literature on Oprah's Book Club, which has tended to measure the club's success or failure based on the normative standard of a collegiate literary education.[9]

In the first section of this chapter I examine claims that Winfrey and the book club have transformed the culture of books and reading in the United States. My point here is that while the book club's success definitely has something to do with Winfrey's personality and opinion leadership, at least as important are its branding strategies and the ways in which it exploits the idiosyncrasies of contemporary TV programming. The next two sections focus directly on book club participants who have appeared on *The Oprah Winfrey Show*.[10] Taken together, they chart the norms, rules, and procedures through which the book club has articulated a unique economy of bibliographic value centered on everyday life. The final section spotlights Winfrey's highly publicized disputes with authors Jonathan Franzen and James Frey, providing occasions to reflect on the politics of the book club's value system.

Oprah's Book Club has undergone several transformations throughout its existence. It began by featuring contemporary works by living authors, a trend that continued from its inception in September 1996 until May 2002. Following a year's hiatus, the club returned in mid-2003 and began featuring so-called classic literary works two to four times a year. Since 2005 the book club has become a more sporadic aspect of *The Oprah Winfrey Show*, often convening once or twice annually. As of this writing, it's again begun featuring more contemporary works by living authors. Rather than focusing on these shifts, I wish to explore why, regardless of which books Winfrey chooses, Oprah's Book Club has maintained its popularity. This has to do with the distinctive way in which it interfaces both practically and meaningfully with the everyday lives of its participants. Although I do not wish to suggest that the book club has created the basis for broad-ranging progressive political action, nonetheless it has interjected circumspection, reflection, and creativity into the everyday lives of at least some of those who have participated.

O®

Love her or loathe her, it is difficult to deny that Oprah Winfrey spans a broad cultural landscape. Ratings estimates vary, but her flagship production, *The Oprah Winfrey Show*, reaches as many as forty-nine million domestic viewers each week during the regular television season, a majority of them women between the ages of eighteen and fifty-four. Worldwide, the show airs in 136 different countries, representing more than two thirds of all countries on earth.[11] As impressive as those figures may be, *The Oprah Winfrey Show* represents just a fraction of Winfrey's involvement in the mass media, popular arts, and education.

Of course, ratings explain little about a celebrity's authority and power. Winfrey possesses ample amounts of both. In 2007 *Forbes* listed her as number 462 among the wealthiest individuals worldwide and number 165 among the richest individuals in the United States, with an estimated net worth of $2.5 billion. She also ranked number 21 on the *Forbes* 2007 list of the world's most powerful women, one notch below U.S. Supreme Court justice Ruth Bader Ginsburg, two above Queen Elizabeth II, and four ahead of Senator Hillary Rodham Clinton. Winfrey topped the magazine's 2007 list of the most powerful celebrities, clocking in ahead of golfer Tiger Woods and pop music provocateur Madonna, who rounded out the top three.[12]

Some have gone so far as to suggest that Winfrey has leveraged her celebrity and substantial media holdings to force a sea change in religion, politics, culture, self-expression, mental health, and other spheres of everyday life. This phenomenon, called "Oprahfication," has occurred since her talk show debuted in national syndication in September 1986. For good or bad, neither personal nor social life has seemed the same since. Oprahfication functions as an umbrella term—often a demeaning one—in popular discourse, encompassing all of the following: a perceived excess of emotionality; the popularization of suffering, public confession, therapy, and self-help; the privileging of image over depth; a lack of intellectualism; and, more generally, the debasement of culture.[13] Criticisms of the book club epitomize these sorts of critiques since its success would appear to mark nothing less than the Oprahfication of literacy within and beyond the United States.[14] Indeed, scholars routinely speak of Winfrey and the book club's "influence" and "impact" on people's everyday attitudes toward books and book reading, as well as on the choices the book trade routinely makes about what it ought to publish.[15]

All these dynamic-sounding words and the accounts in which they appear embody certain assumptions about Winfrey's capacity to effect change in diverse industries and social settings. Granted, she's an astonishingly wealthy media mogul who possesses remarkable authority both inside and outside the culture industry. People clearly respond to her preferences, practices, and opinions; the consistency with which book club selections have topped the best-seller lists attests to this. Nevertheless, we need to be cautious about slipping too easily into an unreconstructed language of cause and effect, one that attributes to Winfrey, Oprah's book club, and/or *The Oprah Winfrey Show* a singular capacity to induce change in people's reading habits—or anything else, for that matter.

Since 1996 the phrase "an Oprah book" has resounded throughout the book industry and across everyday book culture. What function, precisely, does the phrase perform? Like "the Book-of-the-Month Club," "Harlequin Romance," and the "for Dummies" series, "Oprah" is an abstract label under which more or less unique books can be rendered commensurable. Oprah, in short, is a brand that fulfills an important economic and cultural function in the book industry and beyond. Branding permits publishing firms partially to sidestep the time-consuming, costly, and often haphazard work of identifying or creating a unique audience for each and every title in their catalogs. By permitting publishers to target audiences already familiar with particular brand names, the costs of advertising individual titles can be spread across multiple volumes.[16] As Janice A. Radway has explained, in the twentieth century branding emerged as a crucial and, indeed, transformative marketing strategy for the U.S. book industry insofar as it reoriented "the principal activity of [mass market] publishers . . . significantly from that of locating or even creating an audience for an existing manuscript to that of locating or creating a manuscript for an already-constituted reading public."[17]

The success and visibility of Oprah's book club could thus be explained, in part, as a sophisticated implementation of this century-old marketing strategy.[18] Publishers are quick to capitalize on the brand's symbolic and economic power, as witnessed by their custom of reissuing titles immediately after being selected. Usually the reprinted editions feature the club's official logo—the words "Oprah's Book Club" encircled by a graceful letter O—on the volume's spine, cover, or both.

Just as branding has been an integral component of the book club's success, so have the idiosyncrasies of television programming. A key shift, which coincided with the book club's launch in the fall of 1996, was the switch from a single topic to a segmented program format for *The Oprah*

Winfrey Show. The change permitted a more flexible daily program schedule, including the possibility of addressing several topics for as much or as little time as each one seemed to warrant.[19] Indeed, Winfrey and her producers have been unusually adept at "align[ing] their behaviour, their performance, to the nature of the places in which listening and viewing take place."[20] Segmenting, in particular, has helped them grapple with some of the problems they face in a time of proliferating cable and satellite TV channels, competition from other media, and the sheer omnipresence of the TV remote control. Given the fact that changing the channel and finding other programming have become so easy, the challenge of sustaining viewer interest in hour-long programs has grown increasingly difficult.

This can be inferred from an earlier failure. In 1993 Winfrey invited a cohort of her favorite novelists to appear together on *The Oprah Winfrey Show*. The episode "just bombed" in the ratings, she later reported, since viewers were unwilling to watch an hour-long program about books most presumably they hadn't read.[21] The point is obvious, so much so that its significance is easily overlooked: many *Oprah* viewers felt unprepared for this particular show, which led a sizable portion of the audience to tune out for the day. What this suggests is that however savvy Winfrey may be at choosing books, she isn't singularly responsible for their success in her role as a tastemaker. Equally important are the programming and communication strategies whereby Winfrey and her producers prepare viewers at home to commit themselves to watching programs about books. As Paddy Scannell has observed, "Broadcasters *must* organize their affairs by virtue, in the first instance, of the gap between the place of transmission and the place of reception and their consequent inability to control the behaviour of their audiences."[22] To make Oprah's Book Club work, therefore, Winfrey and her producers needed to concoct a recognizable structure and routine whose purpose would be to alleviate the sense of disorientation the proto–book club experiment of 1993 had induced.

Simply put, the book club would need to be more predictable, more everyday. In its first incarnation (1996–2002) Oprah's Book Club met on *The Oprah Winfrey Show* roughly once a month during the regular television season. Though program formats fluctuated from time to time, book club episodes often consisted of six segments: a short montage previewing the episode; a plot summary provided by Winfrey; a videotaped background piece—often shot on location—featuring the author; clips of *Oprah* viewers sharing how they had responded to the selection; a videotaped discussion involving Winfrey, the author, and four or five *Oprah* viewers; and a concluding segment in which Winfrey asked the studio audience to describe their impressions of the book. Show formats have varied since the book club returned to the airwaves in 2003. Earlier in the club's history Winfrey typically announced the next book club selection at the close of that day's telecast. Her doing so certainly engendered "a horizon of expectations, a mood of anticipation, a directedness towards that which is to come,"[23] which is to say a sense of constancy brought on by a recognition that the book club could be counted on to return to *The Oprah Winfrey Show* once a fixed period of time had elapsed. The club has succeeded, in part, because of the way in which it has (until recently) drawn near to the temporality—the periodicity—of everyday life, which proceeds on the basis of scheduled recurrences.

Given the ubiquity of Winfrey's star image, it may be tempting to attribute the success and appeal of Oprah's Book Club directly to her, or perhaps even to a seismic shift she's alleged to have brought about in American culture. While it would be wrong to dismiss Winfrey's influence altogether, the foregoing discussion suggests that the club's popularity ought to be explained, first, by a host of relatively mundane technical and infrastructural changes that preceded or arose alongside Oprah's Book Club. It's also attributable to the club's having been engineered according to a time structure commensurate with the cyclicality of daily life, a programming strategy so utterly assumed that it's easy to forget the degree to which it's a construct. Indeed, the club wouldn't exist as such—perhaps it wouldn't exist at all—were it not for the everydayness of celebrity, branding, TV broadcasting, channel surfing, and a host of other factors. These preconditions provide only part of the story, however. Understanding the "talking life" of Oprah books also helps explain the book club's popularity and its politics, not to mention its willingness to listen closely to the voices of its participants.[24]

"No Dictionary Required"

As popular as the book club may be, it nonetheless worries some commentators who fear its success will tarnish the standards by which books are judged. A 2001 piece by Cynthia Crossen published in the *Wall Street Journal* exemplifies these anxieties. Crossen asserts that "no dictionary is required for most" Oprah's Book Club selections, "nor is an appreciation for ambiguity or abstract ideas. The biggest literacy challenge of some Oprah books is their length."[25] Crossen took Winfrey, the primary spokesperson for the club, to task for failing to challenge readers with the literariness of book club selections or, alternatively, for failing to challenge readers with titles sufficiently literary at all. What Crossen failed to acknowledge, however, is that the success of Oprah's Book Club is built on both Winfrey and the book club's participants intentionally sidestepping discussions of "abstract ideas" and purely aesthetic concerns in favor of articulating a fundamentally different economy of bibliographic value.

The televised book club discussions have admittedly tended to shy away from even the most basic vocabulary of literary criticism (e.g., allusion, imagery, metaphor, symbolism, tone), a trend that continued with the club's return in 2003 and its brief shift to "classic" literary works. Crossen was right in pointing out that page length has been a far more important criterion for making book club selections than, say, a given book's literary qualities. In fact, almost every on-air announcement of new Oprah's Book Club selections has included at least some mention of the book's length. Rather than dismissing a preoccupation with length outright or seeing it as a sign of amateurishness, it might be more constructive to examine why it's played such a crucial role in the book club's selection process.

When Winfrey announced the selection of Barbara Kingsolver's *Poisonwood Bible* in June 2000, just prior to the summer recess of *The Oprah Winfrey Show*, she described it as "a walapalooza of a book." "It's 500 and some pages," Winfrey continued. "Actually, it's—yeah, 546, 546, which is wonderful for the summer, because I didn't want you to, like, just breeze through it and then have to complain to me because you didn't have enough to read." Winfrey then went on to admonish her audience to "take your time with it. Read one of the . . . chapters, come back, let that settle in with yourself, come back and read another chapter."[26] She concluded the day's broadcast by reiterating that *The Poisonwood Bible* was a "great, great, great book for the summer, 546 pages."[27]

Winfrey has framed other selections almost identically. At the beginning of a broadcast in June 1997 she stated: "Today we're announcing a big—I mean B-I-G book."[28] Later, when she revealed the selection, she explained: "I knew back last year when we first started this book club that this was the book that you should be reading for the summer, because it is 740 pages long. Now for a lot of you, that's—that'll be you first time with a book that big—a big accomplishment, OK? So our big book for the summer is *Songs in Ordinary Time* by Mary McGarry Morris—*Songs in Ordinary Time*."[29]

Winfrey used virtually the same language to frame the selection in June 1998, Wally Lamb's *I Know This Much Is True*. Weighing in at 897 pages, she called it "a great, big book for the summer."[30] By contrast, Jane Hamilton's

Book of Ruth appears to have been selected in December 1996 in part because of its brevity. Winfrey explained: "You have two months to finish . . . and it's not even a whole lot of pages. . . . It's only 328 pages in paperback." She then commented on the significance of the book's length: "The next Book Club airs Wednesday, January 22nd of next year, 1997. We gave you extra time over the holidays so you don't have to read at the Christmas table, OK?"[31]

The language Winfrey used to frame every one of these selections suggests that something more than taste in the abstract guides the decision-making process. That she repeatedly referred to specific selections as summer books, holiday books, and so forth, indicates that that both time and page length are criteria she carefully considers. Longer books have tended to coincide with the summer months, when *Oprah* viewers presumably have more time to devote to reading. Shorter books have tended to coincide with occasions (e.g., the winter holidays) when women are assumed to have more responsibilities and thus less time to read. In other words, Winfrey and her producers have been keenly sensitive to how the reading of specific books matches the tempo and variable rhythms of women's lives rather than placing the burden on them to adjust their schedules to accommodate specific reading assignments.

Indeed, *The Oprah Winfrey Show* has been explicitly pedagogical with respect to how women might fit books and book reading into their everyday routines. On several occasions book club episodes have featured segments in which club members—particularly mothers and wives—shared their strategies for finding time for books and reading amid their daily responsibilities. One unidentified woman recalled having finished Jacquelyn Mitchard's *Deep End of the Ocean* by "snatching a few minutes of reading time in the carpool lane and even waiting for red lights."[32] Another woman stated: "Sometimes I'll . . . carry a book with me in the car, and if I get to a stoplight and my state trooper husband's not around, I'll glance down at my book."[33] A third viewer concurred: "My secret is reading in the car, at soccer practice, at the dentist's office."[34] Winfrey has since cautioned viewers against reading in the car, calling it "very dangerous to you and your children."[35] Those risks notwithstanding, cars seem to offer unique advantages for these book club participants over other, more customary settings for book reading. In contrast to the home, automobiles seem to provide these women with something akin to a "room of one's own" and thus a measure of freedom away from—or even in the midst of—their everyday family responsibilities.

Women featured on Oprah's Book Club have consistently stressed that raising children poses perhaps the most formidable challenge to their finding personal time to read books. During the book club's first anniversary party in 1997, a woman named Peggy admitted to not having read a novel in twenty years, explaining: "I didn't read for pleasure at all the whole time I was raising my children."[36] Over the years many women have explained how Oprah's Book Club has occasioned their incorporating books and reading into their daily lives despite—and, in some cases, because of—their parental responsibilities. Consequently, in 2001 Winfrey offered a list of "ways you moms can rescue some reading time." She suggested that "in lieu of gifts ask your spouse and older children for reading time."[37] Her advice seems to have resonated with Karen, a regular participant in Oprah's Book Club, who was interviewed once on the show. Karen described how and when she became interested in the club: "I'm a full time mom now, but when I started I had a business, and it's something I—after I graduated college, I felt I didn't have time, and when you [Winfrey] started with *The Deep End of the Ocean*, I thought, 'Mm, I can do this, I can read this book. Check it out.' I was 38 years old, and I was addicted. I could be the poster child for your Book Club at this point. I've read over . . . 400 books since you've been—started your Book Club"[38] She went on to add: "My children now are trained that when they see Mom with a book, they just don't bother me. . . . And on Saturday and Sunday mornings, my husband knows I'm going to get up early at 5 to read, fall back to sleep, and wake up again and read some more . . . I get up about 1:00 in the afternoon to start my day, because I love to just lay there and read."[39]

For Karen, Oprah books and other selections have helped her to construct imaginary—albeit effective—spatial and temporal barriers with which to modulate her marriage and the demands placed on her by her children. Her having been singled out on *Oprah* is thus significant for two reasons. First, it underscores the degree to which the book club works because of Winfrey and her producers' awareness not only of which abstract demographic groups watch *Oprah* but also of how the specific "life-position" of these viewers bears on the occasions and contexts in which they may or may not read. As Scannell explains: "It is above all *life-position* (that cluster of such factors as age, sex, occupation, and marital status) that shapes the overall 'time-geography'—the when and where—of people's daily routines, including their routine usage" of media.[40] What this amounts to, essentially, is the difference between marketing a book to a particular segment of the reading public (a preferred strategy of the book industry) and finding ways to help any single book, as well as books in general, achieve a fit with living, breathing human beings in their daily lives. Karen's having been featured on *Oprah* also is significant for the didacticism implicit in her story, which Winfrey makes manifest in her suggestion that mothers should ask those around them for reading time. Both women demonstrate that the book club isn't merely interested in talking about the meaning and artistry of books, as is customary in formal literary instruction. Also at stake is a much more mundane—though no less consequential—matter: How, given my daily responsibilities, can I fit the reading of this particular selection into my life?

Clearly, some women have found in Oprah's Book Club resources with which to mitigate the demands placed on them as spouses, mothers, and professionals. Still, the extraordinary success and visibility of Oprah's Book Club cannot be explained solely in terms of that aspect. While many women featured on Oprah's Book Club have attributed their inability to read books to their responsibilities at home, an equal number have admitted to never having developed an interest in books or book reading prior to their involvement with the club.

For example, in September 1997 Oprah's Book Club featured an interview with Candy Siebert, a woman who had written in to *Oprah* to explain her newfound interest in the book club:

WINFREY: Candy Siebert wrote us to say—Candy, wrote us to say she's never read a book in her entire life. Not one?

SIEBERT: Not one. . . .

WINFREY: Until?

SIEBERT: Until—I kept watching the Book Club. And it was like something made me want to do this. I was, like, "I got to take part in this. It looks so wonderful." . . . And finally I bought my first book, and I bought it so I would have to read it. And I did it. I—[Wally Lamb's] *She's Come Undone*—and I—I cried at the end and it was because I finished it and it was a great book.

WINFREY: It was the first book you read at 40 years old?

SEIBERT: Yes.

WINFREY: I could weep for you.[41]

The same program also featured videotaped excerpts from previous episodes of *Oprah* in which one unidentified women admitted to not having read a novel in two decades; another confessed that she had not read any books at all in about a dozen years.[42]

Candy Siebert's provocative statement about "something" compelling her to take up books and book reading raises an important question: What is it about Oprah's Book Club that has motivated women—and presumably some men—to become involved with and read books for the first time in many years, perhaps even for the first time in their lives?

Some critics have expressed dismay over the range of titles chosen for Oprah's Book Club, including Cynthia Crossen of the *Wall Street Journal*. "Taken individually," she writes, "Oprah's books run the gamut from absorbing to vacuous."[43] Crossen appears to have been troubled by the inconsistent demands Oprah's Book Club places on participants in terms of the degree of difficulty of club selections, which have fluctuated between arguably straightforward books like A. Manette Ansay's *Vinegar Hill* and Alice Hoffman's *Here on Earth* to more intricate, lyrical titles such as those of Toni Morrison or Bernhard Schlink's understated yet morally complex novel *The Reader*.

It may be that those who have not read books in many years were drawn to Oprah's Book Club precisely because of this apparent inconsistency. Indeed, the producers of *The Oprah Winfrey Show* have demonstrated remarkable sensitivity to the range of reading abilities of both actual and potential club members. Anticipating that readers might find Toni Morrison's *Paradise* a difficult read, club members were granted seven rather than the customary four weeks between the book's announcement and the televised discussion.[44] Beyond merely acknowledging and making allowances for the fact that certain titles may prove more challenging than others, the choice of specific selections has often been influenced by the relative difficulty of the preceding one. *The Reader* was followed by Anita Shreve's novel *The Pilot's Wife*, which Winfrey repeatedly charactrized as a "quick read" in contrast to the previous selection.[45] Similarly, Kingsolver's "B-I-G" *Poisonwood Bible* was followed by Elizabeth Berg's *Open House*. "As I've been saying," Winfrey revealed, *Open House* "is really going to be a breeze. I thought after reading over 500 pages, we needed something lighter. For those of you who want a break from heavy reading, our Book Club this month is *Open House* by Elizabeth Berg."[46]

The intense frustration many members experienced with the selection in September 1999, Melinda Haynes's *Mother of Pearl*, provides by far the richest example illustrating how the relative degree of difficulty of club selections has affected the choice of subsequent books. When announcing *Mother of Pearl* in June 1999, Winfrey encouraged readers to persevere. *Mother of Pearl* "is layered," she observed, "which means that in the beginning you're thinking, 'Where is this going?'"[47] At the conclusion of the program she reemphasized: "It's not a fast read, again. The first few chapters may challenge you, so stay with it until the flood. Hang in there until the flood, OK? You've got all summer to read it."[48]

When the book club reconvened in September, Winfrey reiterated her caveats from the beginning of summer. "I warned you-all," she stated, "it wasn't an easy book, but my feeling was that you have the whole summer."[49] Still, her warnings didn't manage to defuse readers' strong reactions to the book. Rather than trying to conceal the fact that many club members disliked *Mother of Pearl*, the producers opted to air readers' frustrations in an audio montage:

WINFREY: Some people didn't make it beyond the first word before getting frustrated.

UNIDENTIFIED WOMAN #1: Why is Even's name Even? I am so confused.

WINFREY: Others got stuck a little later in the book.

UNIDENTIFIED WOMAN #6: I've been reading *Mother of Pearl* for a month and I'm only on page 219. . . .

WINFREY: Some of you drove yourself a little cuckoo.

UNIDENTIFIED WOMAN #10: I've had this book in my car for two weeks, thinking I will read this and finish it. I couldn't do it. . . .

WINFREY: One reader even used it as a sleep aid.

UNIDENTIFIED WOMAN #12: It was a great book to read before going to bed because I always fell asleep quickly.[50]

Airing readers' negative reactions was a clever strategy for reframing the confusion and frustration many women felt toward *Mother of Pearl*. What this incident reveals, in effect, is that reading on Oprah's Book Club doesn't connote the act of humbling oneself before the "genius" of an intractable book as it might in a more traditional context of literary instruction. Rather, it connotes, on the one hand, doing one's best to engage with challenging books and, on the other, recognizing that one's dissatisfaction with specific selections stems not from any personal intellectual defect but rather from Winfrey and her producers' having failed to choose a book that meets the needs, tastes, and desires of the club's members. Reading should offer a trajectory to challenge, in other words, but shouldn't simply be a challenge in and of itself.

This isn't to suggest that all book club members were turned off by *Mother of Pearl*, or that "faster reads" like *Tara Road* are the only fare they find appealing. Indeed, during the book club broadcast in September 1999 several women expressed how much they enjoyed and were moved by

Mother of Pearl. One woman commented: "A friend asked me if I was leaving this planet, what three books would I take with me. My second choice was *Mother of Pearl*."[51] Another woman confessed: "*Mother of Pearl* is the only book that when I finished reading it, I immediately began rereading it because I was captivated."[52] At the end of the *Mother of Pearl* broadcast, Winfrey asked a guest in the studio audience who belonged to a women's book club to share some of the group's favorite selections. "Truthfully, *Mother of Pearl*, we all agreed was . . . four-star. We loved it. We would read passages just to anyone walking by that's how much we loved it."[53]

There's no single level, then, at which members of Oprah's Book Club read, and their range of reading interests and abilities goes a long way toward explaining why the club's book list might seem inconsistent at first glance. In fact, it's quite consistent, assuming one takes the time to locate its underlying unity, which is driven by the book club's spirit of inclusiveness. It welcomes prolific, seasoned readers with the same heartfelt "hello" as it does newcomers. This commitment, however, shouldn't be mistaken for a facile pluralism or a sense in which anything goes and nothing in particular is valued. The book club's express openness to newer or more hesitant readers and the selections best suited to them is ultimately grounded in an ethic of challenging them to become involved in lengthier and more difficult texts in the long term.

In a more mundane sense, Oprah's Book Club adds value to books by sorting and classifying them assiduously, and by matching them up with appropriate readers at opportune moments in their lives. As such, it fills a major gap in the adult end of the book trade. Books intended for children and adolescents routinely carry special labeling indicating age range, grade level, or reading ability for which a given title is best suited. Yet, with the exception of some category fiction and the "for Dummies" series, comparable labeling practices largely don't exist for adults. For those disengaged from books, picking one up can be bewildering. Jacket copy, however useful it may be to those already in the know, can amount to an interminable exercise in referentiality for those otherwise unacquainted. The sheer volume of books can also be overwhelming. Where should one start? Oprah's Book Club has succeeded where the book industry has tended to come up short. In making the demands of a particular title explicit, it embraces the type of useful information the book trade usually provides only indirectly—even somewhat cliquishly. What's more, the club has done so in a way that spares new or unpracticed readers the potential embarrassment of having to buy a book labeled "adult/easy reader" without disparaging the value of longer or more complicated books.

"It's More About Life"

The preceding section largely focused on Oprah's book selections them-selves and how women have found creative ways to integrate them into their everyday lives. Beyond merely sorting and classifying who should be reading what, where, and when, the questions I now wish to consider are: How has Oprah's Book Club helped connect the *content* of specific book club selections to the lives of women? How have women made use of what these books have to say? What, if anything, has their content helped women achieve?

The book club discussion in March 2001 included an intriguing message from Winfrey directed at those members who hadn't read that month's selection, Joyce Carol Oates's *We Were the Mulvaneys*. "Don't worry if you haven't read . . . *We Were the Mulvaneys*," she advised, "because as with all our Book Club shows, it's more about life than about a novel."[54] What this statement suggests—and what's emerged time and again on episodes of Oprah's Book Club—is that Winfrey and her viewers/readers perceive the content of specific books as valuable to the extent that it demonstrates a clear connection with life, or that it resonates with their everyday interests, personal experiences, and concerns.

One way in which the book club has established and maintained this connection to life is through its constant emphasis on the actuality—not merely the realism—of the settings, events, and people featured in each book. Nearly every episode of Oprah's Book Club has included interviews in which authors describe the creative process and how they have been inspired by real places and people. This pattern began at least as far back as the beginning of the club's second season, when it featured Mary McGarry Morris's *Songs in Ordinary Time*. "Even though the people were made up," Winfrey explained, "some of the places in Atkinson, Vermont [the setting of the book], are not far from [Morris's] hometown." The program then cut to a videotaped interview with Morris conducted while walking along the streets of Rutland, Vermont:

> There is so much of Atkinson, Vermont in Rutland, Vermont. I don't think much has changed at all here since I was a child along this section of Main Street. On the corner is the funeral home I imagined when I was writing the funeral of Sonny Stoner's wife, Carol. And I naturally thought of this little restaurant when I was writing the book. This is the Rutland Restaurant. It's been here since 1917. This beautiful old Victorian house on Main Street was

the house where old Judge Clay sat dead in the window for a few days. . . . The character of Sam is very much like my father. He—he was a very intelligent man, an educated man, who was cursed with the disease of alcoholism. . . . I've created my own Rutland, I guess.[55]

Similarly, the book club episode in January 2001 focused on the inspiration behind *House of Sand and Fog* by Andre Dubus III. The author described how he drew inspiration for the novel from an article he had read in the *Boston Globe*, in which a young woman, like the lead character Kathy Nicolo, was evicted from her house for failing to pay an erroneous tax bill.[56] Dubus also disclosed that he had based the other main character, Massoud Amir Behrani, on the life of a friend's father who had been a colonel in the Iranian Air Force before the shah was deposed and who, like Behrani, lost nearly everything after immigrating with his family to the United States.[57] Dubus went on to note that the man who had purchased the house in the *Boston Globe* article was of Middle Eastern descent, prompting him to wonder, "What if my colonel bought this house?"[58]—a question that summarizes the basic storyline of the book.

Because the characters and settings to which Oprah's Book Club selections refer sometimes no longer exist, producers of *The Oprah Winfrey Show* have turned to authors, invited guests, and particular textual elements to bear witness to their actuality. For example, in November 1999 the program on Breena Clarke's *River, Cross My Heart* dwelled extensively on the actuality of the novel's setting and main character. The book is set in the Georgetown area of Washington, D.C., in the 1920s, when the neighborhood largely consisted of working-class African Americans (in contrast to the mostly white, petit-bourgeois population of today). In order to demonstrate the actuality of "Black Georgetown," the episode included a videotaped interview with centenarian Eva Calloway, whom Winfrey described as "one of the last living witnesses" of the old Georgetown community.[59] Calloway's oral testimony was clearly meant to evidence a Georgetown that once existed. The episode also featured an on-camera interview with Edna Clarke, the author's mother, who, Winfrey revealed, "was the inspiration behind 12-year-old Johnnie Mae," the novel's main character.[60]

The videotaped interview with Lalita Tademy, author of *Cane River*, the book club selection in September 2001, likewise bore witness to the disappearance of people and places while underscoring their actuality. Spanning 1834–1936, *Cane River* chronicles the lives and stories of four generations of Louisiana Creole slave women, Tademy's ancestors, whom she came to "know" after conducting exhaustive genealogical research.[61] Although *Cane*

River was marketed as a novel, the videotaped author interview repeatedly stressed the fact that it was anchored in concrete settings and experiences. "Cane River is a real place," Tademy observed, adding: "A lot of the areas that were plantations that I talk about in the book no longer exist. For one thing, so much of it was burned during the Civil War."[62] Tademy's videotaped tour thus affirmed not only the actuality of the place, Cane River, but also its historicity as it relates to the novel. Near the end of the discussion, Winfrey referred to the photographs included in the book: "That's one of the fascinating things, didn't you all think, about the book? When you turn the page, there are the pictures of the people you've been reading about."[63] Both Tademy and Winfrey thus drew attention to the indexical nature of these photographs, the fact that they couldn't have been produced without the women and places of *Cane River* having been present. Taken together, the videotaped author tour and the photographs invited book club participants to think about the characters and setting of *Cane River* as actual despite their novelization.

Although novels figure prominently in the Oprah's Book Club catalog, four of the sixty-four selections (as of this writing)—Maya Angelou's *Heart of a Woman*, Malika Oufkir's *Stolen Lives: Twenty Years in a Desert Jail*, James Frey's *A Million Little Pieces*, and Elie Wiesel's *Night*—are memoirs; Sidney Poitier's *Measure of a Man* is an autobiography.[64] By stressing the grounded actuality of *Songs in Ordinary Time*; *River, Cross My Heart*; *Cane River*, and other novels, the book club complicates any straightforward generic categorization of these works as mere fiction. Eva Illouz sees this as the book club's penchant for "cutting across the distinction between fiction and truth."[65] There may be something more subtle going on here, however, given how actuality often seems to trump the designation of specific books as fiction in the book club's routine patterns of conversation. Fiction, in effect, falls out, leaving "truth" as the overarching framework according to which club members are encouraged to approach and make sense of any and all titles. *The Heart of a Woman*, *Stolen Lives*, *A Million Little Pieces*, *Night*, and *The Measure of a Man* therefore make perfect sense alongside all the novels chosen for Oprah's Book Club. Virtually all of these selections have been presented as stories that actually happened, despite the fact that authors, book publishers, booksellers, critics, and others persist in labeling them either fiction or nonfiction.

Oprah's Book Club producers and participants have connected books with life by rejecting this generic framework. Collectively they've articulated book club selections—especially novels—from the realm of the imagined to the actual or, more accurately, from the fantastic to the everyday.

Indeed, the televised Oprah's Book Club broadcasts regularly go beyond framing the selections as stories that actually happened by highlighting how the characters, events, and themes correspond to women's personal experiences and daily lives.

During the first anniversary episode of the book club, Winfrey remarked, "I love books because you read about somebody else's life but it makes you think about your own,"[66] a point she reaffirmed eighteen months later during a discussion of *The Reader*: "We love books because they make you question yourself."[67] Thus, book reading has been valued on Oprah's Book Club because of its capacity to provoke critical introspection or, more significantly, because it provides audiences with both practical and symbolic resources for challenging reified conceptions of their own subjectivities.

Herein lies the book club's dialectic with the everyday. On the one hand, the material facticity of the books themselves has provided at least some participants with much-needed time and space away from their daily obligations as partners, mothers, and professionals. On the other hand, the club has marshaled the content of the books to serve a seemingly contrary purpose, namely, that of facilitating a more intense, introspective engagement with women's everyday realities vis-à-vis the main characters and events of the selections. This dialectic, together with the book club's explicit instructions for acquiring books and time-management techniques, might well account for the group's appeal. Indeed, the club demonstrates how women can carve out a safe harbor of sorts for themselves, one adjacent to but ultimately distinct from everyday life's repetitive routines. Through books they find the necessary perspective to reflect on how their needs correspond with others' expectations of them, and perhaps even to invent new possibilities for repeating everyday life differently.[68]

The way in which the December 1999 selection, Ansay's *Vinegar Hill*, was discussed and framed illustrates this dialectic in practice. The novel describes the tensions between a married couple and their in-laws. Specifically, it focuses on Ellen Grier's struggle to assert herself after she, her husband James, and their two young children are forced to move in with James's overbearing parents. Ansay explained that the novel was inspired by actual events. She and her parents moved in briefly with her paternal grandparents when she was five, and she drew some of the scenes in the book directly from that experience.[69] Although Ansay claimed that Ellen was not her mother,[70] she did reveal that "my mother's own story inspired Ellen's transformation because my mother is someone who does not give up."[71] The program thus stressed how *Vinegar Hill* was grounded in the experiences of a woman who had overcome the unreasonable expectations of her in-laws.

Winfrey had already touched on the actuality of *Vinegar Hill* when she announced its selection for Oprah's Book Club a month earlier: "The author does a really outstanding job of showing us a real-life family and common problems. When finished, I thought, 'We need to get that family on *The Oprah Show*.'"[72] Her comment led her producers to break temporarily with what was then the show's dinner-discussion format. Instead, they invited married women and their mothers-in-law to the studio to share how living together had affected their relationships with one another and with their families. One guest, a woman named Valerie, explained that she was "amazed at how similar Ellen's experience was to something that happened to me 18 years ago," when she was forced to move in with her mother-in-law while her husband completed his degree.[73] Another guest, Cherie Burton, who eight months earlier had moved in with her in-laws, also identified with Ellen Grier. "I wouldn't say it feels like a prison here, but there are some moments where I do feel trapped."[74]

The program in March 2001, on Joyce Carol Oates's *We Were the Mulvaneys*, provided some of the most moving examples of this process of identification and self-reflection. Winfrey indicated that numerous readers had written in to the show explaining how they had seen themselves and their families in the book. "What's so exciting about *We Were the Mulvaneys*" was that "we've gotten so many letters from . . . people who were members of families who say, 'We were the Grants,' or 'We were the Pullmans.' 'We were'—a lot of people started their letters that way."[75] The segment followed a poignant videotaped interview with the Hanson family, who, like the Mulvaneys, were ostracized from their community after they filed suit against a young man who had raped their daughter, Susan.[76] As Jayne Hanson, Susan's mother, explained, "It dawned on me reading this book, we have all been—we've all been raped."[77]

A member of the *Oprah* studio audience once asked Winfrey why she chose books with so much "angst" in them.[78] Winfrey responded, "All the stories I . . . choose, in one way or another, are always ultimately about triumph."[79] Her comment affirms Illouz's observation that "the awful end" has a tendency to occur at the start of many book club selections, thereby leaving their narratives open to exploring "how a character will cope with something already known to be awful."[80] Interestingly, the one novel in which Winfrey promised "a total escape from your own life—escape, escape, escape,"[81] *House of Sand and Fog*, met with significant resistance on the part of those viewers invited to participate in the videotaped discussion. All but one of the guests were particularly disgusted by Kathy Nicolo's character, whose lying, promiscuity, theft, substance abuse, racism, and inattention to her daily responsibilities appear to have disturbed them deeply.[82] While the exact source of their distress remains unclear, it might have been a function of the book's escapist tenor. Its deeply tragic conclusion—all of the leading characters wind up either dead or imprisoned—might have further reinforced this sense of disconnect. Perhaps *House of Sand and Fog* upset these readers because it failed to tell a story that resonated sufficiently with their own daily lives. As such, it may have run afoul of the book club's ethico-aesthetic imperative to connect literature and life. By concluding on a tragic note rather than proceeding from one, *House of Sand and Fog* offered readers little hope in overcoming desperate circumstances. For all that, the controversy surrounding Dubus's book remained a matter more or less internal to the club. Other controversies would bring its discussion and decision-making practices under intense public scrutiny.

A Million Little Corrections

On September 24, 2001, Winfrey announced the inaugural book club selection for the 2001–2002 TV season: Jonathan Franzen's third novel, *The Corrections*, his meditation on family, contemporary culture, and the lengths to which people will go to achieve happiness. Normally enthusiastic when announcing new selections for the book club, she seemed particularly exuberant about this one: "The phrase 'the great American novel' is often overused," she noted, but *The Corrections* "is the closest I've come to it in contemporary fiction in a long, long, long, long time."[83] Critical reviews published on the occasion of the novel's debut only seemed to confirm what Winfrey had surmised about the book months earlier: it was a genuine "masterpiece."[84]

Typically, authors whose books have been selected for Oprah's Book Club have effused publicly about how thrilled they are to receive such a unique honor and have jumped at the chance to discuss the book on the air. Franzen reacted differently. In a series of interviews he gave while on tour in the autumn of 2001, he expressed misgivings about having been brought into the Oprah's Book Club fold. He seemed troubled, first of all, by the allegedly mediocre company he and *The Corrections* henceforth would be compelled to keep as associates of the book club. Winfrey "picked some good books," Franzen told an interviewer at Powell's Books in Portland, Oregon, "but she's picked enough schmaltzy, one-dimensional ones that I cringe myself, even if I think she's really smart and she's really fighting the good fight."[85] Franzen elaborated on the reasons underlying this sense of conflict in an interview published in the *Oregonian*: "I feel like I'm solidly in the high-art literary tradition," he remarked, and as such he fretted about being "misunderstood" by audiences who possessed aesthetic sensibilities different from his own—people who, presumably, wouldn't have bothered with *The Corrections* without Winfrey's endorsement.[86] Franzen later claimed to have misspoken, suggesting that he had "conflate[d] 'high modern' and 'art fiction,'" even as he went on to praise the work of Marcel Proust, Franz Kafka, and William Faulkner, hypostases all of highbrow literary fiction.[87] Although Franzen recognized how Oprah's Book Club had energized interest in books and reading, and although he might have welcomed an expanded readership in principle, he seemed to shrink from the more popular connotations that flowed from his association with the club.

Franzen also worried about the alienation that might ensue as a consequence of his having become a certified Oprah author. Would the book club's stamp of approval turn off men who otherwise might be interested in *The Corrections*? In an October 2001 interview on National Public Radio's *Fresh Air*, Franzen explained to host Terry Gross that this was precisely the trend he had gleaned from interactions with readers. "I had some hope of actually reaching a male audience," Franzen confessed, "and I've heard more than one reader in signing lines now in bookstores say, 'You know, if I hadn't heard you, I would have been put off by the fact that it is an Oprah pick. I figure those books are for women, and I never touch it.' Those are male readers speaking."[88] While his anecdote suggests that Franzen actually seemed to be bridging whatever gap might have existed between women who followed Oprah's Book Club and men who ordinarily wanted nothing to do with it, he still seemed disturbed by the prospect of his novel failing to reach sufficient numbers of men.[89]

The novel's association with TV in general vexed Franzen even more. A few weeks before appearing on *Fresh Air*, he had taped what was scheduled to be his *Oprah* author interview. He described the awkward and unpleasant experience to Terry Gross as "the sort of bogus thing where they [the producers] follow you around with a camera and you try to look natural. And I've done a two-hour interview, which will be boiled down to three minutes or so."[90] TV's contrivances clearly discomforted Franzen, but he was most upset by the connection the show's producers had attempted to draw—or compel, as far as he was concerned—between the book and his life growing up in St. Louis, Missouri. "I'm a Midwesterner who's been living in the East for twenty-four years," Franzen wrote in a plaintive essay published that December in the *New Yorker*. "I'm a grumpy Manhattanite who, with what feels like Midwestern eagerness to cooperate, has agreed to pretend to arrive in the Midwestern city of his childhood to reexamine his roots."[91] The book club experience was becoming too much about biography—or what he gathered the producers wanted his biography to look and sound like—and not enough about the imagination he had put into crafting his novel.[92]

Finally, Franzen's consternation also derived from the custom of reissuing titles selected for Oprah's Book Club with the group's distinctive, trademarked logo. Immediately upon learning of his novel's nomination, Farrar, Straus and Giroux, Franzen's publisher, returned the book to press. The new Oprah edition—totaling half a million copies in all—featured the book club insignia prominently on the cover.[93] The redesign irritated Franzen. In a series of interviews with the *New York Times*, he explained that adding the logo constituted a breach of tradition, given how new hardcover fiction published in the United States has tended to be free of advertising.[94] Worse, he felt the logo implied that Harpo Productions, the powerhouse media organization to which Oprah's Book Club is appended, henceforth effectively controlled the rights to his work. "I see this as my book, my creation, and I didn't want the logo of corporate ownership on it," he told the *Oregonian*.[95] For all the hard work, creativity, and physical and psychological anguish he had experienced while trying to write a meaningful, socially engaging novel, Franzen now felt inconsequential alongside the demonstrative letter O emblazoned on the cover of his latest book. (The fact that global media giant Holtzbrinck owns Farrar, Straus and Giroux apparently didn't faze him.)

After several weeks of indulging Franzen's kvetching, Winfrey had heard enough. On October 23, 2001, his comments earned him the dubious distinction of being the first and only book club author to have an invitation to *The Oprah Winfrey Show* rescinded. *The Corrections* would remain on the book club roster, but Franzen's dis-invitation meant that viewers/readers would never have the chance to discuss the book on the air, nor would they ever see him traipsing awkwardly about St. Louis trying to discover how to rediscover his roots. The controversy also prompted Farrar, Straus and Giroux to begin issuing two editions of *The Corrections*—with and without the book club logo—presumably as a gesture to placate both parties. The seal for the National Book Award for fiction, which Franzen took home in November 2001, would replace the Oprah insignia on all subsequent editions.

Contrition soon kicked into high gear, however, leading Franzen to make some corrections of his own. "Both Oprah and I want the same thing and believe the same thing," he told the *New York Times* in late October 2001, adding that "the distinction between high [art] and low [art] is meaningless."[96] He even acknowledged Winfrey's "enthusiasm and advocacy" upon his receiving the National Book Award for fiction.[97] It remains an open question whether these gestures constituted a genuine apology on Franzen's part or just some hasty backpedaling.

Recriminations and regrets aside, the whole Franzen–book club meltdown might have exposed the arbitrariness of value hierarchies, but it also reinforced how distinctions—between low and high art, women and men, TV and books, corporate and independent media production—are anything but meaningless in the late age of print. Much of the controversy can be attributed to the misunderstanding of the relationship of books to everyday life on—and beyond—Oprah's Book Club on the part of commentators and critics. The club's success and appeal aren't mere symptoms of the triumph of sentimentality in the book world, much less that of pop psychology; nor are they evidence of the "dumbing down" of American culture, a claim Todd Gitlin has levied against trade fiction in general.[98] The popularity of Oprah's Book Club underscores the fact that readers might well be buying books in larger quantities if only authors, publishers, critics, and booksellers communicated more effectively not only in terms of highlighting specific titles but also in achieving a better fit with readers' experiences, needs, and daily routines. The Franzen affair crystallized just how much the book club "scramble[s] the 'high' and the 'low,'" and how the recalcitrance of that distinction in other cultural domains ultimately hinders rather than helps a pedagogy for daily life.[99] The distinction prioritizes abstract aesthetic deliberations and consequently marginalizes more practical considerations, such as: How can I find the time to read? Where should I do it? Which books are best suited to my abilities and interests? Where can I find them?

The kerfuffle surrounding the book club's selection in September 2005— James Frey's *A Million Little Pieces*, a graphic account of drug addiction and recovery—brings the politics of the group's value system into even sharper relief. Winfrey billed the book as "a gut-wrenching memoir that is so raw and . . . real."[100] Like those that had come before it, the televised discussion, which aired that October, stressed the book's actuality or grounding in concrete events. Frey told Winfrey how he had referred to "400 pages of very detailed, day-to-day, hour-to-hour documentation" of his stay in rehab to help him compose the book with utmost accuracy. He added that this information was especially important since drug addiction had so affected his memory that it no longer could be relied upon to render such details accurately.[101] The episode also featured a segment in which Frey toured his hometown of St. Joseph, Michigan, pointing out places he had allegedly purchased drugs and alcohol as a teenager, plus another clip in which he visited a drug-addicted woman who, having been moved by *A Million Little Pieces*, checked herself into rehab. Once again the connection was clear: what matters on Oprah's Book Club is life and the ways in which the reading of books can give one pause to reflect on unhealthy patterns of behavior in order to correct and thereby triumph over them.

Toward the end of the telecast Winfrey turned to Frey to express her astonishment at his having survived multiple overdoses, bouts of alcohol poisoning, uncontrollable vomiting, blackouts, incontinence, clashes with police, arrests, imprisonment, his girlfriend's suicide, and a harrowing oral surgery for which, as a patient in rehab, he was denied painkillers. "The first time you start reading," Winfrey told the author, "you're like, 'Is this real?' Okay, this isn't a novel."[102] Within a matter of months, however, Winfrey's question would return to haunt her.

The Smoking Gun, an investigative news magazine owned by Court TV, collects celebrity mug shots for an online rogues' gallery. Frey's newfound notoriety as an Oprah's Book Club honoree led the magazine to take an interest in him, especially since he made no bones about having been arrested fourteen times. His shots would be a first for the Web site since no other Oprah author had appeared there. After some initial searching, the magazine was puzzled by the dearth of information concerning Frey's criminal record. It decided to delve deeper into his alleged arrests, as well as other claims he had made in the memoir.[103] A more extensive search of police and court records unearthed photos and documents pertaining to just two of Frey's many purported arrests.[104] These happened to correspond to episodes chronicled in *A Million Little Pieces*, but the stories hardly matched up.

In the first Frey claimed to have been arrested in 1988, at age eighteen, for driving while under the influence. His blood alcohol level of 0.36 was not only more than three-and-a-half times the legal limit but, according to Frey, the highest ever recorded by authorities in Berrien County, Michigan.[105] While police and court records confirmed his arrest, they showed a significantly lower blood alcohol level. According to *A Million Little Pieces*, the incident landed Frey in jail for a week, whereas the magazine's research revealed that police had released him into his parents' custody soon after his arrest. Frey eventually pleaded to a lesser charge that stipulated no jail time.[106]

Frey's second documented arrest occurred in Ohio in 1992 and stemmed from a similar incident. In the book he claims he hit a police officer with his car, brawled with arresting officers, and was found to be carrying crack cocaine. A slew of charges were filed, ranging from driving without a license to assault with a deadly weapon and "felony mayhem."[107] A conviction could have landed Frey in prison for more than eight years, but he claims that some shady, behind-the-scenes maneuvering landed him a ninety-day stint in the Licking County, Ohio, correctional facility and three years of probation on a misdemeanor conviction.[108] Despite all this drama, the magazine's own investigation turned up quite a different series of events. Frey reportedly never had struck a police officer with his car, tussled with authorities, or spent significant time in jail. The arresting officer, who had witnessed Frey commit a minor traffic infraction, cited him for a series of misdemeanors, the most serious of which was driving while under the influence. The twenty-three-year-old spent all of five hours in custody and later paid an undisclosed fine to settle the case.[109]

In addition to detailing these and other major factual inconsistencies in *A Million Little Pieces*, the magazine noted a conspicuous lack of witnesses to corroborate aspects of the story. "Almost every character in Frey's book that could address [these issues] has either committed suicide, been murdered, died of AIDS, been sentenced to life in prison, gone missing, landed in an institution for the criminally insane, or fell off a fishing boat never to be seen again."[110] In the course of its investigation the magazine also learned that Frey had shopped an early draft of *A Million Little Pieces* around to publishers as a novel and that only after receiving seventeen rejections did he revise the manuscript and begin billing it as a memoir.[111] This unusual move provided additional cause for concern. Despite Frey's threats of a defamation suit, in early January 2006 the magazine went public with its report, calling it "The Man Who Conned Oprah."

Days before the story broke, Frey learned that *A Million Little Pieces* had become the second best-selling book of 2005, trailing the penultimate installment of author J. K. Rowling's phenomenally successful Harry Potter franchise. More good news: *A Million Little Pieces* was declared *the* best-selling trade paperback of 2005.[112] Here was a book whose gritty realism had lifted it to the top of the year's best-seller lists, a book that had so moved Winfrey that she decided to give it the book club's coveted endorsement. Short of receiving a Pulitzer Prize or a National Book Award, this type of success was about the best that a writer could hope for—sort of, for surely Frey's success magnified the seriousness of *The Smoking Gun*'s allegations of deceit and braggadocio.

On January 11, 2006, Frey appeared on CNN's *Larry King Live*, where he responded to charges of having fabricated key characters and events. The disputed sections, he insisted, constituted a paltry 5 percent of his memoir. He insisted that the magazine's allegations of impropriety had been blown out of proportion. In a last minute phone call to the show, Winfrey stated that she found all the quibbling over details to be "irrelevant" and affirmed that the book's "underlying message of redemption . . . still resonates with me."[113]

She quickly reversed course, however, as the controversy continued to foment. On January 26 Frey returned to *The Oprah Winfrey Show* for what can only be described as a grueling inquisition. That Winfrey had taken the unusual step of broadcasting live seemed to underscore the program's gravity. She began by admitting she had erred in defending Frey on *Larry King Live*. "I regret that phone call," she told the audience. "I made a mistake and I left the impression that the truth does not matter. And I am deeply sorry about that, because that is not what I believe." She then confronted Frey, telling him how she felt "duped" and that he had "betrayed millions of readers." Frey was contrite, though he was also clearly at pains to acknowledge, once and for all, having lied. Nevertheless, when Winfrey asked him flat out about *The Smoking Gun*'s dossier, he finally admitted that "most of what they wrote was pretty accurate, absolutely."[114]

Franzen's misdeeds had resulted in his becoming the only Oprah author ever to have his invitation to appear on the show withdrawn. Why, then, did she invite Frey not once but twice to discuss *A Million Little Pieces*? The Franzen controversy had broken weeks before his scheduled book club appearance, whereas in Frey's case revelations of impropriety came to light only afterward. Surely timing played a role in how Winfrey and her producers managed the fallout from each scandal. Still, their markedly different responses to Franzen (shunning) and Frey (confrontation) suggest that more was at stake than mere timing. The book club could ignore Franzen precisely because the trope around which so much of the controversy had turned—the distinction between high and low culture—was more or less irrelevant to the book club's worldview and ways of operating. Responding at length would have been tantamount to validating what are, in effect, exogenous categories. Indeed, this would explain why Winfrey, when asked about the controversy four years later, responded by saying that Franzen was "not even a blip on the radar screen of my life."[115]

In Frey's case, however, his fabrications contravened what is probably *the* core value of Oprah's Book Club: the grounding of books in actual events. Rather than reinforcing the intimate connection between literature and life, as almost all previous book club selections had been made to do, *A Million Little Pieces* embodied the possibility of a disconnect. It thus cast doubt on a fundamental principle according to which the club has inspired legions of people to engage with books both meaningfully and practically. Furthermore, the controversy highlighted the degree to which the book club refuses to trade in moral ambiguity. Despite what some academic analysts may say about *Oprah*, truth is an inviolable category and lying constitutes a serious moral breach—at least where the book club is concerned.[116] Letting Frey's falsehoods and exaggerations go unchallenged would have implied that actuality is just as acceptable and virtuous as the more pliant category of "truthiness."[117] Since this would have been an unthinkable conclusion for the book club to have reached, Frey and his lies needed to be confronted and purged in order to restore homeostasis to the group and reassert its moral order.

An Intractable Alchemy

Oprah Winfrey doesn't make best sellers, nor has she changed the way in which Americans read—at least not single-handedly. Rather, she is an important link within a complex assemblage of individuals, agencies, institutions, technologies, and communication media that has made Oprah's Book Club the success it clearly is. It's important not to lose sight of this bigger picture lest one slip into an overly simplistic, causal model of media effects. In other words, one shouldn't confuse the marketing and ubiquity of Oprah® for the flesh-and-blood individual, Oprah Gail Winfrey. While it would be problematic to suggest that she wields no—or even minimal— authority within and beyond the book industry, whatever success Oprah's Book Club has enjoyed shouldn't be reduced to vague assertions of Winfrey's influence or impact.

Nevertheless, what's clear is that, since 1996, Oprah's Book Club has emerged as a powerful arbiter of bibliographic taste in the United States. This is significant for many reasons, not the least of which is the fact that an African American woman serves as its titular figurehead. Given the country's shameful history of excluding women, people of color, and the poor from the cultures of books and reading, the success of Oprah's Book Club perhaps bears witness to a long (-overdue) revolution in the gendered and racialized structures of bibliographic authority.[118] The book club's success has also challenged what many presume to be the agonistic relationship that books and TV seem to share. This refrain can take many forms, most often with TV serving as a scapegoat for why people seem to be reading fewer and fewer books.[119] Oprah's Book Club has shown that whatever the relationship of books and TV may be, it's neither necessary nor inherent in these media forms. Books can indeed play well with TV.

The book club's authority, moreover, has accrued from its pragmatic disposition toward books and reading—embodied in the clever and diffuse forms of social pedagogy by which it engages both actual and potential readers at the level of the everyday. These include not only discussing the content of specific selections but also sharing tips about finding time to read, the book club's distinctive sorting/classifying/labeling practices, and more. Those for whom books and reading already form part of their daily lives may forget that making a lasting entrée into the world of letters, which can be an intimidating foray for those looking in from the outside, requires background and skill sets beyond the intensive task of learning to read. Unfortunately, many who have assumed the mantle of formal literary education have tended to find such details too trivial, rudimentary, digressive, or vulgar to warrant sustained attention and commentary. Their comparative indifference to the pragmatics of book acquisition and other mundane concerns partially explains why Oprah's Book Club has succeeded and why it should refuse to make itself over in the image of, say, a college literature class.[120] If anything, those engaged in formal literary instruction might consider taking a few more cues from Oprah's Book Club.[121]

The book club's success certainly owes a great deal to the unique ways in which it's helped imbue books with a vital "talking life." Another key to its success has been its remarkable willingness to listen. This quality is especially important, given how a powerful multimedia corporation, Harpo Entertainment Group, stands behind the book club. One could easily attribute people's enthusiasm for the club to the manipulations of the culture industry. To whatever extent that might be accurate, top-down ideology alone cannot account for its popularity. Its direction and, ultimately, its success have been fueled from the ground up by those who look to Winfrey, *The Oprah Winfrey Show*, and the book club. *Oprah* producers reportedly have waited to hear from viewers/readers before crafting at least some book club programs, and they've done so with an eye toward identifying what readers have found particularly challenging, provocative, salient, or vexing about a given book.[122] I'm reluctant to call this kind of input "cultural democracy" since doing so connotes a level of transparency essentially free of all traces of corporate power and control. At the very least, however, this ethic of active listening underscores the degree to which people's everyday lives and their actual concerns form a creative basis for the book club's ways of operating.[123]

Commonplace generic distinctions (e.g., fiction vs. nonfiction) and value hierarchies (e.g., low vs. high culture) seem to have little place on Oprah's Book Club. All these categories operate, as it were, from the wrong common place—that of the book industry, or perhaps that of professional literary criticism, but certainly not that of a majority of book club participants. The group's refusal to repeat and reaffirm categories handed down from credentialed bibliographic authorities, however, shouldn't be taken as a sign of its having abandoned the work of distinction. "Anything goes" is hardly a mantra of Oprah's Book Club. Since its inception the book club has engaged in copious amounts of creative work, fashioning a unique set of standards and protocols by which to assess a given book's worth. Life, actuality, a dialectic with the everyday—these form the crux of its evaluative framework. Part of the reason why the book club has been misunderstood by some is precisely the groundedness of these categories in the exigencies of everyday life—indeed, in the facticity of everyday life itself. The controversy over A Million Little Pieces demonstrated how these categories constitute more than just aesthetic criteria; they form a moral threshold by means of which club members differentiate truth from falsity and right from wrong in their daily lives. Ultimately, identifying good books is less important for Oprah's Book Club than finding books that fit—an intractable alchemy that's vexed the book industry for a century.

Does all this listening, creative work, and groundedness in the concrete demands of daily life mean that the book club has been an unqualified success? No. It undoubtedly has established a remarkable synergy with the lives of hundreds of thousands—perhaps millions—of readers in the United States. Oprah's Book Club also has had much to say about recalcitrant social problems such as racism, misogyny, economic injustice, colonialism, child abuse, and genocide. As such it's helped to show how antagonism suffuses what for some participants might otherwise seem like dull routine. For these reasons it deserves to be commended. What remains worrisome, however, is whether the group's confrontation with some of the most compelling political concerns of our time will press beyond the purchasing and reading of books and develop into even more engaged, broad-ranging acts of intervention.[124] On this matter, one might find some solace in the fact that Oprah's Book Club is what it is—a club—which by definition implies some degree of sociality or, more optimistically, a willingness on the part of participants collectively to engage social problems. The larger challenge consists in finding ways to further politicize these relations and, in doing so, in refusing to close the book on Oprah's Book Club.

As of this writing, two books about Oprah's Book Club have been published and more are likely to follow.[125] Neither carries a disclaimer about Winfrey not having endorsed its contents, this despite Oprah having become such a commercially lucrative, trademarked brand name. Why, then, do so many books about the popular Harry Potter book series carry warnings of this kind? What is it about the magic of Harry Potter that compels writers, publishers, and a host of other cultural producers to defer to its creators and intellectual property rights holders? How has the aura of originality, authenticity, and sanctity surrounding the series been produced—and for whose benefit? The next chapter will answer these and other questions by tracing Harry Potter's circulation, proliferation, and transfiguration within and beyond the borders of the United States.

5 Harry Potter and the Culture of the Copy

WHEN IT COMES to books these days, there are few names more recogniz-able to the public than Oprah, but Harry Potter is surely one of them. Since 1997, when author J. K. Rowling's *Harry Potter and the Philosopher's Stone* first landed in British bookstores, the adventures of the boy wizard have gone on to become nothing less than an international sensation. Prior to the July 2007 release of the final installment of the book series, *Harry Potter and the Deathly Hallows*, the total number of authorized copies in print reached an estimated—and staggering—325 million worldwide. They are sold in over two hundred countries and have been translated into more than sixty different languages, ranging from Afrikaans to Welsh.[1] While the list of translations doesn't quite stretch from A to Z, there is an uncon-firmed—and, if true, unauthorized—Harry Potter edition in Zulu. They've also spawned lucrative movie and product franchises, making Harry Potter iconic well beyond the book world.

Another way of putting this would be to say that Harry Potter prolifer-ates—often in ways exceeding the control of his creators and rights holders. Rowling and company have profited handsomely from Potter's reproduc-ibility but fear for the effects of his unauthorized reproduction within and beyond the print media. The explosive popularity of the book series and its growing unwieldiness consequently have moved Rowling and her associ-ates to begin building elaborate walls around their Potter empire. Witness, for example, a recent flurry of scholarly treatises on the Potter phenom-enon. Nowhere on any of their covers is the boy's trademarked visage to be seen, though many carry a disclaimer indicating that neither Rowling nor her associates have created or endorsed the contents.[2] The closest analog to these disclaimers might well be the Surgeon General's warning, which reminds you of the dangers lurking inside your pack of cigarettes. Why do Rowling and company seem to think that unauthorized Potter products can prove hazardous to your health?

Potter's creators and rights holders are, of course, hardly the first to take issue with those attempting to ride the wave, legally or otherwise, of a popular artifact. What may be unusual, however, are the ways in which intellectual property concerns and even broader issues pertaining to security and logistics—matters typically discussed in the book industry's back office—have surged to the forefront, becoming facets integral to the everyday relationship of Rowling's fans to the Potter books. Think about the long line you or someone you know may have waited on, anxiously anticipating the stroke of midnight when the newest Potter tome would be released at long last. What purpose, exactly, did all that waiting serve beyond helping to ensure that no one would be able prematurely to reveal the book's twists and turns?

Neither demand nor accident can fully account for this type of response. Indeed, inasmuch as Harry Potter's enchanting spell might seem to derive from Rowling's ability to tell engaging stories, the series owes its success and popularity to far more than what lies within its pages. Crucial, too, are the conjuring acts that happen behind the scenes. In fact, the painstaking efforts by Rowling and her associates to control exactly when, where, how, and among whom the Potter books circulate, coupled with the often punitive measures they exact on those who deviate from their wishes, constitute a story almost as spellbinding as the Potter books themselves. It's a tale full of twists and turns that I'm calling "Harry Potter and the Culture of the Copy." In case you're wondering, it's completely unauthorized.[3]

This tale concerns the enabling conditions and the politics of the astonishing global popularity of the Harry Potter book series. It raises important questions about the originality, repetition, and circulation of commodities in the late age of print. The cast features illicit Potter volumes—early releases, knockoffs, imposter editions, soundalikes, contested copies, and more—that exist on the margins of, and constantly threaten to cross over into, legitimate consumer culture. The drama revolves around the rights holders' compulsive efforts to chase down and suppress these errant Potter volumes wherever and whenever they appear. In this chapter I will examine the political-economic relations within which an increasingly transnational book industry operates, the global uptake of and resistance to Western intellectual property law, and the relationship of both to broader practices of everyday life.

The first section focuses on publishers' efforts to coordinate the release of each new volume in the Potter series and the lengths to which they will go to secure millions of copies of each book prior to their authorized on-sale date. These measures, I contend, produce artificial conditions of scarcity in the global market for Potter books and happen to be a convenient way in which to promote each new release in the absence of advance reviews. The second section looks at a flurry of unauthorized Potter editions that in recent years have cropped up in, among other places, East and South Asia and eastern Europe. It takes issue with the discourses that Western media outlets use to frame the Potter piracy pandemic, which consistently obscure the conditions whereby piracy has come to thrive in these contexts.

Although this chapter does engage directly with the texts of the Harry Potter book series to a limited degree, it's more concerned with tracing what Dilip Parameshwar Gaonkar and Elizabeth A. Povinelli have called their "cultures of circulation and transfiguration."[4] The concept of transfiguration is particularly intriguing, for it has uptake not only in critical theory but also in the Harry Potter books. According to Gaonkar and Povinelli, it denotes the material and social processes through which objects change their form. Transfiguration basically means the same thing in Potter's universe, except there the process is a purely magical one. In any case, the connection is fortuitous. I will argue that what's at stake in the runaway global success of the Harry Potter book series is precisely the power of transfiguration and who gets to wield it legitimately and authoritatively.

Securing Harry Potter

The management of closely guarded stories can be an awfully mean business, a lesson Harry Potter learns only too well in *Harry Potter and the Order of the Phoenix*. Among those leading the effort is Dolores Umbridge, a manipulative Ministry of Magic policy wonk who launches Harry's fifth year at Hogwarts School of Witchcraft and Wizardry as its newly appointed instructor of Defense Against the Dark Arts. A daring day-one dustup with Dolores over Harry's claim to have witnessed the return of the evil Lord Voldemort (a.k.a. He-Who-Must-Not-Be-Named) earns the lad a weeklong detention in the clutches of the odious teacher, who concocts what seems like a hackneyed punishment. Like countless students before him, Harry is forced to transcribe, to his teacher's satisfaction, an abiding moral lesson, in this case the ironic refrain "I must not tell lies." Professor Umbridge provides young Harry with a special quill pen but curiously denies him any ink. He soon discovers why. The sadistic professor has put a spell on the quill so that it carves whatever Harry writes directly into the back of his hand, rendering the words he sets down on parchment in blood magically extracted from the wound. Each iteration of "I must not tell lies" tears deeper and deeper into Harry's flesh, leaving the boy with a grisly reminder of the hazards of circulating stories without proper authorization.[5]

As fantastic as this scene may seem, in a way it is a fitting parable for the measures authorities have taken to control Harry Potter's circulation and proliferation. The print run for the first American edition of *Harry Potter and the Sorcerer's Stone*, (published by Scholastic in 1998), the initial installment of the series, was an admirable—but by today's Potter standards comparatively meager—50,000 copies.[6] The next volume in the series, *Harry Potter and the Chamber of Secrets* (Scholastic, 1999), had a first printing of .25 million. That figure doubled with the release of *Harry Potter and the Prisoner of Azkaban* (Scholastic, 1999), which in turn increased to 3.8 million with the publication of *Harry Potter and the Goblet of Fire* (Scholastic, 2000). The first printing of the next installment, *Harry Potter and the Order of the Phoenix* (Scholastic, 2003), eclipsed that of all of the previous books combined, totaling 8.5 million. The first printing of the penultimate volume in the series, *Harry Potter and the Half-Blood Prince* (Scholastic, 2005), reached 10.8 million copies. With an initial print run of 12 million copies, the series finale, *Harry Potter and the Deathly Hallows* (Scholastic, 2007), edged out its predecessor to become the most extensively reproduced new release in the history of book publishing.[7]

Unsurprisingly, the steep upsurge in print runs occurring over the life of the book series has brought with it dramatic changes in the way Potter's trademark and copyright holders—Warner Bros. and Warner Bros./J. K. Rowling, respectively—allow the volumes to be sold. In 1998, before most American readers had even heard or uttered the name "Harry Potter," Scholastic released advance copies of *Harry Potter and the Sorcerer's Stone* to booksellers. Its editors hoped that doing so would lead store owners and staff to take an interest in the otherwise obscure British children's book and begin promoting it among their patrons.[8] Sure enough, booksellers hand-sold the volume and helped create a groundswell of interest in the burgeoning series.

Now, compare the slow and deliberate work that went into peddling the first book with that of *Harry Potter and the Half-Blood Prince*. Barnes & Noble anticipated selling the volume at the rate of about fifty thousand copies—the equivalent of *Sorcerer's Stone*'s entire first print run—per *hour* on the first day of its release in the United States. On the other side of the Atlantic, the British supermarket chain Tesco projected that first-day sales of the book would reach three hundred copies per minute, or eighteen thousand copies per hour.[9] Despite—or perhaps because of—the publishers' absolute refusal to circulate any advance copies of *Half-Blood Prince*, it reportedly sold 6.9 million copies in just the first twenty-four hours of its release in the United States.[10]

The issue of prereleasing titles has become a troubling one as far as Potter's publishers and rights holders are concerned. Scholastic, in particular, began running into trouble with the release of *Harry Potter and the Chamber of Secrets*. Publisher Bloomsbury had issued the latter in the United Kingdom about a year before its release in the United States and was able to do so because of the nature of territorial publishing rights, which empower the rights holder to issue a given title in a specific country or region whenever it chooses to do so. Most American Potter fans who had read and enjoyed *Sorcerer's Stone* anxiously anticipated the follow-up volume, but some grew impatient as Scholastic slowly churned out an edition of its own. Thus, an indeterminate number of American Potter fans contacted British booksellers and had them ship Bloomsbury editions to the United States well in advance of Scholastic's release.[11] They realized, in effect, how they could leverage an imbalance in the distribution of books in space—itself a result of legal contract—to correct an imbalance in the distribution of books in time. Suddenly and rather unexpectedly the everyday practice of buying and selling books had come to resemble the world of international arbitrage, where commodities brokers exploit these and other types of market inconsistencies for profit.

The asynchronous selling of Potter books posed both a legal and an economic quandary for the lad's rights holders, for if territorial rights were to mean anything, they needed to remain sovereign. Otherwise the value of those rights and, just as important, their status as such would (depending on your point of view) lead to welcome competition or nerve-racking volatility in the book market. Another way of putting this would be to say that in trying to overcome legally manufactured conditions of scarcity, fans of the Potter series de facto floated publishers' territorial rights on the open market. Their having done so certainly provided a short-term financial and competitive boost to Bloomsbury and to at least some Potter purveyors based in the United Kingdom. In the long term, however, the prospect of territorial rights becoming subject to the vagaries of consumer demand seemed like a recipe for fomenting uncertainty in an industry regarded by insiders on both sides of the Atlantic as having too much of it already.

Potter's rights holders had concluded that the time was out of joint and needed to be stabilized. Hence, the millennial release of *Harry Potter and the Goblet of Fire* brought with it major changes in terms of how it and the three remaining installments in the series would be issued in the English language. Bloomsbury, Scholastic, and Raincoast (Potter's Canadian publisher) would guarantee one another's territorial publishing rights by agreeing to what the book industry calls a "global lay-down date." Together they would agree on a single day on which they would release their respective editions simultaneously, thereby denying shoppers the opportunity to exploit systemic imbalances in the global market for Potter books that would accompany a more traditional rollout. While it's unclear whether *Harry Potter and the Goblet of Fire* was the first book to be issued in this way, it undoubtedly was among the very first to follow what's gone on to become a common industry practice for hotly anticipated titles.[12]

Intuitively, publishers' accession to global lay-down dates would seem to be consistent with the book trade's drive toward global interconnectedness and consolidation, a tendency underscored by the fact that revenues from more than three quarters of all books sold in the United States wind up in the coffers of just five multinational corporate media giants: Time Warner, Disney, Viacom, Bertelsmann, and News Corporation.[13] Globalization seems to be the order of the day not only in the book trade but also in countless other industries. This characterization is only partially accurate, however. Global lay-down dates certainly demand cooperation and coordination on a global scale. Yet their purpose is precisely to modulate a potentially more open, global, and asynchronous circuit of books and book culture in the name of maintaining territorial—often national—sovereignty and the rights corresponding to it.

Of course, it's one thing for three more or less like-minded publishers to agree to abide by a global lay-down date. Getting all those involved to acquiesce—from printers to shippers, warehousers, wholesalers, and retailers—in moving a popular book like Harry Potter to market is another matter entirely. Hence, from *Harry Potter and the Goblet of Fire* on, publishers demanded that any bookseller or librarian in Britain, Canada, or the United States wishing to distribute copies of the latest Potter release sign an embargo agreement stipulating that the book would not be sold or loaned prior to its lay-down date. For its part, Scholastic further insisted that all booksellers designate secure staging areas in which to store shipments of unreleased Potter books. It also recommended that booksellers prohibit employees from bringing anything into the area that would allow them to abscond with, or duplicate parts of, the rarified volumes.[14] In the event of a breach, Scholastic informed its clientele, the offending party could expect to face a costly lawsuit; have its supply of additional Harry Potter books restricted or cut off altogether; and lose the privilege of receiving other embargoed Scholastic titles prior to their street date.[15]

The contract for the final volume in the series, *Harry Potter and the Deathly Hallows* (2007), stipulated even more exacting terms. As if to underscore the magnitude of the volume's secrets—Is Professor Dumbledore alive or dead? Is Severus Snape good or evil? Will Lord Voldemort triumph? Will Harry or any of his closest friends die?—the document contained two new sets of provisions omitted from preceding agreements. The first set, which the document refers to benignly as "third party access guidelines," is perhaps better described as a gag order. It required booksellers not to disclose when they had received supplies of *Deathly Hallows*, where they were storing the much sought-after volumes, or their methods of securing them. This particular set of guidelines also delineated precise terms under which booksellers would be expected to manage the inquiries of journalists reporting on the run-up to the final Harry Potter release. Both a bookseller and security personnel would be required to accompany members of the press while they researched their stories, a measure designed to ensure that some overzealous reporter wouldn't try to swipe an advance copy of *Deathly Hallows* from a bookseller's storeroom. Photojournalists and videographers were only permitted to shoot pictures from beyond secure staging areas and could only take images of the sealed boxes containing copies of the book. Names and photos of bookstore employees were to be excluded from all press reports, presumably to protect them from threats, blackmail, or other methods by which "third parties" might coerce them into stealing advance copies. Finally, the contract required booksellers to guarantee that the press would refrain from releasing any photographs or video footage until five days before the lay-down date of July 21, 2007.[16]

Everyone was considered a potential thief—at least from Scholastic's viewpoint. Consequently no one could be trusted to preserve the book's secrets without a certain modicum of compulsion. This may help to explain not only the second set of provisions Scholastic included in its *Deathly*

Hallows embargo agreement but also the publisher's righteously indignant tone:

> We [the bookseller] acknowledge and agree that any such Violation [of the terms of the contract] will cause irreparable harm to Scholastic and the author, J. K. Rowling, and that monetary damages will be inadequate to compensate for Violations and that, in addition to any other remedies that may be available, at law, in equity or otherwise, Scholastic and/or J. K. Rowling shall be entitled to obtain injunctive relief against any Violation, without the necessity of proving actual damages or posting any bond.[17]

The language used here is worth examining. Though an early release of *Deathly Hallows* surely would result in the proverbial genie escaping from its bottle, and hence would entitle both the publisher and Rowling to some form of compensatory damages, it is difficult to grasp in exactly what sense violating Scholastic's sales contract would cause either party *irreparable* harm. Would Scholastic plunge into bankruptcy if the secrets were revealed prior to the official release date? Would a leak so damage Rowling's reputation as an author that she would be unable to profit from this work or publish any future work? Would all twelve million copies of *Deathly Hallows* go unsold? The answers to these questions are obvious.[18] Scholastic's proviso about "obtain[ing] injunctive relief" in the absence of its ability to "prov[e] actual damages" may even have suggested as much. That didn't stop the publisher from setting up a special toll-free hotline in advance of the volume's lay down, however, in the hope that upstanding members of the book world would tip off the company to miscreants who had breached their contracts.[19]

One American librarian offhandedly suggested that "we sign the pledge in blood," thereby drawing an eerie connection between the publishers' embargo agreements and the gruesome blood oath Dolores Umbridge forced on young Harry Potter in the fifth installment of the book series.[20] Potter's publishers, like Umbridge, clearly understood the stakes involved in letting stories circulate without what they considered to be the proper oversight. In fact, the embargo agreements comprised but one facet of a much broader set of both formal and informal guidelines Potter's publishers expected those involved in the boy wizard's lay down to abide by.

In addition to enforcing global lay-down dates, representatives from Scholastic performed stringent security inspections at every facility involved in the book's manufacture before each new Potter volume went to press. A company executive who toured one particular printing house took issue with its paper shredders, which the printer used to destroy errant pages. They didn't work well enough, Scholastic's inspector claimed, since the sample shreds he had seen were relatively thick and, worryingly, still readable. The printing house landed the lucrative Scholastic contract only after if it agreed to implement a new document shredding system consistent with the publisher's specifications.[21]

If creating a reliable and efficient distribution apparatus counted among the book industry's major problems in the first half of the twentieth century, then fine-tuning and securing that apparatus comprise two of the industry's most pressing concerns today. In the case of *Harry Potter and the Half-Blood Prince*, the time between Rowling's completion of the manuscript and its lay-down date was a scant seven months.[22] The breakneck pace of production, coupled with the publishers' almost maniacal interest in keeping the books under wraps, compelled them to implement unique just-in-time delivery systems to ensure that all copies of the book get to market safely and efficiently. This process begins at the bindery, where the finished Potter volumes are shrouded in high-test opaque plastic and placed into steel shipping containers, which are then tightly sealed.[23] Instead of warehousing them, as is the custom with most as yet unreleased books, the majority of Scholastic's editions is loaded directly onto a fleet of trucks waiting at the bindery. They're then hauled either directly to national chain stores or to one of several hundred secure hubs from which the publisher will supply smaller stores across the United States roughly thirty-six hours before the book's official release to the public.[24] Thus, behind every celebratory Potter release there lies a logistical operation whose pace, intricacy, and tight controls were, until recently, quite alien to the book industry.

In a move worthy of Mad-Eye Moody, the surly hunter of evil wizards whose magical, all-seeing eye lets no misdeed go unnoticed, Scholastic has outfitted all the trucks it uses to haul the sacred Potter volumes to market with global-positioning devices. The real-time, satellite-based tracking system allows the publisher to monitor the whereabouts of each one of the more than sixteen hundred trucks in its fleet to an exacting degree. Because Scholastic can find out instantly if a driver's made an unauthorized stop or has deviated from the precise route it's prescribed, it can summon the appropriate authorities to the scene within moments of a lapse having occurred. The tracking system also features a unique "electronic fence" function, which guards against the theft of Scholastic's trucks—and, more important, that of their precious cargo—once they've reached their designated delivery destinations.[25]

Despite the publishers' painstaking efforts at locking up new Potter stories, security breaches have still managed to occur. In 2003 New York's *Daily News* purchased a prematurely released copy of *Harry Potter and the Order of the Phoenix* from Karrot, a whole foods store in Brooklyn. The shop's owner, Carlos Aguila, claimed that neither Scholastic nor his regular book distributor, Ingram, had informed him of the Potter embargo. He therefore proceeded to unpack, display, and sell the four copies of *Harry Potter and the Order of the Phoenix* he had received, just as he would any other book. The *Daily News*, intent on demonstrating how easily Scholastic's supposedly stringent security system could be thwarted, published a two-page excerpt together with an explanation of how it had acquired its copy of the coveted novel before the global lay-down date.[26] So incensed was Scholastic that it threatened the newspaper with a one hundred-million-dollar copyright infringement suit, which the newspaper eventually settled out of court on undisclosed terms.[27]

Similar incidents occurred in the United States around the time of the release of *Harry Potter and the Half-Blood Prince*. Several copies of the book surfaced at a pharmacy in Kingston, New York, less than a week before the book officially went on sale. Nine-year-old Sylum Mastropaolo of nearby Rosendale and his mother, Mandy Muldoon, were thrilled to find the illicit stack lying on the store shelf while running errands on the evening of July 11—five days before the book was meant to go on sale to the public. They purchased a copy of *Half-Blood Prince*, took it home, but promptly had a change of heart. The boy and his family decided to alert Scholastic to the mishap and return the book. Much to the publisher's relief, Mastropaolo only had read a couple of pages in the ensuing days, for he had not yet finished the preceding installment of the series. According to the boy's stepfather, Mike Muldoon, the family wanted "to do the right thing [since they didn't] want to ruin it for other kids and take away from the experience of reading it together."[28]

A pair of Indiana businessmen, on the other hand, experienced little or no guilt after managing to pick up copies of *Half-Blood Prince* later that week at an undisclosed store near their workplace in Indianapolis. The seller, who reportedly was oblivious to the lay-down date, sold Tim Meyer and Andrew Rauscher each a copy of the book. By July 13, when the media caught wind of Meyer having bought the book, he had already read more than half of *Half-Blood Prince* and showed no sign of stopping, much less returning the book to Scholastic. Meyer wouldn't divulge any story details, but he did reveal the title of the eighteenth chapter, "Birthday Surprises," and called what he had read "pretty shocking."[29]

Britain has seen its share of Harry Potter security failures, too. In May 2003 Donald Parfitt, an employee of one of the printing outfits with which Bloomsbury had contracted, was arrested, fined, and sentenced to community service after he had attempted to hock the first three chapters of *Harry Potter and the Order of the Phoenix*. The man, who claimed he discovered the unbound pages in a parking lot near his workplace, absconded with the sheets and offered them unsuccessfully to the London tabloid the *Sun* for £25,000 prior to the book's June 21 release.[30] A month later an unidentified man made off with a truck containing 7,680 copies of *Order of the Phoenix* whose total retail value of £130,000 likely couldn't compare with what they'd be worth on the street in advance of the release date. Police recovered the truck thirty-six hours later, sans books, but in the meantime Bloomsbury had secured an injunction barring anyone, under threat of criminal prosecution, from publishing or discussing the contents of the book before the release date.[31]

Another incident in Britain preceded the 2005 release of *Harry Potter and the Half-Blood Prince*. About six weeks before its lay-down date, Aaron Lambert swiped two copies of the book from the warehouse facility where he worked—ironically as a security guard. He and an accomplice, Christopher Brown, then tried but failed to sell a copy of the book to a *Sun* reporter at gunpoint for £50,000. Lambert also attempted to blackmail Bloomsbury, threatening to divulge key aspects of the novel unless the publisher agreed to a payoff. Police eventually arrested the two men on theft, extortion, and firearms charges before either had managed to go public with the books. Lambert later pleaded guilty on all counts. Meanwhile, Bloomsbury obtained a court order enjoining anyone who had come in contact with the books from revealing any aspects of the story before July 16.[32] At his sentencing Lambert attributed his criminal behavior to the side effects of excessive steroid use, but Judge Richard Bray was unmoved. "It was only through the good services of the press and police that fans of Harry Potter—both young and old—were able to read the book without their pleasure being polluted by the premature publication of the plot," he pedantically propounded. Lambert's participation in the pernicious plot to peddle the purloined Potter earned him a four-and-a-half-year sentence in prison.

For its part, Canadian publisher Raincoast went into lockdown mode after it had discovered copies of *Harry Potter and the Half-Blood Prince* circulating in Coquitlam, a Vancouver suburb, nine days before its authorized release. Customers, overjoyed to have discovered the hotly anticipated volume already on sale, swept up fourteen copies before the seller realized its error and pulled the rest of the offending volumes from the shelf. Raincost reportedly learned of the mix-up from a man who, like young Sylum Mastropaolo, was overcome with buyer's remorse and decided to contact the publisher "to preserve the spirit of Harry Potter."[33] That good deed led to the company's securing an injunction from Justice Kirsti Gill, who ordered everyone who had purchased copies of the book to return them immediately to the publisher or face contempt charges and a costly lawsuit. The injunction also barred this small contingent of Potter fans from sharing aspects of the book with anyone, including "displaying, reading, offering for sale, selling, or exhibiting [it] in public" prior to July 16. Raincoast attempted to soft-pedal the whole affair by offering incentives—a commemorative bookplate autographed by J. K. Rowling, a souvenir T-shirt, and, once it was released officially, a complimentary copy of *Half-Blood Prince*—to any individuals who returned the books. A few apparently followed through.[34]

All these leaks paled in comparison with what happened in the week leading up to the July 21, 2007, release of *Harry Potter and the Deathly Hallows*. Whatever anxieties the book industry may have been harboring about the reproducibility of books in an age of accessible digital media came to a head when digital photographs showing the complete contents of *Deathly Hallows* surfaced on the Internet on July 16. The images quickly made their way onto popular file-sharing and social networking sites such as Gaia Online, MediaFire, Photobucket, and The Pirate Bay, where users, eager to learn how the series concluded, duplicated and exchanged them at an exponential rate. Suddenly the contents of *Deathly Hallows* were traveling through the same circuits that earlier had prompted the music and movie industries to file tens of thousands of copyright infringement lawsuits against file traders. Worse, their appearance there seemed to confirm—and probably augment—publishers' long-standing concerns about the pass-along book trade. Instead of acquaintances swapping relatively minute quantities of books back and forth within small, generally localized interpersonal networks, *Deathly Hallows* found itself coursing through a global electronic network at a speed that far exceeded Scholastic's ability to issue takedown notices.[35]

The situation escalated when, on or about July 16, online retailer Deep Discount.com mistakenly shipped about twelve hundred copies of *Deathly Hallows* to customers who had placed advance orders for the book. The volumes began arriving at their doorsteps within twenty-four hours. Scholastic promptly caught wind of the mishap and filed suit against DeepDiscount for having violated the publisher's sales agreement. Officials from Scholastic also pleaded with those who had received advance copies of the book to hide theirs until the July 21 release date.[36] Some may have complied, but at least one customer—Will Collier of Atlanta, Georgia—opted to resell his copy using the online auction site eBay. He verified the book's authenticity by photographing it atop the July 18, 2007, edition of the *Atlanta Journal-Constitution*—a presentation not unlike the proof-of-life photos typical in hostage cases (fig. 9). Robin Lenz, an editor at *Publishers Weekly*, rescued the captive copy at the "Buy It Now" price of $250 that Collier had set, its secrets apparently still intact. (Collier claimed not to have read the book, for which he had paid just $18.)[37] Meanwhile, the *New York Times* and the *Baltimore Sun* scooped their rivals with advance reviews of *Deathly Hallows*, the former having acquired its copy from an unidentified vendor in New York City, the latter from the relative of a *Baltimore Sun* reporter who had ordered it from DeepDiscount.[38]

The enormous lengths to which Harry Potter's publishers and an army of those in their employ have gone to synchronize his sales in the English language have left some wondering to what extent these measures are actu-

FIGURE 9 Photo of *Harry Potter and the Deathly Hallows* as it appeared on eBay July 18, 2007, three days before the book's on-sale date.

ally necessary to secure the newest installments of the book series. Indeed, several press reports have noted how, given the relative lack of anything substantive to say about the books prior to their release, journalists have been forced to report on distribution decisions, sales agreements, and security measures. For example, *Newsweek* asked, "Why all these embargoes and 'shock and awe' laydowns?", and proceeded to answer its own question by calling them "the most elaborate publicity stunt ever."[39]

American television channel Comedy Central's fake news program *The Daily Show with Jon Stewart* seemed to have reached a similar conclusion when, just days before the release of *Half-Blood Prince*, it set its sights on the lengths to which the boy wizard's publishers had gone to control the book's circulation. On July 14, 2005, "Senior Literary Security Analyst" Rob Corddry filed a mock investigative report entitled "Harry Potter Terror: Could It Happen Here?" in which he compared the security lapses in Canada and elsewhere to a successful terrorist campaign—which, if left unchecked, threatened to spread to (cue the overly dramatic music and reverb) *the United States of America!* The piece opened with Corddry barging into an unidentified bookstore, whereupon he noted how the many thousands of books on display there evidenced a reckless disregard for security. "What I saw shocked me," Corddry declared, feigning indignation. "No plot was safe from being spoiled." As if to underscore the point, he then wandered around the store, revealing juicy details about Dan Brown's *Da Vinci Code*, F. Scott Fitzgerald's *Great Gatsby*, and Edward Klein's *Truth About Hillary* to unsuspecting patrons. Next, Corddry went undercover to see if a disguise might help him to abscond with an advance copy of *Harry Potter and the Half-Blood Prince*. Despite putting on a halfhearted J. K. Rowling drag show (fig. 10) and posing as a representative from the Make-a-Wish Foundation (complete with a healthy-looking "dying" child in tow), booksellers rebuffed his repeated requests to see a copy of the book. Undeterred, Corddry confronted the store manager about the efficacy of the Potter security plans and pushed him to admit that ninjas conceivably could steal a copy of the book before the authorized on-sale date. The segment concluded with an on-screen graphic that read, "Harry Potter Terror: Could It Happen Here?" across which the word "YES" appeared in bright-blue bold letters.[40]

This pithy commentary on consumer culture illustrates both misplaced priorities and the politics of everyday fear. Corddry's report suggests that the publishers' efforts to secure Potter were excessive. Journalists, commentators, and critics amplified the absurdity of the whole situation through the complicity of their reporting. In treating the guarding of Harry Potter

FIGURE 10 *Daily Show* correspondent Rob Corddry, posing as J. K. Rowling, attempting to abscond with an early copy of *Harry Potter and the Half-Blood Prince.*

like a matter of national security, they exaggerated the gravity of the novel's secrets and the consequences of their premature revelation. Worse, they engaged in a banal yet effective kind of fear-mongering, given how they spun the security issue—actually a problem of asynchronous bookselling—in the service of promoting the boy wizard's continuing adventures. In a society where advertising, journalism, and political culture increasingly make a fetish of surveillance and security, it literally pays for everyone to be a potential terrorist, literary or otherwise.[41]

That said, one still wonders whether it was unreasonable for Scholastic, Bloomsbury, and Raincoast to take steps to protect their lucrative investments. Either way it's clear that the publishers saw security as integral to their Potter marketing campaigns and was thus an issue they could exploit for profit.

Nowhere was this strategy more apparent than in a short promotional video Scholastic produced for *Harry Potter and the Half-Blood Prince*, which follows a copy of the book on a transatlantic voyage from the United Kingdom to the United States.[42] The video opens in J. K. Rowling's office in

Scotland, where she autographs the volume and hands it off to an executive from Scholastic. He then places it in a camera-friendly clear plastic briefcase before locking the package up tight. Next, the executive delivers the book "under tight security" to the captain of the *Queen Mary 2* cruise liner, who ceremoniously places it into a sturdy shipping container.[43] A tight close-up follows in which the captain seals the container with a massive padlock, whereupon the box is loaded by crane onto the ship. After a quick montage of scenic shots in which the *Queen Mary 2* crosses the Atlantic, the ship arrives in New York City on July 2, 2005. There, as if to reemphasize the book's value and rarity, a forklift loads the still-sealed shipping container into a waiting armored car. The vehicle then drives off "to a secure and undisclosed location," as though its cargo were not one of 10.8 million copies of a popular publication but rather one adept-at-disappearing former vice-president of the United States, Dick Cheney, who found himself similarly whisked off in times of national emergency.[44]

Beyond Scholastic's treatment of a Potter book as though it were a beleaguered head of state, what's so noteworthy about this and the other publishers' efforts to promote every new series release since *Goblet of Fire* significantly through the efforts to guard them? First, their strategy shines a rather public light on the tedious logistical work, technical minutiae, and legal wrangling that have tended to transpire in the book industry's back office. With Harry Potter, this office, in effect, has been turned inside out. No longer does distribution consist simply of the behind-the-scenes, blue-collar business of slogging books to market. Now, suddenly, it offers a shining example of the book industry's progress as an industry, one capable of servicing a global clientele with astonishing efficiency and unprecedented oversight. Second, the security campaign is a testament to the enfolding of two previously distinct aspects of mass culture, namely, advertising and control. In chapter 3 I showed how, in the second quarter of the twentieth century, publicity campaigns competed with logistics and other such distributional concerns to mitigate systemic uncertainties in the book market. At the time they offered distinct yet complementary solutions to what amounted to a crisis of overproduction. Today, in the case of Potter's global lay-down dates, we may be witnessing a synthesis of these spheres such that publicity becomes a form of control (e.g., Judge Richard Bray's praising the press for turning in a would-be Potter despoiler) and control becomes a form of publicity (e.g., the video documenting the *Half-Blood Prince*'s heavily guarded transatlantic voyage).

Moreover, the publishers' efforts to secure Potter and hence to synchronize his sales in the English language illustrate both the range and intensity of the labor necessary to create conditions of scarcity. This point bears repeating: *scarcity takes work to produce*. In the case of Harry Potter, this work begins in the sphere of cultural production, but it's aided and abetted by the police, the courts, journalists, and a bevy of those working in the book industry's back office. Together they've managed to transfigure tens of millions of mass-produced consumer goods into what become, for all practical purposes, coveted rarities until the moment they're released to the public. In other words, they've become adept at making Potter disappear at decisive moments. Potter's rights holders and those they've annexed to their cause have thus engaged in a form of mass production complementing that of consumer goods—paradoxically the mass production of scarcity. Their efforts, in fact, have helped strengthen something akin to the magical aura of exclusivity that, as Walter Benjamin argued, mass reproduction should have obviated.[45]

What's striking, finally, is the way in which Potter's rights holders have conscripted fans to the cause of securing the boy wizard's stories. Those who obtained and subsequently returned early Potter book releases have tended to do so in good faith, believing that their principled acts uphold egalitarian conditions of access to stories that have enthralled millions of readers—including me. They're right in holding fast to their convictions, even though their honesty has served the publishers' less altruistic purpose of synchronizing the global market for Potter books. In helping to secure Harry Potter, in effect fans have been laboring to produce the very conditions of scarcity that, from an economic standpoint, might well be contrary to their own interests. Oligopoly, gag orders, and some commemorative bric-à-brac—what an odd way in which to repay such sincere expressions of goodwill! Yet the fact that at least some Potter fans have returned the books they've acquired in advance of specific lay-down dates suggests that they, too, have embodied something of the lesson the sadistic Dolores Umbridge forced young Harry to gouge into his own flesh: never, under any circumstances, allow unauthorized stories to circulate. This moral continues to be challenged not only at the site of distribution but also at that of production.

Pirating Potter

The world of books has been overrun by fakes, and nowhere is this lesson clearer than in *Harry Potter and the Chamber of Secrets*. There Harry and his cohort meet the enigmatic Gilderoy Lockhart, hero and heart-throb, who, as Lockhart recounts in his numerous best-selling books, has vanquished a surfeit of rampaging magical creatures. Despite Professor Lockhart's throng of swooning fans, Harry senses that something's a bit off about him. His classes seem more like self-promotional infomercials than rigorous instruction, and in a friendly public duel with Professor Snape, the ambiguously evil potions master at Hogwarts, Lockhart seems incapable of repelling even the most simple spell.[46] In other words, his private actions don't mesh with his intrepid public image.

Professor Lockhart's dubious public persona crumbles at the climax. There Harry and Lockhart find themselves stranded in the foreboding Chamber of Secrets, deep below the surface of Hogwarts, about to face an evil basilisk that's been terrorizing the school all year. Instead of confronting this rampaging magical creature, however, the alleged hero turns to Harry and announces that he's decided to flee:

> "You mean you're *running away*?" said Harry disbelievingly. "After all that stuff you did in your books—"
>
> "Books can be misleading," said Lockhart delicately. . . . [Mine] wouldn't have sold half as well if people didn't think *I'd* done all those things. No one wants to read about some ugly old Armenian warlock, even if he did save a village from werewolves. . . . "
>
> "So you've just been taking credit for what a load of other people have done?" said Harry incredulously.
>
> "Harry, Harry," said Lockhart, shaking his head impatiently, "it's not as simple as that. There was work involved. I had to track these people down. Ask them exactly how they managed to do what they did. Then I had to put a Memory Charm on them so they wouldn't remember doing it. . . . No, it's been a lot of work, Harry."[47]

Thus, the revelation that's been foreshadowed throughout the book is finally divulged, appropriately enough, in the Chamber of Secrets. Professor Lockhart's an impostor whose only real skill is his ability to repackage the good deeds of less charismatic witches and wizards from whom he's expropriated them.

The rise and fall of Professor Lockhart is a fitting parable for the history of books. As Adrian Johns, Susan Stewart, and Siva Vaidhyanathan have shown, fakery, dissimulation, and liberal amounts of borrowing—along with practices that many would decry as publishing piracy and textual corruption—have been the custom rather than the exception during the period of mechanically and electronically reproduced books.[48] In this respect Lockhart's statement that "books can be misleading" raises some of the major questions at stake in the political economy of book production, distribution, exchange, and consumption today: What counts as an original or a copy? How is that distinction determined? By whom? For whose benefit? Under what conditions?

Nowhere do these questions become clearer than in the controversies surrounding the global circulation of the Potter book series, in particular what Western media outlets typically describe as pirated Potter editions. These include a dizzying array of knockoffs, counterfeits, imposters, and unauthorized translations whose proliferation and popularity ought to be telling us less about the misdeeds of so-called publishing pirates and more about Western complicity in creating the cultural and economic conditions that have led to a flourishing of these "duplicates" in the first place.

Consider, for example, the imposter volume *Harry Potter and Leopard Walk Up to Dragon*. Here's what you see on the cover: a characteristically bespectacled Harry dressed in a black wizard's robe, holding on tight to a muscular centaur that defends him from a rather cross-looking dragon. Near the center are the initials "J. K.," followed by a series of simplified Chinese characters, indicating that the book was penned by J. K. Rowling. At the bottom right one finds an English-language logo, the letters "HP" rendered in the golden lightning bolt font familiar to most American Potter fans, followed by the two smaller but no less important letters, "TM," indicating the book's common law trademark (fig. 11). Turn to the next page and you'll encounter, along with the usual publication and electronic indexing information (in simplified Chinese), a series of assertive, legalistic statements (in English): "Text copyright C 2002 by J. K. Rowling"; "Harry Potter, names, characters and related indicia are copyright and trademark Warner Bros. C 2002." On the back cover there is a portrait of Rowling. The book even has a legitimate ISBN. (I checked the math.)

By the looks of things, it seems reasonably authentic. About a year before the release of the English-language edition of *Harry Potter and the Order of the Phoenix*, the 198-page *Harry Potter and Leopard Walk Up to Dragon* began selling in bookstores and street markets in Beijing, Hong Kong, Guangzhou, and other cities throughout China for anywhere between $1.00 and $2.80.[49] Given the book's design—including official logos, visual elements drawn from previous Harry Potter stories, ISBN information, and official-looking trademark and copyright declarations—it clearly was intended to be passed off as the legitimate fifth installment in the series. Reports are spotty, but estimates suggest that as many as a million copies

FIGURE 11 The cover of *Harry Potter and Leopard Walk Up to Dragon*. The imposter Harry Potter volume circulated in China in the summer of 2002.

of the bogus Potter books were sold before an official crackdown began a few weeks later.[50] Two additional Potter fakes, *Harry Potter and the Golden Turtle* and *Harry Potter and the Crystal Vase* (presented as, respectively, the sixth and seventh/final installments of the series) also reportedly surfaced and sold briskly in China around the same time.[51]

By early summer 2002 Rowling, Warner Bros., the Christopher Little Literary Agency, and Rowling's publishers had caught wind of the fake Potter volumes selling in China and promptly dispatched a team of lawyers and investigators to track down those responsible for producing them. They began by visiting the Inner Mongolia Printing House, the publisher to whom *Harry Potter and Leopard Walk Up to Dragon* had been attributed, but there they hit a dead end. Company executives vehemently denied having pirated Potter. The publication information appearing in the book, they maintained, had to have been a smokescreen meant to throw off the investigators Rowling and her representatives undoubtedly would send to quash the bogus volume. The team finally managed to secure a copy of *Harry Potter and Leopard Walk Up to Dragon* in Guangzhou. This edition evidently had been printed by Bashu, a publishing house based in Chengdu. When pressed, representatives of the firm confessed to having published *Leopard*, though they claimed ignorance of having violated any laws in doing so. Restitution consisted of a $3,000 fine and Bashu agreeing to issue a public apology, which was published in China's *Legal Times*. In a telling postscript to this story, it was later discovered that Bashu had not, in fact, published the edition of *Harry Potter and Leopard Walk Up to Dragon* that led Rowling's lawyers and investigators to its doorstep. Another still unknown firm had pirated the pirate Potter.[52]

So ends just one well-publicized example of Harry Potter's transfiguration, where copies produce copies and frauds beget frauds, resulting in a recursive spiral of illegitimacy, inauthenticity, and deceit. Despite Rowling, Warner Bros., and other authorities' intensive global efforts to police their coveted Harry Potter copyrights and trademarks,[53] fakery has proven to be endemic to the book series. Consider what *China Today* calls "The Chinese Harry Potter Epidemic," or a spate of "Harry Potter read-alikes" circulating in and around the country.[54] These include books like *Harry Potter's Sister*, author Serge Brussolo's book *Girl Wizard Peggy Sue*, which Chinese publishers retitled and repackaged—apparently without the author's consent—hoping to cash in on China's Pottermania. Then there's *The Magic Violin*, a novel purportedly written by nine-year-old Bian Jinyang. As with *Harry Potter's Sister*, Bian's publisher attempted to capitalize on the explosive popularity of the Harry Potter series by reissuing the book under the title *China's Harry Potter*.[55]

South Asia, too, has seen its share of Potter knockoffs. Because Harry Potter's official release in Hindi only occurred in November 2003—six years after the first Potter book's official release there in English—Indian translators had ample time to produce and circulate their own unofficial translations of the series for free (to those with access) over the Internet. In contrast, the authorized Hindi translation of *Harry Potter and the Philosopher's Stone*, published by Bopal-based Rakheja, reportedly sells for 165 rupees, or about $5.00.[56] Meanwhile, *China's Harry Potter* seems to have found its Indian counterpart in *Harry Potter in Calcutta*, where, in author Uttam Ghosh's story, our hero interacts with a host of classic "characters from Bengali literature." Harry's adventures in Calcutta were cut short, however, after his publisher, under pressure from Warner Bros., decided to discontinue the book.[57]

Still another Potter interloper has surfaced, this one in Russia: Tanya Grotter, the eleven-year-old title character of the country's briskly selling book series. The first and most obvious point of comparison is the names, Harry Potter and Tanya Grotter, which share a similar syllabic and phonic structure. Thematically Tanya, like Harry, is an orphan who attends an exclusive school for up-and-coming wizards and witches—not Hogwarts, but the Tibidokhs School of Magic. And like her Anglo counterpart, Tanya's preferred mode of transportation is an enchanted object; whereas Harry prefers the traditional broomstick, Tanya travels atop a flying bass (the musical instrument, not the fish).[58] The similarities of Potter and Grotter also extend into the realm of design, with the fonts and color schemes featured on the covers of the Grotter volumes clearly borrowed from the American editions.

In 2002 author Dmitry Yemets penned the first installment in the series, the 413-page *Tanya Grotter i Magicheskii Kontrabas* (Tanya Grotter and the Magical Double Bass), and over the next four years he and his Moscow-based publisher, Eksmo, released an astonishing ten more Grotter volumes (fig. 13). The books typically sell for about $2.50, or less than half the going rate for the officially sanctioned Potter books published in Russia; in many stores they are placed alongside the authorized Potter volumes.[59] Although Tanya's sales figures trail those of Harry's, her numbers are nonetheless impressive. During a nine-month period between 2002 and 2003, Russian booksellers reportedly sold 600,000 copies of Tanya's adventures, compared to about 1.5 million copies of Harry's escapades.[60]

FIGURE 12 The cover of the Russian edition of *Tanya Grotter and the Magical Double Bass*. Note the design similarities with Scholastic's Harry Potter volumes.

Further complicating matters for Potter's rights holders is Porri Gatter, Belarus's adolescent hero, whose first adventure, *Porri Gatter I Kamennyj Filosof* (Porri Gatter and the Stone Philosopher), was published in November 2002.[61] The title clearly pays homage to Rowling's *Harry Potter and the Philosopher's Stone*, yet the name only scratches the surface of the many similarities between the books. Like Harry, young Porri is born of and lives predominantly among enchanted people in England, and both boys are hounded by relentless evil nemeses. Potter's archrival, Lord Voldemort, finds a doppelgänger of sorts in Gatter's world in the anagrammatic Mordevolt, a.k.a. He-Whose-Name-Shouldn't-Be-Pronounced-in-Public-Places, a.k.a. You-Know-Who-I-Mean.[62] Beyond the oftentimes tongue-in-cheek mood and thematic appropriations, *Porri Gatter and the Stone Philosopher* contains its share of embellishments. For instance, Porri is born a non-magical "Muddle" to parents who, unlike Harry's, survive the evil Mordevolt's initial attack. Unlike Voldemort, moreover, Mordevolt long ago opted out of wizardry after a chance encounter with Leonardo da Vinci's ghost led him to develop an almost cartoonish fascination with high technology—one which, along with his magical powers, imprint themselves on young Porri during a botched murder attempt.[63] Authors Ivan Mytko and Andrei Zhvalevsky acknowledge having read and been inspired by Rowling's books, though they insist that theirs is a parody—a permissible use under some international intellectual property paradigms—rather than an illicit derivation. Rosman, Harry Potter's Russian publishing rights holder, has concurred, perhaps in part because of Porri Gatter's first printing of just seven thousand copies and the fact that Potter has yet to be translated into Belarusian.[64]

Still, the same can't be said for the Tanya Grotter series, whose popularity, financial success, and borrowings from the Potter series have landed it squarely in Rowling's and her associates' crosshairs. Like his Belarusian counterparts, Yemets openly admits to having drawn inspiration for his title character and key aspects of the young heroine's adventures from the Potter book series. Similarly, he insists that his books are parodies that, suffused with Russian culture, deserve to be exempt from international intellectual property restrictions.[65] The cases of Gatter and Grotter differ, however, in at least one important respect: Yemets's claims about the legitimacy of his appropriation have failed to persuade Potter's rights holders. Rowling and her associates have repeatedly demanded that both author and publisher discontinue production of the book series, though their threats of legal reprisal have yet to slow the momentum of the Russian Grotter machine.

Not only have Yemets and his publisher continued to produce installments of the Grotter books in Russia, but they've also inked licensing and translation deals that, in principle, would allow them to expand and profit from the girl wizard's sale abroad. "In principle" is the operative phrase here, since Potter's rights holders have been unrelenting in their drive to quash all Potter pretenders they consider to be damaging to their intellectual property rights. Though Rowling and her associates may have failed to halt Grotter's triumphant march through Russia, the latter's forays abroad are another matter. Her westward expansion has opened up new opportunities for Rowling and her team to score the legal victories they felt they had been denied, given the fact that western European nations have a longer and more substantial tradition of upholding international intellectual property rights compared to the former Soviet republics.[66] Grotter's internationalization has also presented Rowling and her associates with a chance to send a stern message to all would-be Potter piggybackers: cease and desist—or don't start copying Potter in the first place—unless you want to face a costly and time-consuming lawsuit. Books, after all, shouldn't be misleading.

The parties finally squared off in the Netherlands after publisher Byblos announced in early 2003 its intention to produce the Dutch translation of *Tanya Grotter and the Magical Double Bass*. The company began by making the already delicate situation even worse when, in its spring 2003 sales circular, it boldly described young Tanya as the "Russian 'sister' of Harry Potter."[67] Potter's rights holders were outraged. They already had serious qualms about Grotter's originality, and now they were incensed by her prospective publisher's attempt to hock the offending translation by drawing a familial link between the title characters. The boy wizard's rights holders promptly filed suit in the District Court of Amsterdam, citing a long list of similarities they insisted overstepped the bounds of creative propriety. By early April, Rowling and her team had managed to secure an injunction barring Byblos from producing any Grotter translations, though the publisher quickly responded by filing an appeal.[68]

The briefs that Byblos's attorneys filed with the Court of Appeal of Amsterdam held firm to Yemets's contention, namely, that the Grotter novels parodied Potter and thus deserved to be exempt from any copyright or trade rights restrictions. They went on to describe *Tanya Grotter and the Magical Double Bass* as "an ironic polemic" by means of which Yemets intended to expound his unique worldview and asserted that the novel was more "philosophical" and morally ambiguous than any that had been published thus far in Rowling's series. As such, they suggested, the Grotter books ultimately were more adult-oriented than were those of Potter.[69]

Byblos's attorneys weren't content merely to defend Yemets's book. They went on the offensive, challenging the substance of Rowling's own copyright. Like numerous scholars and critics before them, the attorneys noted that Rowling had appropriated many elements of the Potter stories—orphan tales, British boarding school dramas, fantasy stories—from already existing literary materials, only some of which were in the public domain.[70] At worst, they contended, Yemets's novel was a derivation of an already derivative work. If that were the case, what would be the point of adjudicating the legitimacy of one author's acts of appropriation over those of another? At best, they insisted, *Tanya Grotter and the Magical Double Bass* was a substantially original work whose differences flowed from Yemets's *creative acts of appropriation*.

The court's decision, which was handed down on November 6, 2003, reads like an assiduous work of literary criticism. It adjudicated the originality and distinctiveness of *Tanya Grotter and the Magical Double Bass* largely by conducting a side-by-side close reading of the Potter and Grotter stories. Having made a detailed inventory of the similarities, the court moved on to address the issue of their differences by critiquing Rowling's and Yemets's writing styles. It called the former's more "sober and subtle" and the latter's "superfluous," "complex," and digressive. It indicated that these differences, though apparent, were insufficient to distinguish Rowling's and Yemets's stories from one another in any substantive way.[71] The court added that most of the differences specific to the stories—such as the sex of their respective title characters—"seem[ed] rather artificial."[72]

Still, the court needed to contend with Byblos's assertion of the polemical and parodic character of *Tanya Grotter and the Magical Double Bass*. It began by noting the book's genre, which it described as a fairy tale, and asserted that such works don't lend themselves well to making polemical arguments.[73] (The court evidently hadn't read Gregory Maguire's *Wicked: The Life and Times of the Wicked Witch of the West* or John Gardner's parody of *Beowulf*, *Grendel*, two exemplars that mobilize the fairy tale genre for the sake of polemic.) Concerning the matter of parody, the court shifted its focus from the book's content to its context: "Byblos mentions that Yemets had wanted to tell the story of Harry Potter *anew* and that the 'very convincing story about Tanya Grotter' was unique and authentic. The only conclusion one can draw from these facts is that Byblos . . . took [Tanya Grotter] entirely serious[ly], and not as a parody of [Harry Potter]."[74]

Where the court did admit to Grotter's parodic dimensions, it immediately downplayed them. In particular, it took issue with those moments in which the novel seemed to "wink at the hype surrounding Harry Potter." A true parody, it insisted, would rail more directly "against the book [*Sorcerer's Stone*] itself."[75] Parodies should, of course, home in on the distinguishing elements internal to a given text, but why must their doing so exclude a text's conditions of reception? Indeed, wouldn't any parody worthy of the name be hard pressed *not* to comment on Potter's unusual success?[76] The court nevertheless was unequivocal in its findings: Yemets was "free to build on earlier literature, but then with his *own* story. The conclusion must be that [Tanya Grotter] is an unauthorised adaptation of [Harry Potter]."[77]

The language that pervades both the Grotter decision and the foregoing analysis of Potter fakery in South and East Asia and eastern Europe—

imposter, knockoff, pirated edition, fake, unauthorized adaptation—suggests the primacy or originality of Rowling's books over books like *Harry Potter and Leopard Walk Up to Dragon, Harry Potter in Calcutta, Porri Gatter and the Stone Philosopher, Tanya Grotter and the Magical Double Bass*, as well as other titles published after her series. Both the temporality and crypto-moralism implied in this language is unfortunate, unwanted, perhaps even unwarranted. Yet it's difficult to avoid for at least two reasons: first, because of an epistemological proclivity prevalent in Western philosophy (at least since Plato) to see the world in terms of originals and copies; and, second, because of a flaw inherent in the English language, which provides a rich vocabulary for differentiating so-called real objects from fakes, but which is less helpful in positing a world populated by, and in differentiating only among, fakes. Equally important, the language of originals and copies tends to direct attention toward specific objects while deflecting it from their conditions of production, circulation, and transfiguration.

For instance, consider how Western media outlets have tended to frame the phenomenon of global book piracy in general and acts of Potter fakery in particular. By many accounts book publishing piracy in South and East Asia, South and Central America, eastern Europe, and the Middle East has reached epidemic proportions, resulting in a devastating economic impact on Western publishers. U.S. book publishers' estimated losses due to foreign book piracy—an umbrella term that encompasses professionally printed illegal editions, illicit photocopying of copyrighted materials, unauthorized translations, and online peer-to-peer file sharing of copyrighted texts—reportedly topped five hundred million dollars in 2003 alone.[78] One uncorroborated estimate places the global book industry's losses due to piracy as high as seven billion dollars.[79]

Among the many culprits, the People's Republic of China (PRC) is the bête noire of the book industry, not to mention the culture industry at large. One U.S. critic has described it as "the piracy capital of the world."[80] Indeed, U.S. book publishers estimate a net loss of about $40 million to Chinese pirates in 2003 alone,[81] although this figure appears to have fallen significantly since the PRC's entry into the World Trade Organization in December 2001. Before then, American and British publishers reportedly lost $150 million to piracy in the PRC, a number that's all the more startling in that it only accounts for losses due to the unauthorized reproduction of academic and professional journals.[82]

A 2003 report broadcast on the *CBS Evening News* had this to say about the implications of book piracy in the PRC and elsewhere: "Millionaire authors like 'Potter' writer J. K. Rowling may not miss the lost income, but in parts of the world where books mean knowledge and knowledge means progress, the pirates are stealing more than money; they're stealing the future."[83] What's odd about this statement—and about Western reporting on intellectual property concerns in South and East Asia, eastern Europe, and elsewhere—are the contradictions and reversals of accountability they embody. While unauthorized reproduction may militate against some generally smaller publishers taking risks on unproven authors or book projects, the suggestion that pirate publishers somehow "steal the future" by forestalling the production and distribution of knowledge is absurd. In many instances they facilitate those practices, often in places where historically embedded power structures and bad economies conspire to limit the creation and flow of knowledge-based goods through legitimate channels. As Ravi Sundaram has written of cultural piracy in India: "This is a pirate modernity, but one with no particular thought about counter-culture or its likes. It is a simple survival strategy."[84]

Consider, for example, the price of so-called Harry Potter rip-offs, which often is about half that of the legitimately produced installments of the Potter book series. Now consider the price differential alongside the Asian financial crisis of the mid-to-late 1990s. The crisis was brought on in no small measure by Western financial institutions calling in loans en masse they had made to their East Asian counterparts, resulting in the substantial devaluation of currencies throughout the East Asian region and a corresponding decline in consumer spending. Russia felt the effects of the crisis, too, in the form of a steep falloff in its oil exports to East Asia and a resulting decline in the value of the ruble.[85] As Shujen Wang has noted, these conditions forced many legitimate DVD and VCD manufacturers—and, presumably, other cultural producers—either to start producing cheaper (i.e., pirated) goods or stop producing altogether since in many cases those whom they hoped would purchase their legitimate goods no longer possessed sufficient economic capital to do so.[86]

Moreover, because legitimacy can be such a tenuous state of affairs, the producers and sellers of errant cultural goods aren't necessarily—or, at least, simply—the malicious pirates that most Western media make them out to be. Granted, some of those who operate in the shadows of legitimate cultural production are out to turn a quick profit by exploiting intellectual property rights they don't own or by taking advantage of unsuspecting consumers. Yet the conspicuous absence of any shades of gray in this portrait of piracy suggests that it amounts to little more than a caricature of those who trade in counterfeits, imposters, and the like. For instance, Ziauddin Sardar has shown how at least some purveyors of pirated cultural goods genuinely look out for the interests of their customers by helping them to differentiate between more or less acceptable versions of the illicit items in which they're interested. The seller in Sardar's case study even offers a no-hassle return policy in the event that a purchaser finds a particular item to be of unacceptably low quality.[87] At least some of those who produce and sell pirated cultural goods also trade in legitimate goods in part to service, economically speaking, the broadest possible clientele. They are, in other words, legitimate businesspeople who also happen to trade in pirated goods.[88] Western discourses about publishing and other forms of piracy often fail to account for the vast gray market in cultural goods in which fakes, frauds, and illicit editions blend in easily with the "real thing" and generally above-board business practices. Nor are buyers simply the unsuspecting prey of conniving pirates. Many seem to understand perfectly well that they're buying what Sardar calls "genuine fakes,"[89] or objects that, for whatever reason, prove to be acceptable alternatives to authorized cultural goods.

The global outsourcing of factory labor from the West (see chapter 2) and related economic imbalances may help to account for why at least some people opt to buy unauthorized cultural goods. As Sardar writes of the situation in Kuala Lumpur, Malaysia: "Those who labour in the factories to produce all the consumer desirables often earn too little money to buy the genuine branded end products. . . . The fake economy . . . enables those with little money to keep themselves in the game of social presentation and fashion permutations."[90] Whether intended or not, the ubiquity of Western products within the context of their foreign manufacture helps to stimulate a demand—even an expectation—among those charged with producing them. This isn't a problem in itself, but it becomes one when Western and local rights holders are unwilling to make their goods available at prices consistent with manifest economic conditions. The producers and sellers of pirated cultural goods may take advantage of buyers at times, but if that's the case, they're certainly not the only ones guilty of exploiting people's consumeristic desires and pushing them toward illicit goods.

Then there is the thorny legacy and persistence of British and American imperialism, a factor that's startlingly absent from many discussions in the West about the popularity of pirated English-language books, especially those circulating throughout East and South Asia.[91] To put it bluntly, mainstream Western discourses about publishing piracy tend to be profoundly amnesiac. They almost unilaterally sidestep the reprehensible acts that have helped lead, either directly or indirectly, to the formation of what Wang calls a global "shadow economy."[92] This legacy has been compounded by the propagation of Western development schemes in East and South Asia and parts of eastern Europe, which both implicitly and explicitly demand that people living in these locales model their social, cultural, and economic behavior on patterns established elsewhere. These schemes generally are premised on a logic of repetition whose parameters are quite narrowly—and often ethnocentrically—defined.[93] Bricolage, indigenization, parody, and other forms of appropriation are frequently perceived by Western journalists, intellectual property rights holders, and others to be insufficiently or inappropriately transfigurative acts. This perception, in turn, places those who have assumed the task of development in an impossible position. On the one hand, they're charged with repeating foreign values, styles, and culture, while, on the other, they are condemned for having done so under existing economic and infrastructural conditions. Despite their complaints, Western authorities tend not to admit their part—our part—in both creating and sustaining the conditions leading to book piracy and other forms of intellectual property piracy on the world scene.[94]

Western intellectual property owners' presumptive claims about sales lost to pirates also are worth examining more closely. Wang has noted that Western estimates of financial losses due to piracy tend "to be based on extrapolation from very limited information."[95] A typical calculation for computing these losses assumes that every Potter imposter or knockoff means one less sale of a legitimate edition. According to this logic, Potter fakes necessarily devalue and degrade the original series on a one-to-one basis. This reasoning is flawed if for no other reason than it assumes a zero-sum economy of cultural and economic value. It's virtually inconceivable for, say, *Harry Potter and Leopard Walk Up to Dragon* or *Tanya Grotter and the Magical Double Bass* to maintain a more synergistic relationship to the authorized Potter books by generating continuing enthusiasm for the series while anxious fans await the next legitimate installment.[96]

Similarly, this reasoning allows one to forget the myriad ways in which alleged pirates potentially add value to cultural goods through the tedious work of translation, as well as creating Web sites and other promotional materials. For instance, Berlin is home to an eight-hundred-member Harry Potter translation collective where group members eager to read new Potter installments in their native language agree to translate or proofread portions of each new book for the privilege of accessing the final (unofficial) translation online—often months before the release of an official translation. The group's Web site (www.harry-auf-deutsch.de) also hosts a discussion forum where members exchange ideas about or work through specific problems in translation; they also confer about mistakes and oversights that they've found in the official German-language Potter translations.[97] The point I am trying to make is that Western intellectual property law/jurisprudence may very well be working against itself, especially when rights holders assume that they must use the law to militate unilaterally against the production of value forms other than those they've authorized.

Ironically, *Harry Potter and the Chamber of Secrets* contains within itself an apt lesson about popular books and the lengths to which people will go to gain access to them. Upon discovering that brothers Ron, Fred, and George Weasley all would need to buy the complete works of Gilderoy Lockhart to fulfill their studies at Hogwarts, George states: "That won't come cheap. . . . Lockhart's books are really expensive." Conscious of her family's meager income, Mrs. Weasley turns to him and resignedly replies, "Well, we'll manage."[98] Like many consumers hamstrung by limited economic mobility, the Weasleys are forced to make do in the face of a resplendent array of enthralling books that they're expected to buy but cannot really afford. So goes the tale of the pirated Potters. It is, at least in part, a tale about managing, of finding creative ways of getting by in the face of global economic uncertainty, imperial legacies, development pressures, and a profound lack of distributive justice. Books can be misleading, but even the misleading ones can tell us a great deal about how the global book industry—and this world of ours—works and for whom.

He-Who-*Must*-Be-Named

Harry Potter proliferates. He moves. He changes. He escapes.[99] So goes "Harry Potter and the Culture of the Copy," a strange tale about the transfiguration of the boy wizard's forms and meanings as he circulates the world over. From the orphan characters alleged to have inspired J. K. Rowling to Tanya Grotter and her ilk, our hero certainly is a shifty fellow. And yet his shiftiness is only half the story. Inasmuch as "putting culture into motion" may be a useful methodological technique by which to "foreground the social life of" a given object "rather than reading social life *off* of it,"[100] we also need to be vigilant in identifying the many administrative, legal, material, practical, procedural, and technical encumbrances that impinge on an object's capacity to move and change. Shifty he may be, but, as we've seen, sometimes Potter's rights holders insist that he stay still.

In chapter 3 I demonstrated the growing economic importance of the book industry's capacity to distribute its wares quickly and reliably. Here the obverse may be true as well. Friction, deflection, and stasis constitute key tools by means of which authors, publishers, and other interested parties try to increase their profits and lay claim to a greater market share. What's at stake in the global success of the Potter book series is not only its circulation and transfiguration but also its embeddedness in an increasingly complex circuitry of control. Control monitors and regulates, permits and forbids, legitimates and condemns. Its purpose is to confront and exploit the capacity of specific artifacts to move and to permute. Accordingly, it forms a crucial locus of power for those engaged in the production, distribution, exchange, and consumption of books. Though Potter's publishers clearly have flaunted it, control also operates more subtly, suffusing the everyday practices and routines that are constitutive of contemporary book culture. In short, control encompasses a broad set of conditions and techniques affecting how one wields the power of transfiguration—or whether one gets to wield that power at all.

We've witnessed the union of circulation, transfiguration, and control in the rather duplicitous relationship Potter's publishers seem to share with the mass-production process. According to *Newsweek*, Scholastic's initial print run for *Harry Potter and the Order of the Phoenix* required 30,000 pounds of ink, about 13.5 tons of paper, and approximately 120,000 "man-hours" for workers to print and bind all 8.5 million copies of the book. Similarly, its first printing of *Harry Potter and the Half-Blood Prince* consumed 16,000 tons of unrecycled paper, for which an estimated 220,000 trees had to be felled. (The latter prompted a Greenpeace boycott, which resulted in Scholastic's decision to publish *Harry Potter and the Deathly Hallows* on more environmentally friendly paper.)[101] These examples clearly underscore the book industry's enormous productive capacities. What they obscure, however, is the way in which the industry simultaneously manufactures scarcity in order to regulate demand. This process begins in the abstract, when Potter's rights holders artificially manipulate the availability of the books in space and time. In more concrete terms, it's manifested in the publishers' lay-down agreements, the rights holders' injunctions and lawsuits, and the good old-fashioned guilt some people feel when they happen upon a prematurely released Potter book. In other words, Potter's publishers have become quite adept not only at making millions of Potter books but also at making them vanish—save for the few, disquieting appearances that anticipate their arrival en masse at the stroke of midnight.

Despite the book industry's history, which evidences an avowedly uneasy and sometimes ambivalent relationship to commerce, it clearly has the capacity to become an astonishingly complex, well-coordinated, business-savvy enterprise; in some ways it already has become one. I do not, however, wish to paint a one-dimensional portrait of the contemporary book industry. Barnes & Noble might have expected to sell fifty thousand copies of *Harry Potter and the Half-Blood Prince* each hour on the first day of its release, but as company CEO Steve Riggio observed, "Less than one percent of all books published sell that many copies in a lifetime."[102] Harry Potter is thus an exceptional case when it comes to the book industry's everyday operations. The series is a best seller's best seller, with unusually broad-ranging appeal, but its success—or, more precisely, the conditions surrounding its success—aren't yet applicable across the book industry as a whole. This doesn't mean that we should dismiss Harry Potter as an anomaly. Other than providing entertaining stories, the value of the series lies in the many opportunities it affords to glimpse the growing entanglement of circulation, transfiguration, and control, and, more specifically, emerging values and practices that may be becoming normalized in the book industry at large. These include everything from the use of GPS and other tracking technologies to uniform selling agreements, security standards, and product authentication.

The global ebb and flow of the Potter book series also calls for a more contingent understanding of what's often referred to as piracy and, for that matter, of cultural appropriation and creativity. To put it bluntly, you don't know much about mass culture unless you come to grips with the intricate imbrications of legitimacy and illegitimacy prevalent throughout the entire circuit of production, distribution, exchange, and consumption. The challenge consists in figuring out how the boundary separating cultural legitimacy from illegitimacy is determined and by whom, and to view such acts as efforts to control the circulation and transfiguration of books and book-related products.

The point of all of these efforts to map instances of Potter book piracy is not simply to valorize these deeds as heroic acts of resistance. Rather, it is to identify some of the conditions under which people are willing to risk fines, imprisonment, public humiliation, and other forms of punishment for the sake of writing, manufacturing, disseminating, reading, and otherwise consuming books—objects that at some level they feel are vital to their well-being. In this chapter I have attempted to convey some sense of how cultural legitimacy and illegitimacy might be allowed to mingle a bit more freely. Since it's not always clear, for example, that unauthorized uses of a given party's copy or trade rights produce negative repercussions for the rights holder, those who make their livelihoods producing or trading in books and other cultural goods might do well to loosen up on the controls a little rather than arbitrarily threatening lawsuits or securing injunctions.

There may be no more fitting moral to the story of "Harry Potter and the Culture of the Copy" than the following exchange in *Harry Potter and the Sorcerer's Stone*. "Call him Voldemort, Harry," Albus Dumbledore instructs his charge as the boy clumsily attempts to circumlocute the name of his nemesis. "Always use the proper name for things. Fear of a name increases fear of the thing itself."[103] The young wizard's rights holders have benefited handsomely from his name, visage, and adventures circulating and proliferating on the world scene. At the same time, however, they also clearly fear for the ways in which these copyrighted and trademarked materials can be transfigured, that is, used and altered by parties without their consent, or in ways inconsistent with their plans. They want us to share their fears and to respect the fences they've built around Harry Potter's world. Those fences, they claim, protect us from illicit Potter pretenders and guard the significant investments they've made in bringing the beloved book series to market. Yet those fences stretch too far and encompass too much when they make us question whether we can even utter the name Harry Potter in public without jinxing ourselves. It's up to us to find the courage not to be intimidated and, where appropriate, to fight for what lies on the other side.

Conclusion From Consumerism to Control

I INITIALLY POSITED a perceived crisis, a decline in the quantity of literature being read that threatened to corrupt the quality of culture. From laments about the negative impact of e-books on the authority of printed books to concerns about the predatory business practices of corporate booksellers on- and offline, and from Oprah Winfrey's power to determine which books deserve to be read to the lockdowns resulting from the premature release of Harry Potter volumes, crises seem to abound in the late age of print. Does this mean that the latter represents a crisis period in book history? Not necessarily, for those who sound the alarm bells have a tendency to exaggerate or misconstrue what's at stake. The late age of print hardly portends cultural homogeneity, the end of printed books, or the complete upending of literary authority, though more modest changes in these and other spheres undoubtedly have occurred and will continue to do so.

In other words, the late age of print isn't a period in which familiar aspects of books and book culture are nearing their final and definitive moment of reckoning. Rather, it's a more dynamic and open-ended moment characterized by both permanence and change. Elizabeth Eisenstein has summed up the situation, noting how those who proclaim the end of what's often referred to as "print culture" tend to do so in ways that reinforce modes of thought, conduct, and expression long associated with printed books. "Premature obituaries on . . . the end of the book," she writes, "are themselves testimony to long-enduring habits of mind. In the very act of heralding the dawn of a new age with the advent of new media, contemporary analysts continue to bear witness, however inadvertently, to the ineluctable persistence of the past."[1] Accordingly, the late age of print is a period rife with consistency and contradiction, tradition and transformation, deference and discord. Although it's not a crisis period per se, it's definitely an uncomfortable period in which to live, if for no other reason than everyday book culture seems deeply and profoundly unsettled.

The preceding chapters illustrated how the late age of print lurches forward and backward, slowly and spasmodically. Every few years or so an e-book revolution seems to flare up, only to fizzle out within a relatively short period of time. In a little over a decade Oprah's Book Club has come, gone, metamorphosed, returned, and (as of this writing) seems to be going strong and barely holding on at the same time. The Harry Potter series has shaken up nearly all facets of the book trade, and one can only wonder what will happen now that the book series has ended. Participants in Laura J. Miller's study of retail bookselling expressed similar feelings when they described "a sense in which one era was coming to a close, but no one had yet developed absolute certainties about the future."[2] Something nebulous appears to be on the horizon, though determining what that "something" is and how it will affect established ways of producing, distributing, exchanging, and consuming books remains something of a mystery.

What, then, are we to make of the late age of print, given all the starts, stops, and frustrations that pervade everyday book culture today? James Carey has provided a clue when he wrote that "we are living . . . in a period of enormous disarray in all our institutions and in much of our personal life as well. We exist on a 'verge,' in the sense Daniel Boorstin gave that word: a moment between two different forms of social life."[3] If Carey is correct, then the late age of print may not be a determinate historical period but rather an indeterminate time *between* periods, a protracted moment in which we find ourselves straddling two different but imbricated configurations of reality. The tension between what I've been calling consumerism and control would seem to suggest that this is a plausible hypothesis. Here I want to suggest that whatever discomfort may arise from living in the late age of print is the result of these two ways of life colliding with one another, like tectonic plates jostling for position. Their convergence places new constraints on political action, while at the same time opening up unique opportunities for repeating everyday life differently.

On the Verge

Economically the first half of the twentieth century was a deeply troubled time in the United States, and mass consumerism arose in part as a way of rectifying the situation. Crises of overproduction, depressive economic conditions, and persistent labor unrest combined to produce an uncertain future for the country's budding industrial economy.[4] An expanding middle class emerged from these troubled circumstances, an alternative to the "bloody capitalism" that for the better part of a century had pitted workers against both the owners of the instruments of production and the state. Lizabeth Cohen has summarized the historic bargain that produced not only this new middle class but also a new, consumer-oriented economy:

> What social scientists have since labeled the "embourgoisement" of workers also implied a trade-off: rewards of material prosperity and social integration in return for ceding shopfloor control and company governance to management, and for accepting private corporate welfare such as pensions and health insurance in place of an expanded and more social democratic welfare state. . . . Corporate America got stability, and workers learned to derive increasing satisfaction and status from the lives they created outside of work, thanks to high wages and generous fringe benefits.[5]

From the 1940s through the 1960s places like Barnes & Noble in New York City simultaneously reflected and reinforced these larger changes taking place in the nation's economy and class structure. They were places that made books and other mass-produced goods abundantly available for consumption by middle-class people and those who aspired to be so. Perhaps unintentionally they brokered in possibilities for social democracy vis-à-vis the advancement of working people, but they did so without a sustained critique of the basic tenets of capitalist accumulation.

This history isn't meant to suggest the complete enervation of those whose claims to social, political, and economic power have rested on their ability to consume books and other commodities. Far from it. The widespread availability of mass-produced consumer goods and the concomitant rise of consumer capitalism helped fuel the growing importance of what was then a relatively novel form of politics—cultural politics—beginning somewhere around the middle of the twentieth century. Cohen has described how African Americans pressed for equal rights as citizens not only through organized protests and other forms of social activism but also through their increasing ability to interact with consumer goods: "As war administrators increasingly moved consumption into the civic realm, African Americans, like white female citizen consumers, made it a new ground upon which to stake their claim to fuller political participation. Citizenship came to be defined more broadly to encompass new kinds of political rituals beyond traditional voting and military service, and in the process the potential for political discontent and the grounds for mobilizing against discrimination grew."[6]

During the Second World War and in the following decades the political field in the United States began enlarging and realigning. As mass culture came to pervade the fabric of daily life, it ushered in new forms of political mobilization centered on and around consumer goods and people's everyday consumptive practices. Hence, when Raymond Williams wrote in 1958 that "any account of our culture which explicitly or implicitly denies the value of an industrial society is really irrelevant; not in a million years would you make us give up this power," the latter referred to more than just the sense of convenience these new consumer goods afforded.[7] Although formal political processes and social activism remained crucial vehicles by which to effect change, they increasingly intersected with and were inflected by people's investments in the mass-produced objects that surrounded them.

Chapters 2 and 4 underscored the continuing efficacy of both consumerism and cultural politics in the late age of print. In chapter 2, for example, I showed how the city of Durham, North Carolina, leveraged the construction of a shopping mall, which included a Barnes & Noble superstore, in an attempt to redress disparities that had long disadvantaged Durham's African American population, as well as the city's population as a whole, relative to Chapel Hill, its wealthier, whiter neighbor. Similarly, in chapter 4 I examined how Oprah's Book Club has helped to open possibilities for women both to distance themselves from and to reflect on the conditions of their daily lives. The club's willingness to embrace veteran, sporadic, and nonreaders has resulted not only in a dynamic book list but in a distinct economy of bibliographic value. On Oprah's Book Club, categories of truth and actuality supersede the more traditional—and traditionally divisive—canons of high and low culture that have sustained a certain literary authority for well over a century.

In this respect consumer capitalism isn't simply a mode of production significantly driven by, and whose well-being largely depends on, the conspicuous consumption of mass-produced commodities. While it would be ludicrous to suggest that it hasn't been successful at exploiting consumeristic desires, in the end we're more than one-dimensional people or mere cogs in the system. Consumer capitalism repeatedly produces repeated things, and while these objects can and do foster a strong sense of routine, they also serve as common resources by means of which individuals and groups can reshape their lives. As Michel de Certeau has stated: "To a rationalized, expansionist and at the same time centralized, clamorous, and spectacular production corresponds *another* production, called 'consumption.' The latter is devious, it is dispersed, but it insinuates itself everywhere, silently and almost invisibly, because it does not manifest itself through its own production, but rather through its *ways of using* the products imposed by the dominant economic order."[8] To consume isn't simply to use up, in other words, but to make do in unique and unexpected ways. Consumer capitalism thus implies at least a modicum of agency, given how its products and the institutions associated with them can help facilitate our acting creatively in the world. This is why cultural politics mattered—and why it continues to matter to this day.

The preceding chapters have related another story as well. They've shown how some of consumer capitalism's defining attributes have been challenged in recent decades and how, consequently, the enabling conditions of cultural politics have themselves come under attack. For example, in chapter 1 I explored how the digital rights management schemes embedded in some e-book technologies restricted the circulation of e-book content—in extreme cases by erasing it altogether. It's worth remembering that these technologies emerged, in part, as responses to the proliferation of printed books after 1930 and what the book industry considered to be the problems associated with their more or less unfettered circulation. Similarly, in chapter 3 I explored how, following a crisis of overproduction in the 1920s and 1930s, the book industry improved its capacity to distribute its wares. Since then the International Standard Book Number, machine-readable bar codes, and related back-office systems have not only helped to mitigate a good deal of the guesswork associated with book production and selling but also to create a book-distribution apparatus that's carefully monitored and intensively micromanaged. Finally, in chapter 5 I examined how Harry Potter's rights holders have attempted to regulate when, where, how, and among whom the Potter books and Potter-related indicia circulate. Coordinated lay-down dates, tracking technologies, threats of legal reprisal, and other measures modulated the global proliferation of the Harry Potter series and restricted how various transfigurations of the boy wizard could be put to use.

Collectively these and other examples point to a persistent problematizing of activities that were and continue to be quite common under consumer capitalism, not to mention an insurgent desire among agents of capitalist accumulation to police the disposition of consumer goods more rigorously than they ever have previously. These examples point to the gradual and as yet incomplete emergence of what Henri Lefebvre has called a "society of controlled consumption."[9]

Lefebvre arrives at this phrase after surveying a range of shibboleths social theorists have advanced to characterize postwar Western societies. Among those he rejects are "industrial society" (too totalizing), "technological society" (too deterministic), "affluent society" (too optimistic), and "society of leisure" (too misleading).[10] Lefebvre also tellingly refuses to accept that modern Western societies are clearly consumer societies, owing in part to the persistence of both ideologies and practices of thrift from the nineteenth to the twentieth centuries.[11] He also hesitates to use the phrase "consumer society" because of what he takes to be the growing organization and regimentation of consumeristic practices after about 1960.[12] In the end, instead of rejecting the phrase outright, as he does the aforementioned terms, he offers a more tentative assessment. The phrase is "not entirely satisfactory" in that it foregrounds the dominance of consumer capitalism at the cost of obscuring that formation's own historicity.[13] Consumer societies encompass both residual and emergent elements that aren't altogether commensurate with—and may even be antagonistic toward—some of consumer capitalism's core strategies. Any effort to name the postwar period must therefore confront the dynamic becoming of capitalism itself.

Lefebvre admittedly does get a bit ahead of himself. One gets the impression that consumer capitalism is completely on the skids, and that a society of controlled consumption has all but supplanted it. Lefebvre was writing in the late 1960s, right around the time ISBNs, machine-readable bar codes, stricter copyright statutes, and other instruments of control were only starting to be implemented within and beyond the book industry. Thus, he didn't glimpse the emergence of a society of controlled consumption as much as he beheld its "pre-emergence," to borrow a term from Raymond Williams. Control was "active and pressing but not yet fully articulated" when Lefebvre began his initial inquiry.[14] As such, it surely hadn't edged consumer capitalism out of existence—nor has it done so thus far, for that matter. Nevertheless, the brilliance of Lefebvre's analysis resides in his having discerned the rudiments of this formation before it coalesced more fully in the final quarter of the twentieth century.

A society of controlled consumption both operates and attempts to organize social life pursuant to a general logic of control, which according to Lefebvre is actuated in four specific ways. First is a critical infrastructure consisting not only of enormous industrial capacity but, equally important, of cybernetic systems that manage key aspects of commodity production, distribution, exchange, and consumption.[15] The managerial dimension of cybernetic systems is vital, for it's what sets them apart from more run-of-the-mill communication and information technologies. The words "cybernetics" and "governor" share the common Greek root κυβερνήτης, or "steersman."[16] Hence cybernetic systems aren't mere technical infrastructure whose purpose is to convey information, nor are they neutral pathways leading from the "real" world into the "virtual" world. Rather, they're directive and regulatory apparatuses, like the elaborate computer controls that orchestrate workflow in Amazon.com's distribution facilities.

Second, control operates through a process Lefebvre calls programming.[17] To be sure, ideology is a tricky business. Though it may work, there's no guarantee that it will. The fact of advertising isn't enough to ensure that someone will buy a particular consumer good or use it in a prescribed way, try as advertising agents might to convince us otherwise. This is reflected in the old saw bandied about the ad industry: "I know that half of my advertising budget is wasted, but I'm not sure which half."[18] Programming, on the contrary, attempts to minimize—and, ideally, to eliminate—whatever freedom of choice may still exist in the realm of consumer culture. It does so by causing certain things to happen automatically. In chapter 1 I showed how some e-book technologies literally have been programmed with locks, time limits, usage caps, and more, all of which allow hardware developers, software engineers, and digital content providers to oversee the circulation and longevity of e-books. Programming need not occur purely in the digital realm, however. The publisher Scholastic, it will be recalled, has tracked the whereabouts of its fleet of Harry Potter delivery trucks using GPS devices, satellites, computers, and electronic fence systems, all of which help to ensure that the drivers follow the company's mandated delivery routes and that the coveted merchandise will arrive in stores on time and without incident.

Third is the related attribute of control Lefebvre identifies as obsolescence.[19] This term may be somewhat misleading since obsolescence in a society of controlled consumption differs from what the term usually designates in consumer capitalism. The latter proceeds mainly by way of planned obsolescence, which consists of the deliberate malfunctioning of consumer goods within a given period of time and of the regular release of new styles into consumer markets.[20] (Think of the mountains of discarded personal computers that now reside permanently in landfills because their processors and hard drives can't accommodate software released even just a few years ago.) Planned obsolescence doesn't guarantee obsolescence, however. Though certain objects may be made to break, and though there may be tremendous psychosocial pressure to replace putatively outmoded consumer goods, nothing can assure their failure or replacement. Controlled obsolescence, on the other hand, turns the cliché "failure is not an option" on its head. In a society of controlled consumption, failure would be the only option for a given item—at least ideally. This is certainly the case with time-limited and disappearing e-books, whose programming undermines whatever permanence the notion of ownership might once have implied.

Finally, societies of controlled consumption secure their power and authority significantly by troubling, acting on, and reorganizing specific practices of everyday life.[21] For example, in chapter 1 I showed how something as banal a bookcase can embody specific dispositions toward commodity ownership, accumulation, and display, which are consistent with consumer capitalism and hence anathema from the standpoint of control. E-books attempt to make bookcases—and hence the ways of life with which they're associated—irrelevant. The same goes for the common practice of passing along books to friends, family, and acquaintances, a practice that people like Edward L. Bernays and other forebears of control tried their best to scandalize. Alternatively, think about the way in which Oprah's Book Club inverts the age-old logic of branding. It used to be that products were branded to help consumers differentiate among similar items in the marketplace. Not so with Oprah®, whose brand is so elastic that it would be more apt to say it's "producted" with books—not to mention magazines, television shows, movies, apparel, baby outfits, fitness programs, dog training systems, and more.[22] Then there are the long lines that millions of Harry Potter fans have waited on, anticipating the release of each new installment of the book series. The lines are more than just a prosaic form of crowd control. They're one way in which Potter's publishers enforce their global lay-down agreements at the level of the everyday and how, by extension, they mitigate what were once more consumer-friendly imbalances in the global marketplace for Harry Potter books.

So why not call this emergent formation "post-consumer capitalism," a name perhaps more in keeping with the current academic fashion? Consumer capitalism, both in name and in practice, places consumers center stage as both objects and subjects of the drama of capitalist accumulation. They are objects insofar as capitalism created an expansive consumer class in the early-to-mid-twentieth century by increasing wages and shortening the work week.[23] They are subjects insofar as consumerism also empowered individuals and groups to politicize themselves in new, more or less meaningful ways, that is, to engage in cultural politics. Yet, as Gary Cross has observed, "The triumph of consumption in the past century [the twentieth] is not a certain model for the next."[24] Notice, for example, how the word "consumer" is nowhere to be found in Lefebvre's phrase "society of controlled consumption." Its absence is more than a matter of semantics. Consumers still play a crucial role in a society of controlled consumption; after all, someone has to do the consuming. On balance, though, this type of society tends to be less consumer-centric compared to consumer capitalism. Indeed, a society of controlled consumption is premised on a transformation of the figure of the consumer from subject to object of capitalist accumulation—this despite the rhetoric of "empowerment" and "interactivity" that pervades contemporary media and consumer culture.[25] This shift is evident in the growing body of legal and technological constraints that today place serious limits on the efficacy—or even the possibility—not only of consumer activism but of cultural politics more broadly defined.[26]

Harry Potter is illustrative in this regard. The popularity of unauthorized Potter books worlwide underscores the persistence and continuing import of cultural politics in the late age of print. Intentionally or not, these books constitute efforts on the part of non-Western cultural producers simultaneously to exploit and challenge the global hegemony of Western cultural goods. By the same token, the vehemence with which Potter's rights holders have policed appropriations of the boy wizard's name, character, story lines, and related indicia underscores the very real constraints on cultural politics today. Their motivations may be largely economic, given how they tend to frame their threats and pursuit of legal action as efforts to protect valuable intellectual property rights. The effects of their actions, however, exceed the economic. They can result in unreasonable terms of access to, and of use of, key resources for engaging in cultural politics. Little wonder, then, that intellectual property has become such a contentious and, indeed, ubiquitous issue during the last twenty or thirty years. Intellectual property disputes often result when a dominant form of consumer capitalism and an emergent society of controlled consumption collide.

This isn't to suggest that books are singularly responsible for or implicated in whatever changes may be occurring in the realm of capitalist accumulation. Rather, these changes are the result of a broader process by means of which reality is actively being reconfigured. In music and video publishing, for example, trade organizations such as the American Society of Composers, Authors, and Publishers (ASCAP) and the Motion Picture Association of America (MPAA) have responded to consumer-centric practices, such as peer-to-peer file sharing, with a swift and formidable crackdown. Like their counterparts in the book industry, these organizations have implemented ever more rigorous legal and technological controls in order to regulate the conditions under which music and video consumption occurs. The changes taking place in everyday book culture constitute but one facet of a constellation of informally interconnected events that are in the midst of transforming the very fabric of social and political-economic reality.

Some writers have classified the phenomena I associate with a society of controlled consumption under a kindred theoretical heading. Drawing on Michel Foucault's lectures at the Collège de France in the late 1970s, they speak of the growing prevalence, in the United States and elsewhere, of "neoliberal governmentality."[27] The phrase refers to a particular form of post-welfare politics in which the state outsources the responsibility of ensuring the population's well-being to individuals, who are expected to look after themselves. It further refers to the subordination of state power to the dictates of the marketplace, so that solutions to "political" problems are increasingly posed in market terms. For example, Mark Andrejevic has shown how the "war on terror" has been prosecuted as much through traditional military might as it has through the U.S. government's injunction to its citizens to purchase plastic sheeting, duct tape, surveillance gear, and other do-it-yourself items to achieve a heightened state of "readiness."[28] Neoliberal governmentality thus puts forth an ethic of self-care in lieu of a broader social consciousness and celebrates individual acts of consumption as evidence of good citizenship.

Neoliberal governmentality, its critics argue, is a diffuse form of rule whose strategies and imperatives of control suffuse even the most mundane practices of everyday life. A relevant example from—although certainly not confined to—the book world would be the customer loyalty cards Barnes & Noble and Borders actively promote. In exchange for personal information (name, postal address, e-mail, phone number, etc.), they offer specialized discounts, targeted news, and other perks as a form of customer appreciation. These programs also promise a more interactive and individualized book-buying experience, as evidenced by the "personal shopping days" that accrue to those who purchase frequently at Borders. There are downsides to these types of programs, however, and in significant ways customer loyalty is only backhandedly rewarded. The bar codes appearing on the reverse side of loyalty cards allow companies like Barnes & Noble and Borders to record information about a customer's specific transactions in their databases. Once this information is cross-referenced with that of other customers, these booksellers are able to create detailed profiles and individuated marketing instruments to better influence the purchasing habits of their customers. In other words, each transaction customers make using their loyalty cards produces valuable data for these booksellers. In effect, they are outsourcing the costly labor of market research to their most loyal customers, who ironically buy back the labor they've freely given with each subsequent purchase.

Andrejevic has dubbed this type of activity "the market analogue" of the forms of self-management typical of post-welfare politics.[29] We're promised unprecedented levels of freedom, interactivity, and customization—which is to say a heightened degree of control over the disposition of our lives—yet the critics of neoliberal governmentality say that in reality this sense of control is an illusion. It masks the extent to which we're surveilled, mined for data, and compelled to act in ways contrary to our own interests—more than even Karl Marx could have imagined. Instead of being in control, these critics suggest, our daily lives are increasingly controlled by the agents of capitalist accumulation.

There's certainly a strong measure of truth to this claim. Consequently, it's easy enough to see the affinities between a society of controlled consumption and the techniques of neoliberal governmentality. I nevertheless hesitate to embrace the latter paradigm since it seems to view control as a given rather than as a major point of contestation in the late age of print. In the preceding chapters I demonstrated how the book industry's grip on consumer activity has been tightening over the last several decades, and how the industry has pioneered in laying the groundwork for controlled consumption. What's also clear from these chapters, however, is that the industry's desire for control is attenuated by a restless public that refuses to be impressed by the industry's tough talk or to defer in every instance to its technological innovations. Indeed, the phrase "control is an illusion" cuts both ways.

The other problem with neoliberal governmentality is that it smoothes over the complex historicity of contemporary social formations, which consist of dominant, residual, and emergent elements. Its exponents want to tell a story about control so unique that they risk underestimating the degree to which consumer capitalism and cultural politics persist in the present—and not as a mere residuum. An important exception to this would be Foucault himself, who cautioned against seeing processes of control as a replacement for, rather than as an addition to, the forms of rule preceding it.[30] In doing so, he indirectly affirmed why a phrase like "the late age of print" is so important. It indexes not a distinct historical moment but rather a point of conjuncture where at least two historical formations meet. Instead of the possibilities for politics diminishing, it would be more accurate to say they're being transformed—or maybe even multiplying.

Politics in the late age of print may assume familiar forms, like the labor activism several years back at Amazon.com (which, as of the present writing, is still percolating over at Borders), the acts of transvaluation evident on Oprah's Book Club, or the many appropriations of Harry Potter circulating globally. To dismiss these deeds as somehow out of step with the times politically or as mere throwbacks to a bygone era is to adopt a rather uncomplicated view of historical reality. Nevertheless, in a time when law and technology increasingly interact to restrict how people can use signs and other such commonplaces that pervade everyday life, more conventional forms of cultural-political struggle will need to be complemented with other strategies. Significantly, it will be necessary to identify and exploit vulnerabilities in the technical and legal infrastructure according to which control sustains itself, as illustrated by the case of *Harry Potter and the Deathly Hallows*. A simple mailing error opened the floodgates to the book's uptake and rampant reproduction online, ultimately leading to the collapse of the intricate web of rules, routes, regulations, and routines Potter's publishers had spent months—even years—constructing. The error also gave Will Collier—who hocked the advance copy of the book he received on eBay—an opportunity to test the integrity of the first-sale doctrine, a key limitation on copyright, precisely when publisher-initiated embargoes were poised to force its rollback.[31]

Collier's action was important, I believe, not only because he took advantage of a Harry Potter security lapse and consequently demonstrated—as many have—control's endemic precariousness. If Tarleton Gillespie is right about control "writing alternatives out of existence" (e.g., the first-sale and fair use doctrines), then politics in the late age of print must do more than just short-circuit certain aspects of a technical-legal system.[32] It must also attempt to restore a sense of the choices that would—or *should*—otherwise be available to us. In this respect I'm inclined to agree with Alexander Galloway, McKenzie Wark, and others who have argued that "hacking" is an apt metaphor to describe this type of political practice. Here the term is understood not in the sense of malicious deeds carried out by rogue computer programmers but rather in the more general sense of the activities individuals and groups may engage in to "leverage possibility."[33] Hacking attempts to actualize absent alternatives, effectively writing them (back) into the realm of everyday existence.

From Heyday to History and Beyond

Clearly books have a great many stories left to tell, although you would hardly know it given the dearth of scholarly investigations of books and book culture on the twentieth century and after. At the risk of oversimplification, academic historians have tended to focus on the early-modern and modern periods, specifically the years 1500–1899. I suspect this may have something to do with the epistemological proclivities of the discipline of history, which understandably tends to be somewhat wary of research that smacks of contemporaneity. The characteristically high quality of this body of research notwithstanding, scholarly book history sees a noticeable falloff at the start of the twentieth century.

As I noted in the introduction, however, there's no shortage of books either celebrating the persistence of print or mourning the technology's alleged decline in the twentieth and twenty-first centuries. These tend to be trade books about books. In contrast to their scholarly counterparts, enough of them have appeared over the last decade or two that it seems safe to say the genre has developed into something of a cottage industry. Their appearance is conspicuous in this regard, which leads me to speculate that it may be motivated as much by an affirmative desire to champion print as it is by a more defensive sense in which printed books no longer possess the authority or relevance they once did. As James Carey states: "Scholarship on the book is, in one sense, another example of the principle of Minerva's Owl: we focus our energies on a phenomenon at the moment it takes flight, at the moment we are about to lose it. Scholarship becomes simultaneously an episode in nostalgia and a way of finding our bearings in a world that seems to be shifting under our feet."[34] Indeed, whether these books about books aspire to celebrate or to defend print, there's something pathetic about them—as though, despite themselves, they were trying to convince readers of the enduring import of printed books.

Paradoxically, both the relative absence and conspicuous ubiquity of research into the recent history of books can reinforce a sense in which the technology has seen its heyday. In the first case, a falloff in book historiography can give the false impression that there isn't much left to say about books and book culture after 1900. In the second case, the recent history of books seems to become—at least on some level—a matter of grasping at straws. I'm especially heartened to see a groundswell of interest in the recent history of books and book culture, particularly among scholars and writers who refuse to accept that books today are anachronistic, less relevant, or represent a type of media in decline.[35] Their work—and, I trust, this book—challenges the sense of heyday-ism and locates books and book culture at the forefront of the contemporary historical process.

Writing a more rigorous recent history of books is important for many reasons, among which is the need to challenge common misconceptions about how other media affect books and book culture. For example, conventional wisdom holds that electronic media jeopardize the existence of printed books and the reading of them. The NEA study *Reading at Risk*, which I cited in the introduction to this book, significantly attributed a two decades-long decline in the reading of literature to the impact of electronic media: "The decline in reading [between 1982 and 2002] correlates with increased participation in a variety of electronic media. . . . While no single activity is responsible for the decline of reading, the cumulative presence and availability of these alternatives have increasingly drawn Americans away from reading."[36] What's striking about this statement is how the NEA simply assumes that electronic media and printed books are agonistic "alternatives." Is that actually the case?

By studying book culture across a variety of sites, guided by the principle of intermediation, I've demonstrated how printed books and electronic media can complement one another. Their synergy was especially evident in chapter 3, in which I explored how computers and other electronic devices facilitated the large-scale distribution of printed books, and in chapter 4, in which I investigated the stunning success of Oprah Winfrey's TV-based book club.[37] In the end, claims about the decline of books and book culture probably tells us more about the gaps in book history that need filling or about popular culture's proclivities toward crisis discourse than it does about the health of books in the twentieth and twenty-first centuries.

The sooner we come to grips with the vitality of books in the late age of print, the sooner we'll be able to explore even more meaningfully how, through the growing prevalence of books in everyday life, present conditions are opening out onto emergent futures. Throughout this study I've demonstrated how crisis discourses about books have for decades obscured how books have been implicated in an active process of problematizing the routines associated with consumer capitalism and in helping to actualize a nascent logic of control. Books have long been at the cutting edge of capitalist development—and they remain so to this day.

Crisis discourses do more than just obscure the political work being carried out through books and book culture. If we're living on a "verge," as Carey says, then we have reason for both pessimism and optimism. The changes currently underway in and beyond book culture threaten to constrain the accessibility, ownership, and potential uses of books and other consumer goods. More perniciously, they appear to be limiting the efficacy of the very kind of politics—cultural politics—in which many scholars active in the twentieth century have invested a great deal of faith. Living life on the verge of something can be a disturbingly unsettled experience as older habits of thought, conduct, and expression appear to give way to newer ones that have yet to fully replace them. This experience, however, can also be regarded as more open-ended and hopeful. Transition implies that the future has yet to be settled once and for all, and that politics, however (re)defined, remains a possibility. Books and book culture can reveal emergent trends and tendencies that may be antidemocratic, but they also should remind us that life may repeat itself differently—and, with any luck, for the better—every day.

Notes

Introduction: The Late Age of Print

1. National Endowment for the Arts, *Reading at Risk: A Survey of Literary Reading in America*, Research Division Report, no. 46 (Washington, D.C.: National Endowment for the Arts, 2004), xiii.
2. Ibid., 1. On the following page of the report one reads: "No distinctions were drawn on the quality of literary works."
3. Ibid., ix.
4. Ibid.
5. Ibid., xiii.
6. National Endowment for the Arts, *To Read or Not to Read: A Question of National Consequence*, Research Division Report, no. 47 (Washington: National Endowment for the Arts, 2007).
7. Ibid., 16–18.
8. In the preface to *Reading at Risk* NEA chairperson Dana Gioia observed: "Although the news in the report is dire, I doubt any careful observer of contemporary American society will be greatly surprised—except perhaps by the sheer magnitude of the decline" (vii).
9. D. T. Max, "The Last Book," *Utne Reader*, March–April 2001, 74–78; David A. Bell, "The Bookless Future: What the Internet Is Doing to Scholarship," *New Republic*, May 2, 2005, http://www.tnr.com/doc-mhtml?i=200502&s=bell050205; Sven Birkerts, *The Gutenberg Elegies: The Fate of Reading in an Electronic Age* (New York: Fawcett Columbine, 1994); Tom Engelhardt, *The Last Days of Publishing: A Novel* (Amherst: University of Massachusetts Press, 2003).
10. John Updike, lecture presented at BookExpo America, Washington, D.C., May 20, 2006, http://bookexpocast.com. The *New York Times* subsequently published a

modified version of Updike's address. See John Updike, "The End of Authorship," *New York Times*, June 25, 2006, http://www.nytimes.com/2006/06/25/books/review/25updike.html.

11. Kenneth Burke, "Literature as Equipment for Living," in *The Philosophy of Literary Form*, 3rd rev. ed. (Berkeley: University of California Press, 1973), 293–304.

12. André Schiffrin, *The Business of Books: How International Conglomerates Took Over Publishing and Changed the Way We Read* (London: Verso, 2001), 2.

13. Jay David Bolter, *Writing Space: Computers, Hypertext, and the Remediation of Print* (Mahwah, N.J.: Lawrence Erlbaum, 2001), 3.

14. Nicholas A. Basbanes, *A Gentle Madness: Bibliophiles, Bibliomania, and the Eternal Passion for Books* (New York: HarperCollins, 1995). See also: Nicholas A. Basbanes, *Patience and Fortitude: A Roving Chronicle of Book People, Book Places, and Book Culture* (New York: HarperCollins, 2001); idem., *A Splendor of Letters: The Permanence of Books in an Impermanent World* (New York: HarperCollins, 2003); Matthew Battles, *Library: An Unquiet History* (New York: Norton, 2003); Lawrence Goldstone and Nancy Goldstone, *Slightly Chipped: Footnotes in Booklore* (New York: St. Martin's Press, 1999); Rob Kaplan and Harold Rabinowitz, eds., *Speaking of Books: The Best Things Ever Said About Books and Book Collecting* (New York: Crown, 2001); Harold Rabinowitz and Rob Kaplan, eds., *A Passion for Books: A Book Lover's Treasury of Stories, Essays, Humor, Lore, and Lists on Collecting, Reading, Borrowing, Lending, Caring For, and Appreciating Books* (New York: Three Rivers Press, 1999); and Jerome Rothenberg and Steven Clay, eds., *A Book of the Book: Some Works and Projections About the Book and Writing* (New York: Granary Books, 2000).

15. See, e.g., Dwight Conquergood, "Rethinking Elocution: The Trope of the Talking Book and Other Figures of Speech," *Text and Performance Quarterly* 20, no. 4 (October 2000): 325–41; Carolyn Marvin, "The Body of the Text: Literacy's Corporeal Constant," *Quarterly Journal of Speech* 80, no. 2 (May 1994): 129–49; Carolyn Marvin, "Bodies, Texts, and the Social Order: A Reply to Bielefeldt," *Quarterly Journal of Speech* 81, no. 1 (February 1995): 103–7; and Laura J. Miller, *Reluctant Capitalists: Bookselling and the Culture of Consumption* (Chicago: University of Chicago Press, 2006), 204–9.

16. William Mitchell has described printed books as "tree flakes encased in dead cow." See his *City of Bits: Space, Place, and the Infobahn* (Cambridge: MIT Press, 1996), 56.

17. Raymond Williams, *Writing in Society* (London: Verso, 1983), 70. Williams is writing about the British context, though I think it's safe to say that his observation is applicable to the United States. See also Paul Star, *The Creation of the Media: Political Origins of Modern Communications* (New York: Basic Books, 2004), 124.

18. The following are among the most important works documenting aspects of this history in the twentieth century: Janice A. Radway, *Reading the Romance: Women, Patriarchy, and Popular Literature* (Chapel Hill: University of North Carolina Press, 1984), esp. 19–45; idem., *A Feeling for Books: The Book-of-the-Month Club, Literary Taste, and Middle-Class Desire* (Chapel Hill: University of North Carolina Press,

1997); and Joan Shelley Rubin, *The Making of Middlebrow Culture* (Chapel Hill: University of North Carolina Press, 1992).

19. Williams, *Writing in Society*, 6.

20. Ibid., 7.

21. I have drawn my notions of "dominant" and "emergent" cultural forms from Raymond Williams, *Marxism and Literature* (Oxford: Oxford University Press, 1977), 121–27.

22. Henri Lefebvre, *Everyday Life in the Modern World*, trans. Sacha Rabinovitch (New Brunswick, N.J.: Transaction Publishers, 1984), 68–109.

23. Miller, *Reluctant Capitalists*, 19.

24. Pierre Bourdieu, *The Rules of Art: Genesis and Structure of the Literary Field*, trans. Susan Emanuel (Stanford, Calif.: Stanford University Press, 1996), 142.

25. Roland Barthes, "From *Mythologies* (1957)," in *A Critical and Cultural Theory Reader*, ed. Anthony Easthope and Kate McGowan (Toronto: University of Toronto Press, 1992), 14–20.

26. See Jason Epstein, *Book Business: Publishing Past, Present, and Future* (New York: Norton, 2001); André Schiffrin, *The Business of Books*. See also Tom Engelhardt's fictional account in *The Last Days of Publishing*.

27. According to Pierre Bourdieu, "There are economic conditions for the indifference to economy." *The Field of Cultural Production: Essays on Art and Literature*, ed. Randal Johnson (New York: Columbia University Press, 1993), 40.

28. Lucien Febvre and Henri-Jean Martin, *The Coming of the Book: The Impact of Printing, 1450–1800*, trans. David Gerard (London: Verso, 1976), 109.

29. Ibid., 248.

30. Ibid., 128–36. See also Marshall McLuhan, *The Gutenberg Galaxy: The Making of Typographic Man* (Toronto: University of Toronto Press, 1962), 228; and cf.Elizabeth Eisenstein, *The Printing Press as an Agent of Change: Communications and Cultural Transformations in Early-Modern Europe* (Cambridge: Cambridge University Press, 1979), 689. For more on the historical constitution of modern labor practices and class relations in general, see E. P. Thompson, "Time, Work-Discipline and Industrial Capitalism," in *Customs in Common: Studies in Traditional Popular Culture* (New York: New Press, 1993), 352–403.

31. Benedict Anderson, *Imagined Communities: Reflections on the Origin and Spread of Nationalism*, rev. ed. (London: Verso, 1991), 39.

32. Cf. Stephen Nissenbaum: "As far as I can determine, Gift Books were the *very first* commercial products of any sort that were manufactured specifically, and solely, for the purpose of being given away by the purchaser." *The Battle for Christmas: A Cultural History of America's Most Cherished Holiday* (New York: Vintage Books, 1996), 143; emphasis in original.

33. Ibid., 141.

34. Ibid., 142.

35. Ibid., 148.

36. Ibid., 140.

37. Ibid., 143.

38. Lendol Calder, *Financing the American Dream: A Cultural History of Consumer Credit* (Princeton, N.J.: Princeton University Press, 1999), 60; see also 20, 167, 176, 180, and 187.

39. On the distinction between productive and frivolous purchases based on consumer credit, see Calder, *Financing the American Dream*, 231.

40. Karl Marx, *Capital*, vol. 1, *A Critique of Political Economy*, trans. Ben Fowkes (London: Penguin Books, 1976), 163.

41. Ibid., 167.

42. Lefebvre, *Everyday Life in the Modern World*, 24.

43. Paddy Scannell, *Radio, Television and Modern Life: A Phenomenological Approach* (Oxford: Blackwell, 1996), 94.

44. Rita Felski, "The Invention of Everyday Life," *New Formations* 39 (Winter 1999–2000): 29. My understanding of everyday life has been influenced by the following: Henri Lefebvre, *Everyday Life in the Modern World*, op. cit.; idem, *Critique of Everyday Life*, vol. 1, *An Introduction*, trans. John Moore (London: Verso, 1991); idem, *Critique of Everyday Life*, vol. 2, *Foundations for a Sociology of the Everyday*, trans. John Moore (London: Verso, 2002); idem, *The Critique of Everyday Life*, vol. 3, *From Modernity to Modernism: Towards a Metaphilosophy of Daily Life*, trans. Gregory Elliott (London: Verso, 2005); Michel de Certeau, *The Practice of Everyday Life*, trans. Steven Rendall (Berkeley: University of California Press, 1984); Meaghan Morris, "Banality in Cultural Studies," in *The Logics of Television: Essays in Cultural Criticism*, ed. Patricia Mellencamp (Bloomington: Indiana University Press, 1990), 14–43; Michael E. Gardiner, *Critiques of Everyday Life* (London: Routledge, 2000); and Gregory J. Seigworth and Michael E. Gardiner, "Rethinking Everyday Life: And Then Nothing Turns Itself Inside Out," *Cultural Studies* 18, nos. 2–3 (March–May 2004): 139–59.

45. In this respect I part company somewhat from phenomenological and ethnomethodological approaches to the study of everyday life. Those who operate within this ambit typically investigate how people's interpersonal ties, nonverbal behaviors, patterns of talk, etc., imbue seemingly mundane interactions with a deep and abiding—even world-building—significance. Within the realm of book studies, this approach is perhaps best exemplified by David Barton and Mary Hamilton's *Local Literacies*, a self-described "critical ethnography" exploring how residents of Lancaster, England, make sense of and implement a range of reading and writing practices within specific social contexts. Here the everyday is simultaneously a domain of lived experience and a staging ground for ethnographic encounters. There's much to gain from this approach in that it compels researchers to examine the minute intricacies of human affairs. On the downside, it may overlook artifacts, forms of knowledge, technologies, and other phenomena that fall outside the immediate domain of an individual or group's lived experience but that nevertheless play a profound role in organizing what they take their lived experience—their everyday lives—to be. See David Barton and Mary Hamilton, *Local Literacies: Reading and Writing in One Community* (London: Routledge, 1998). I consider Janice A. Radway's groundbreaking study *Reading the Romance* to be an exception to this

criticism. While she devotes a substantial portion of the book to an ethnography of female readers of romance novels, her chapter on the "institutional matrix" of romantic fiction (19–45) is all about the technical, industrial, and infrastructural conditions that shape the experiences of her ethnographic informants—often unbeknownst to them.

46. Sannell, *Radio, Television and Modern Life*, 145.

47. He made this remark in his lecture at BookExpo America, 2006.

48. On the closure of printed books, see Walter J. Ong, *Orality and Literacy: The Technologizing of the Word* (London: Routledge, 1982), 133. The phrase "for all practical purposes" is an important caveat. I realize that the claim I am making here, building on Ong, flies in the face of a good deal of poststructuralist literary theory.

49. Eisenstein, *The Printing Press as an Agent of Change*, 45.

50. Febvre and Martin, *The Coming of the Book*, 222; see also 138.

51. Marvin, "The Body of the Text," 134.

52. For an excellent critique of the normative vision of the sedate, solitary reader, see Elizabeth Long, *Book Clubs: Women and the Uses of Reading in Everyday Life* (Chicago: University of Chicago Press, 2003), 2–11.

53. Nicholas Howe, "The Cultural Construction of Reading in Anglo-Saxon England," in *The Ethnography of Reading*, ed. Jonathan Boyarin (Berkeley: University of California Press, 1993), 58–79, esp. 67; Raymond Williams, *Keywords: A Vocabulary of Culture and Society*, rev. ed. (New York: Oxford University Press, 1983).

54. On "furniture books," see Radway, *A Feeling for Books*, 160.

55. Quoted in Radway, *Reading the Romance*, 213.

56. Alberto Manguel provides a vivid, contrasting image of reading, particularly of Holy Scripture, in *A History of Reading* (New York: Penguin Books, 1996), 45–46.

57. "Cultural studies" is neither a theory, a methodology, a perspective, nor a discipline but rather a disposition toward politically engaged intellectual work. It orients researchers to eschew formalism of all kinds as well as simple, causal explanations in favor of embracing the complexity, recalcitrance, and mutability of cultural life. What this means is that while cultural studies typically starts from specific objects, events, or practices, ultimately its concerns are contextual; more important than any given object, event, or practice is the network of relations within which it's embedded. Cultural studies explores how these networks are forged, maintained, and transformed, and how they, in turn, give rise to particular habits of thought, conduct, and expression. Hence the best work in cultural studies engages in a kind of mapping, one that represents the radical connectivity among elements that constitute, in Raymond Williams's phrase, "a whole way of life"—even those that may not seem to share any obvious connection. And yet work in cultural studies isn't just empirically descriptive. Cultural studies is a critical intellectual practice. It produces knowledge in the hope of empowering people to alter their circumstances. In more contextual terms, this amounts to putting forth a kind of strategic knowledge whose purpose is to help us redraw the maps of our lives. See Raymond Williams, *The Long Revolution* (Orchard Park, N.Y.: Broadview Press, 2001), 63.

58. Elizabeth Long, "Textual Interpretation as Collective Action," in *The Ethnography*

of Reading, ed. Jonathan Boyarin (Berkeley: University of California Press, 1993), 190.

59. My understanding of context is largely drawn from Lawrence Grossberg, "Cultural Studies: What's in a Name? (One More Time)," in *Bringing It All Back Home: Essays on Cultural Studies* (Durham, N.C.: Duke University Press, 1997), 245–71, esp. 254–62; and Jennifer Daryl Slack, "The Theory and Method of Articulation in Cultural Studies," in *Stuart Hall: Critical Dialogues in Cultural Studies*, ed. David Morley and Kuan-Hsing Chen (London: Routledge, 1996), 112–27, esp. 123–25.

60. John Frow and Meaghan Morris, introduction to *Australian Cultural Studies: A Reader*, ed. John Frow and Meaghan Morris (Urbana: University of Illinois Press, 1993), vii–xxxii.

61. Robert Darnton, "Communication Networks," in *The Forbidden Best-Sellers of Pre-Revolutionary France* (New York: Norton, 1995), 181–97, esp. 183.

62. Methodologically I am partly following the example of Lynn Spigel, who in *Make Room for TV: Television and the Family Ideal in Postwar America* (Chicago: University of Chicago Press, 1992) explores how representations of television in popular magazines, on TV, and elsewhere in the mid-twentieth century formed "an intertextual context . . . through which people might have made sense of television and its place in everyday life" (2). I am trying to do something similar for books at the turn of the twenty-first century, though my focus clearly exceeds popular representations of books and book culture.

63. Charles R. Acland, *Screen Traffic: Movies, Multiplexes, and Global Culture* (Durham, N.C.: Duke University Press, 2003), x.

64. Jay David Bolter and David Grusin, *Remediation: Understanding New Media* (Cambridge, Mass.: MIT Press, 1999). See also Bolter, *Writing Space*.

65. Dick Higgins, "Intermedia," in *Horizons: The Poetics and Theory of the Intermedia* (Carbondale: Southern Illinois University Press, 1984), 23.

1. E-books and the Digital Future

1. Quoted in David D. Kirkpatrick, "Forecasts of an E-book Era Were, It Seems, Premature," *New York Times*, August 28, 2001, A1. King's novella was encrypted to prevent its being printed, duplicated, or e-mailed.

2. Ibid.

3. Jim Milliot and Calvin Reid, "Reality Check," *Publishers Weekly*, January 7, 2002, 36–38; Kirkpatrick, "Forecasts of an E-book Era Were Premature"; Calvin Reid, "Stephen King Happy About 'The Plant,'" *Publishers Weekly*, August 7, 2000, 57; Calvin Reid, "King to Take Hiatus from 'The Plant,'" *Publishers Weekly*, December 4, 2000, 10; M. J. Rose, "E-Books Live on After Mighty Fall," *Wired*, December 18, 2001, http://www.wired.com/news/culture/0,1284,49184,00.html.

4. Milliot and Reed, "Reality Check," 37; Calvin Reid, "Selling E-books to Academic, Trade Markets," *Publishers Weekly*, March 25, 2002, 13; Calvin Reid, "E-book Sales

Up 30% in First Half of '03," *Publishers Weekly*, September 22, 2003, 12; and Rose, "E-Books Live on."

5. Jeffrey Toobin, "Google's Moon Shot," *New Yorker*, February 5, 2007, 30–35; Kevin Kelly, "Scan This Book!" *New York Times Magazine*, May 14, 2006, http://www .nytimes.com/2006/05/14/magazine/14publishing.html. See also Siva Vaidhyana-than, "The Googlization of Everything and the Future of Copyright," *UC Davis Law Review* 40, no. 3 (2007), http://lawreview.law.ucdavis.edu/articles/Vol40/ Issue3/DavisVol40No3_Vaidhyanathan.pdf.

6. Quoted in Steven Levy, "The Future of Reading," *Newsweek*, November 26, 2007, 57.

7. Jeff Bezos, interview by Charlie Rose, *Charlie Rose Show*, PBS, November 19, 2007.

8. According to Pat Schroeder, president and CEO of the Association of American Publishers, "We've been ready to sell e-books for 10 years . . . [but] everybody still likes physical books." Quoted in Steven Levy, "Rip This Book? Not Yet," *Newsweek*, February 18, 2008, 24.

9. Nicholas A. Basbanes, *Patience and Fortitude: A Roving Chronicle of Book People, Book Places, and Book Culture* (New York: HarperCollins, 2001), 503. See also Nicholson Baker, *Double Fold: Libraries and the Assault on Paper* (New York: Random House, 2001), 65–72.

10. Basbanes, *Patience and Fortitude*, 499; Robert Coover, "The End of Books," *New York Times Book Review*, June 21, 1992, http://www.nytimes.com/books/98/09/27/ specials/coover-end.html.

11. Steve Silberman, "Ex Libris: The Joys of Curling Up with a Good Digital Reading Device," *Wired*, July 1998, http://www.wired.com/wired/archive/6.07/es_ebooks_ pr.html.

12. Walter Benjamin, "The Work of Art in the Age of Mechanical Reproduction," in *Illuminations: Essays and Reflections*, ed. Hannah Arendt, trans. Harry Zohn (New York: Shocken Books, 1968), 217–51.

13. Sven Birkerts, *The Gutenberg Elegies: The Fate of Reading in an Electronic Age* (New York: Fawcett Columbine, 1994), 188.

14. Birkerts, *The Gutenberg Elegies*, 154–55.

15. Ibid., 163, 188. See also Roland Barthes, "The Death of the Author," in *Image, Music, Text*, trans. Stephen Heath (New York: Hill and Wang, 1977), 142–48; Michel Foucault, "What Is an Author?," in *Language, Counter-Memory, Practice: Selected Essays and Interviews*, ed. Donald F. Bouchard, trans. Donald F. Bouchard and Sherry Simon (Ithaca, N.Y.: Cornell University Press, 1977), 113–38; and Jacques Derrida, *Of Grammatology*, rev. ed., trans. Gayatri Chakravorty Spivak (Baltimore, Md.: Johns Hopkins University Press, 1997).

16. Birkerts, *The Gutenberg Elegies*, 28. Note that in the 2006 edition Birkerts admits to having succumbed to using a computer. He does, however, continue to write out his screeds longhand before finalizing them on his laptop. Sven Birkerts, *The Gutenberg Elegies: The Fate of Reading in an Electronic Age*, 2nd. ed. (New York: Faber and Faber, 2006), xi, 231–33.

17. Langdon Winner, *Autonomous Technology: Technics-Out-of-Control as a Theme in Political Thought* (Cambridge, Mass.: MIT Press, 1978), 315.

18. "The IBM Selectric Typewriter Was Introduced on July 31, 1961," http://www.etypewriters.com/se-thumb.htm.

19. For engaging critiques of the spiritual idea in the history of media as well as in media studies, see John Durham Peters, *Speaking Into the Air: A History of the Idea of Communication* (Chicago: University of Chicago Press, 1999), 63–108; and Jeffrey Sconce, *Haunted Media: Electronic Presence from Telegraphy to Television* (Durham, N.C.: Duke University Press, 2000).

20. Martin Heidegger, *Parmenides*, trans. André Schuwer and Richard Rojcewicz (Bloomington: Indiana University Press, 1992), 81. For a perceptive discussion of the typewriter, its relationship to communicative practice, and to changing conceptions of human being, see Friedrich A. Kittler, *Gramophone, Film, Typewriter*, trans. Geoffrey Winthrop-Young and Michael Wutz (Stanford, Calif.: Stanford University Press, 1999), 183–263.

21. Plato, *The Phaedrus: Compiled with an Introduction and Commentary by R. Hackforth* (Cambridge: Cambridge University Press, 1972), 156–64. Of course, Plato goes on to say that human speech itself is a degraded copy of the divine Word, and as such it suffers—and we suffer—for its finitude.

22. For an astute discussion of this problem in relation to the history of sound reproduction, see Jonathan Sterne, *The Audible Past: Cultural Origins of Sound Reproduction* (Durham, N.C.: Duke University Press), 215–86.

23. John Tebbel, *A History of Book Publishing in the United States*, vol. 3, *The Golden Age between the Two Wars, 1920–1940* (New York: Bowker, 1978), 72–73.

24. Edward L. Bernays, *Biography of an Idea: Memoirs of Public Relations Counsel Edward L. Bernays* (New York: Simon & Schuster, 1965), 485–86.

25. Larry Tye, *The Father of Spin: Edward L. Bernays and the Birth of Public Relations* (New York: Crown, 1998), 52.

26. Margaret Harmon, "Housing Your Books," *American Home* (March 1929): 566.

27. Ibid., 527, 566.

28. Ibid., 568.

29. Joseph Wharton Lippincott, "Support the Built-In Bookcase," *Publishers Weekly*, November 2, 1929, 2157.

30. Ibid., 2160.

31. "Mimic Books in Many Colors Are Now Sold by the Yard," *New York Times*, December 25, 1927, 5. See also Dale Warren, "How to House the Growing Library," *House Beautiful* (June 1926): 778.

32. Lynn Spigel, *Make Room for TV: Television and the Family Ideal in Postwar America* (Chicago: University of Chicago Press, 1992), 18. See also Richard M. Ohmann, *Selling Culture: Magazines, Markets, and Class at the Turn of the Century* (London: Verso, 1996), 141–42.

33. Bernays, *Biography of an Idea*, 486–87; Spigel, *Make Room for TV*, 15.

34. Spigel, *Make Room for TV*, 21.

35. Ibid., 24, 29. See John Hartley, *The Uses of Television* (London: Routledge, 1999),

99–107. See also Walter Rendell Storey, "Radio Cabinets in Decorative Schemes," *New York Times*, May 25, 1930, 87.

36. Ohmann, *Selling Culture*, 163.

37. Thorstein Veblen, *The Theory of the Leisure Class* (1899; repr. New York: Dover, 1994), 6. I employ Veblen's terminology with some trepidation since his historical narrative and understanding of "culture" are heavily mortgaged to an ethnological/evolutionary framework with which I am somewhat uncomfortable.

38. Ibid., 43–62.

39. Ibid., 19. See also Janice A. Radway, *A Feeling for Books: The Book-of-the-Month Club, Literary Taste, and Middle-Class Desire* (Chapel Hill: University of North Carolina Press, 1997), 162.

40. Radway, *A Feeling for Books*, 197.

41. It is important to emphasize the unevenness of the growth of consumer culture and "conspicuous consumption" among working people in the United States. This unevenness is particularly evident in Veblen's comments on servants (cooks, housekeepers, domestic caregivers, etc.), who highlight the supposedly superior social standing of their employers by freeing the latter from specific labors. To the extent that historically people of color have constituted much of this servant class, it seems reasonable to assume that they typically were excluded from the emergent consumer culture Veblen described. His is, in effect, a profoundly white history. See Veblen, *The Theory of the Leisure Class*, 36–42.

42. Siva Vaidhyanathan, *Copyrights and Copywrongs: The Rise of Intellectual Property and How It Threatens Creativity* (New York: New York University Press, 2001), 50.

43. Ibid., 51.

44. For an excellent discussion of the relationship of print and republicanism in the United States, see Michael Warner, *The Letters of the Republic: Publication and the Public Sphere in Eighteenth-Century America* (Cambridge, Mass.: Harvard University Press, 1992).

45. Vaidhyanathan, *Copyrights and Copywrongs*, 51.

46. Ibid., 50. According to Vaidhyanathan, "A London reader who wanted a copy of Charles Dickens' *A Christmas Carol* would have to pay the equivalent of $2.50 in 1843. An American Dickens fan would have to pay only six cents per copy."

47. Ohmann, *Selling Culture*, 23.

48. Vaidhyanathan, *Copyrights and Copywrongs*, 53.

49. Ohmann, *Selling Culture*, 23.

50. Vaidhyanathan, *Copyrights and Copywrongs*, 52.

51. Ibid., 54.

52. Ibid., 52–55. See also Ohmann, *Selling Culture*, 24.

53. Lawrence Lessig, *Code Version 2.0* (New York: Basic Books, 2006), 301.

54. These included subscription book clubs (e.g., the Book-of-the-Month Club, the Literary Guild), department stores (which often sold new books as loss leaders), and cigar and drugstores (where the sale of inexpensive mysteries and remaindered books flourished). See Bernays, *Biography of an Idea*, 484.

55. Ibid., 484–85. See also Tebbel, *A History of Book Publishing*, 458.

56. Quoted in Bernays, *Biography of an Idea*, 489.

57. Ibid., 485.

58. Ibid.

59. Ibid., 488. *Oxford English Dictionary Online*, s.v. "scofflaw," http://dictionary.oed.com/cgi/entry/50216052.

60. "Book 'Borrower' Pest Becomes 'Booksneaf,'" *New York Times*, May, 8, 1931, 27; Bernays, *Biography of an Idea*, 488. Note that the report on the contest results published in the *New York Times* lists the wining entry as "booksneaf." Bernays's memoir, on the other hand, lists the winning entry as "book sneak." I suspect the discrepancy may stem from a typographical error in the newspaper.

61. Bernays, *Biography of an Idea*, 488.

62. Of course, an abundance of technologies capable of reproducing printed materials existed prior to the advent of photocopiers. These included the mimeograph, ditto, and even carbon paper. As Hillel Schwartz has shown, however, these technologies tended to be used for what might be described as more "private" purposes (e.g., keeping copies of letters and other important documents on file). Photocopiers certainly fulfilled this function, but Schwartz argues that they facilitated a more widespread, public dissemination of documents as well. See Hillel Schwartz, *The Culture of the Copy: Striking Likenesses, Unreasonable Facsimiles* (New York: Zone Books, 1998), 238.

63. See Ira Flatow, *They All Laughed: From Light Bulbs to Lasers, the Fascinating Stories Behind the Great Inventions That Have Changed Our Lives* (New York: HarperCollins, 1992), 111–18. See also Schwartz, *The Culture of the Copy*, 229–41.

64. Schwartz, *The Culture of the Copy*, 237.

65. The King report, which examined photocopying practices among library staff, library patrons, and private corporations in 1980–81, concluded: "Of library patrons interviewed, the largest percentage, just over 29%, said they had photocopied all or parts of books on one to three occasions within the previous six months. More than 26% claimed more than six times, less than 19% four to six times, and 24% hadn't photocopied at all. The greatest percentage of those averaging at least once a month were in federal libraries, where nearly 40% said they had done so. In corporate libraries, just over 23% claimed that average." Howard Fields, "Copyright Office Report Shows Low Photocopying Payments," *Publishers Weekly*, June 11, 1982, 19.

66. *Basic Books, Inc., CBS Inc., McGraw-Hill, Inc., Nelson-Hall, Inc., Prentice-Hall, Inc., Princeton University Press, and John Wiley & Sons, Inc. v. The Gnomon Corp. and Adam Carley, Individually and as President of the Gnomon Corp.*, Copyright L. Dec. 25, 145 D. Ct (1980).

67. Quoted in Edwin McDowell, "Nine Publishers Sue N.Y.U., Charging Copyright Violation," *New York Times*, December 15, 1982, 1.

68. *Basic Books, Inc., Harper & Row Publishers, Inc., John Wiley & Sons, Inc., McGraw-Hill, Inc., Penguin Books USA, Inc., Prentice-Hall, Inc., Richard D. Irwin, Inc., and William Morrow & Co., Inc. v. Kinko's Graphics Corp.*, 758 F. Supp. 1522, S.D.N.Y. (1991).

69. In the case of the *Kinko's* decision, the U.S. District Court ruled in 1991 in favor of the publishers, ordering Kinko's to pay damages in the amount of $1.9 million. No damages were awarded in the *Gnomon* case. See Calvin Reid, "Kinko's Pays $1.9 Million To Settle Copyright Suit," *Publishers Weekly*, November 1, 1991, 14.

70. Leonard A. Wood, "The Pass-Along Market for Books: Something to Ponder for Publishers," *Publishers Weekly*, July 15, 1983, 20.

71. Ibid.

72. Howard Fields, "Senate Bill to Study U.S. Public Lending Right," *Publishers Weekly*, October 21, 1983, 15. In the case of the United States, the specific terminology used was "author's lending royalty," a deliberate name change emphasizing author entitlement over public welfare. See Herbert Mitgang, "Authors Seek Pay for Loan of Books," *New York Times*, January 2, 1985, 17.

73. By 1983 a public lending right already existed in Britain, Australia, New Zealand, West Germany, the Netherlands, Denmark, Norway, Sweden, Iceland, and Finland; a similar provision, called "Payment for Public Use," was passed in Canada in 1986. In Britain in the early 1980s authors could "receive government-funded royalties of up to $7,500 based upon the records of a representative group of libraries." Authors and publishers shared royalties in the Australian model of public-lending rights. Fields, "Senate Bill," 15.

74. Elie A. Shneour, "A Look into the Book of the Future," *Publishers Weekly*, January 21, 1983, 48.

75. Print on demand refers to a broad range of just-in-time delivery systems for printed books, in which book buyers make requests for editions that are printed while they wait.

76. Shneour, "A Look into the Book of the Future," 48.

77. John F. Baker, "Electronic Art Book . . . for One Read Only," *Publishers Weekly*, June 29, 1992, 28.

78. Ibid.

79. Since its initial release in 1992, the text has become widely available on the Internet, apparently as a result of both illegal hacking and its official release to a series of online bulletin boards in the mid-1990s.

80. An article in *Details* magazine reported: "Ashbaugh is gleeful about the dilemma [*Agrippa*] will pose to librarians. To register the book's copyright, he must send two copies to the Library of Congress. To classify it, they must read it, and to read it, they must destroy it." Gavin Edwards, "Cyber Lit," *Details*, June 1992, http://www.textfiles.com/sf/cyberlit.txt.

81. However, there was still the possibility that someone might possess sufficient technical knowledge and expertise to crack the code illegally, which apparently did happen. See note 79.

82. Paul Hilts, "BookTech Looks at E-Publishing," *Publishers Weekly*, March 5, 2001, 46. Interestingly, Moynahan sees the passing along of books as an untapped marketing opportunity rather than lost revenue. This is a suggestive insight, one the book industry would do well to heed. I would add that the traditionally higher cost of hardbound library editions partly offsets "lost revenue."

83. Paul Hilts, "Locking in with LockStream," *Publishers Weekly*, July 3, 2000, 27.

84. "RosettaBooks to Publish 'Time Limit' Ebook," *Publishers Weekly*, August 13, 2001, 157.

85. Quoted in Scott Carlson, "Online Textbooks Fail to Make the Grade: Students Prefer Handling Pages the Old-Fashioned Way," *Chronicle of Higher Education*, February 11, 2005, A36. For more on digital "locking," see Andrea L. Foster, "In a Pilot Program, 10 College Bookstores Begin Selling Digital Textbooks," *Publishers Weekly*, September 2, 2005, 45.

86. Jennifer Lee, "U.S. Arrests Russian Cryptographer as Copyright Violator," *New York Times*, July 18, 2001, C8; idem, "In Digital Copyright Case, Programmer Can Go Home," *New York Times*, December 14 2001, C4; Steven Levy, "Busted by the Copyright Cops: How a Controversial Intellectual Property Law Got a Russian Programmer Thrown in Jail," *Newsweek*, August 20, 2001, 54. In a stunning decision ElcomSoft was acquitted in December 2002 of having violated the DMCA. Although the jury found that the Advanced eBook Processor program indeed violated the statute, it nevertheless determined that ElcomSoft's violation of the law was not willful.

87. David D. Kirkpatrick, "With Plot Still Sketchy, Characters Vie for Roles: The Struggles Over E-Books Abound, Though Readership Remains Elusive," *New York Times*, November 27, 2000, C1.

88. Levy, "Rip This Book?" 24.

89. "Intellectual property law" refers to a juridical framework consisting of copyright statutes, patent laws, publicity rights, trademark laws, and attendant case law. Outside the United States one would need to include the moral rights of authors.

90. Laurie Stearns, "Copy Wrong: Plagiarism, Process, Property, and the Law," in *Perspectives on Plagiarism and Intellectual Property in a Postmodern World*, ed. Lise Buranen and Alice M. Roy (Albany: State University of New York Press, 1999), 9. Stearns's discussion specifically addresses the relationship between plagiarism and copyright and, as such, I've adapted her argument. See also Tarleton Gillespie, *Wired Shut: Copyright and the Shape of Digital Culture* (Cambridge, Mass.: MIT Press, 2007), 256

91. According to Lawrence Lessig, "Protection by technology can often reach far beyond the protection of the law." *The Future of Ideas: The Fate of the Commons in a Connected World* (New York: Random House, 2001), 256. Peter Jaszi has termed this new set of legal-cum-practical controls "paracopyright." See "Intellectual Property Legislative Update: Copyright, Paracopyright, and Pseudo-Copyright," paper presented at the Association of Research Libraries Membership Meeting, May 1998, 3, http://www.arl.org/arl/proceedings/132/luncheon/jaszi.html. See also Yochai Benkler, *The Wealth of Networks: How Social Production Transforms Markets and Freedom* (New Haven, Conn.: Yale University Press, 2006): 415. Fair use refers to a key exception in copyright law protecting the appropriation of copyrighted material for the purpose of parody, criticism, and education, under specific conditions. The first-sale doctrine stipulates that the purchaser of a copyrighted work, not the copyright holder, possesses the right to sell it or give it away once the

purchaser has legally acquired it. Both provisions were codified in the U.S. Copyright Act of 1976 (17 U.S.C., secs.107 and 109, resp.).

92. "Publishers Sue Google Over Plans to Digitize Books," press release, *Association of American Publishers*, October 19, 2005, http://www.publihsers.org/press/releases. cfm?PressReleaseArticleID=292. See also Toobin, "Google's Moon Shot"; Kelly, "Scan This Book!"; and Vaidhyanathan, "The Googlization of Everything and the Future of Copyright." The litigants settled the lawsuit as this book was going to press.

2. The Big-Box Bookstore Blues

1. Raymond Williams, "Culture Is Ordinary," in *Resources of Hope: Culture, Democracy, Socialism*, ed. Robin Gable (London: Verso, 1989), 10.
2. Author Barbara Kingsolver, always sensitive to the local, echoes this sentiment: "I know that in some small towns that have never before had the privilege of a real bookstore, the nationally run stores now turning up may be a godsend." She goes on, however, to mourn the passing of one of her favorite Tuscon, Arizona, bookshops, the Book Mark, which was an early promoter of her work and which apparently fell victim to chain store and Internet bookselling. Barbara Kingsolver, "Marking a Passage," in *Small Wonder* (New York: Harper Perennial, 2002), 218–19.
3. Penny Singer, "A Nonchain Bookstore Bucks the Tide," *New York Times*, September 8, 1996, 8.
4. Betty Ann Bowser, "Retail Book Bind," *The NewsHour with Jim Lehrer*, PBS, August 18, 1997, http://www.pbs.org/newshour/bb/entertainment/july-dec97/books_8-18.html.
5. Lynne Tillman, *Bookstore: The Life and Times of Jeanette Watson and Books & Co.* (New York: Harcourt Brace, 1999), xxii.
6. Karen Angel, "Are Independents Making a Comeback?" *Publishers Weekly*, June 8, 1998, 21; Yvonne Zipp, "The Tomes, They Are A-Changing," *Christian Science Monitor*, June 7, 1999, 1; Kyle York Spencer, "A Closing Chapter for Wellington's," *Raleigh News and Observer*, January 11, 1999, 1B. See also André Schiffrin, *The Business of Books: How International Conglomerates Took Over Publishing and Changed the Way We Read* (London: Verso, 2001), 125.
7. Singer, "A Nonchain Bookstore Bucks the Tide," 8.
8. Chet Bridger, "Small Bookstores Fear Writing Is on the Wall," *Buffalo News*, February 8, 1999, A1.
9. Angel, "Are Independents Making a Comeback?" 21; Ric Manning, "Book Stores Fight Back Against Online Goliaths," *Boardwatch*, June 1999, 90–92.
10. Jim Milliot, "Study Shows Chains Had Biggest Share of Book Market in '94," *Publishers Weekly*, June 12, 1995, 14.
11. John Mutter, "More Than Half Now Buy Their Books in Chains—'PW' Survey," *Publishers Weekly*, May 12, 1997, 13; Angel, "Are Independents Making a Comeback?" 21; Manning, "Book Stores Fight Back"; Schiffrin, *The Business of Books*, 124.

12. Josh Getlin, "Chain Reaction: As Mega-Bookstores Move into Their Neighborhoods, Independents Worry About the Future," *Los Angeles Times*, May 24, 1993, E1.
13. Ibid.
14. William Grimes, "Book War: Shops vs. Superstores: As Chains Grow, Struggling Small Stores Stress Expertise," *New York Times*, August 3, 1995, B1.
15. Bowser, "Retail Book Bind."
16. David Rhode, "As Barnes & Noble Looms, Two Bookstores Consolidate," *New York Times*, June 22, 1997, B1.
17. Bridger, "Small Bookstores Fear Writing Is on the Wall," A1.
18. Karen Angel and John Mutter, "Sad Tidings of the New Year," *Publishers Weekly*, January 29, 1996, 24.
19. Steve Sherman, "An Owner's Story: The Closing of the Oldest Bookstore," *Publishers Weekly*, May 31, 1993, 20.
20. Karen Angel, "NYC's Oldest New Age Bookstore Closes," *Publishers Weekly*, March 13, 1995, 23.
21. Robin Pogrebin, "A Shakespeare & Co. to Exit the Scene," *New York Times*, June 12, 1996, B1.
22. Dinitia Smith, "Epilogue for Another Bookstore," *New York Times*, January 18, 1997, A15. See also Tillman, *Bookstore*, 242–77.
23. Judith Rosen, "Bookland of Maine to Close Four Stores," *Publishers Weekly*, March 20, 2000, 26.
24. Schiffrin, *The Business of Books*, 125.
25. George Myers Jr., "Turning a Page: What Gets Published Is Determined, Increasingly, by Fewer Minds," *Columbus Dispatch*, December 28, 1999.
26. Manning, "Book Stores Fight Back," 90–92. See also Bridger, "Small Bookstores Fear Writing Is on the Wall," A1.
27. Mark Feeney, "Pumping Up the Volumes," *Boston Globe*, December 11, 1997, C1.
28. Meaghan Morris, "Things to Do with Shopping Centers," in *Too Soon Too Late: History in Popular Culture* (Bloomington: Indiana University Press, 1998), 86.
29. Janice A. Radway, *A Feeling for Books: The Book-of-the-Month Club, Literary Taste, and Middle-Class Desire* (Chapel Hill: University of North Carolina Press, 1997), 244. See also: Lendol Calder, *Financing the American Dream: A Cultural History of Consumer Credit* (Princeton, N.J.: Princeton University Press, 1999); Lizabeth Cohen, *A Consumers' Republic: The Politics of Mass Consumption in Postwar America* (New York: Knopf, 2003); and Gary Cross, *An All-Consuming Century: Why Commercialism Won in Modern America* (New York: Columbia University Press, 2000).
30. See Radway, *A Feeling for Books*, 152, 161. See also Joan Shelley Rubin, *The Making of Middlebrow Culture* (Chapel Hill: University of North Carolina Press, 1992), 144, 231.
31. For two "coming of age" narratives that exemplify this moment of institutionalization in book publishing, see Jason Epstein, *Book Business: Publishing Past, Present, and Future* (New York: Norton, 2001); and Schiffrin, *The Business of Books*. From a more critical standpoint, see Radway, *A Feeling for Books,* and Rubin, *The Making of Middlebrow Culture*, 266–329.

32. See Nicole Stoops, "Educational Attainment in the United States, 2003" (Washington, D.C.: United States Census Bureau, 2003), 2, http://www.census.gov/prod/2004pubs/p20-550.pdf. See also Cohen, *A Consumers' Republic*, 139–40. Laura J. Miller notes that changes in mass higher education didn't alter the book market substantially. Laura J. Miller, *Reluctant Capitalists: Bookselling and the Culture of Consumption* (Chicago: University of Chicago Press, 2006), 38.
33. Allene Symons, "Interview with Ken White: Blueprint of a Career in Bookstore Design," *Publishers Weekly*, March 23, 1984, 34–35.
34. White is president of Ken White Associates, Inc., a consulting firm that specializes in designing bookstores. Since the 1950s his firm has been involved in redesigning over a thousand of these stores across the United States, including the famous Barnes & Noble store on Fifth Avenue and Eighteenth Street.
35. Symons, "Interview With Ken White," 34. See also "Ken White: Renaissance Man of Architecture," *Publishers Weekly*, February 3, 1969, 54–56.
36. Rachel Bowlby, *Carried Away: The Invention of Modern Shopping* (New York: Columbia University Press: 2002), 194.
37. Ibid., 193.
38. Symons, "Interview with Ken White, 34.
39. Ibid.
40. Ibid.
41. Ken White, "Display and Visual Merchandising," in *A Manual on Bookselling: How to Open and Run Your Own Bookstore*, 3rd ed., ed. Robert D. Hale, Allan Marshall, and Jerry N. Showalter (New York: Harmony Books, 1980), 330–47; see esp. 330.
42. E. P. Thompson, "The Moral Economy of the English Crowd in the Nineteenth Century," *Past and Present* 50 (February 1971): 126.
43. Thompson notes that marketplace riots were not altogether unheard of. See "The Moral Economy," 119–20.
44. Ibid., 84.
45. Ibid., 85.
46. Ibid., 90.
47. Ibid., 101.
48. Cross, *An All-Consuming Century*, 28.
49. "Barnes & Noble, Educational Bookstore, Celebrates 75 Years of Service," *Publishers Weekly*, February 12, 1949, 901. There are some discrepancies concerning when the company was founded. Although this source indicates the year as 1874, most available evidence points to 1873. It's possible that Barnes began selling used books from his home in 1873 and expanded the business into a formal secondhand book wholesaling outfit the following year, although I've yet to find any evidence to corroborate that speculation.
50. See "Wheaton, IL," *The Encyclopedia of Chicago*, http://www.encyclopedia.chicagohistory.org/pages/1350.html. See also Mary Anne Phemister, *32 Wheaton Notables: Their Stories & Where They Lived* (Wheaton, Ill.: Prairie Publications, 2003), 7.
51. See "Follett History," http://www.follett.com/FollettHistory.cfm.
52. "Barnes & Noble . . . Celebrates 75 Years of Service," 902.

53. Ibid.

54. Ibid. See also "Sixty-Five Years of Bookselling," *College Store*, April 1939, 10.

55. "Barnes & Noble . . . Celebrates 75 Years of Service," 902–3. See also the article "Increase in Serious Reading Causes Book Firm to Expand," *New York Times*, April 23, 1932, 30.

56. "Barnes & Noble . . . Celebrates 75 Years of Service," 902.

57. Ibid., 904.

58. Ibid.

59. "Barnes & Noble Remodels Its Quarters for Efficiency," *Publishers Weekly*, December 6, 1941, 2091.

60. See Stephen H. Barnes, *Muzak: The Hidden Messages in Music* (Lewiston, Me.: Edwin Mellen Press, 1988). See also Joseph Lanza, *Elevator Music: A Surreal History of Muzak, Easy-Listening, and Other Moodsong* (New York: St. Martin's Press, 1994), 22–30, 38–54.

61. "Barnes & Noble Remodels Its Quarters for Efficiency," 2092.

62. "Sixty-Five Years of Bookselling," 10.

63. "Barnes & Noble . . . Celebrates 75 Years of Service," 903.

64. "Barnes & Noble Remodels Its Quarters for Efficiency," 2090–91. See also "Barnes & Noble . . . Celebrates 75 Years of Service," 903.

65. "Barnes & Noble . . . Celebrates 75 Years of Service," 903.

66. "Barnes & Noble's Revitalization Program," *Publishers Weekly*, September 28, 1970, 69–70.

67. "Barnes & Noble Success Spawns New Mall Stores," *Publishers Weekly*, August 5, 1974, 43.

68. Ibid.

69. "Barnes & Noble Success," 43.

70. David D. Kirkpatrick, "Barnes & Noble's Jekyll and Hyde," *New York*, July 12, 1999, http://nymag.com/nymetro/news/bizfinance/biz/features/47/infex3.html. There is some discrepancy with regard to the exact sales figure, which Kirpatrick quoted as $750,000. For additional accounts of the deal, see: Lila Freilicher, "Barnes & Noble: The Book Supermarket, of Course, of Course," *Publishers Weekly*, January 19, 1976, 73; "Literary Supermarket," *Forbes*, May 15, 1976, 49.

71. I. Jeanne Dugan, "The Baron of Books," *BusinessWeek*, June 29, 1998, http://www.businessweek.com/1998/26/b3584001.htm.

72. John Mutter, "A Chat with Bookseller Len Riggio," *Publishers Weekly*, May 3, 1991, 36.

73. Ibid. Coincidentally, brothers Tom and Louis Borders founded the first Borders Bookstore in Ann Arbor, Michigan, in 1971, the same year Riggio purchased Barnes & Noble from Amtel.

74. Freilicher, "Barnes & Noble: The Book Supermarket," 71–72.

75. Ibid., 72. See also Dugan, "The Baron of Books."

76. Freilicher, "Barnes & Noble: The Book Supermarket," 72.

77. Radway, *A Feeling for Books*, 166.

78. On the matter of fungibility and printed books, see Radway, *A Feeling for Books*, 154–86.

79. Freilicher, "Barnes & Noble: The Book Supermarket," 73.
80. "Literary Supermarket," 49.
81. Bowlby, *Carried Away*, 31.
82. Freilicher, "Barnes & Noble: The Book Supermarket," 72.
83. Ibid., 71.
84. Mutter, "A Chat with Bookseller Len Riggio," 36; "Barnes & Noble Success," 43–44.
85. Allene Symons, "Barnes & Noble to Buy B. Dalton; Will Become Largest Chain," *Publishers Weekly*, December 12, 1986, 17.
86. Ibid.
87. Ibid., 17, 23. See also Dugan, "The Baron of Books"; Mutter, "A Chat with Bookseller Len Riggio," 36.
88. On "local instances" and "general models," see Morris, "Things to Do with Shopping Centers," 86. On corporate strategies for localizing book superstores, especially community-oriented events, see Miller, *Reluctant Capitalists*, 124–29; and K. D. Trager, "Reading in the Borderland: An Ethnographic Study of Serious Readers in a Mega-Bookstore Café." *Communication Review* 8, no. 2 (April–June 2005): 210.
89. John Mutter, "Location: B & N's Challenge," *Publishers Weekly*, September 27, 1993, 22.
90. The phrase "New South" has been used at least twice to describe the South's efforts to reinvent itself. It was purportedly coined by the journalist and orator Henry W. Grady, who, following the Civil War, called on the southern states to modernize. The latter-day incarnation of "New South" reflects the region's transformation in the 1970s into a sprawling, postindustrial economy. My use of the term here refers to the latter sense. See James G. Leyburn, *The Way We Lived: Durham, 1900–1920* (Elliston, Va.: Northcross House, 1989), 19.
91. Jean Bradley Anderson, *Durham County: A History of Durham County, North Carolina* (Durham, N.C.: Duke University Press, 1990), 154. Durham County, to which the city of Durham now belongs, was founded in 1881.
92. Leyburn, *The Way We Lived*, 22.
93. Ibid., 23.
94. Anderson, *Durham County*, 93, 142; Leyburn, *The Way We Lived*, 22.
95. Anderson, *Durham County*, 175. See also Dolores E. Janiewski, *Sisterhood Denied: Race, Gender, and Class in a New South Community* (Philadelphia: Temple University Press, 1985), 69
96. Anderson, *Durham County*, 144; Janiewski, *Sisterhood Denied*, 72–73.
97. Janiewski, *Sisterhood Denied*, 6.
98. Quoted in Christina Greene, *Our Separate Ways: Women and the Black Freedom Movement in Durham, North Carolina* (Chapel Hill: University of North Carolina Press, 2005), 1.
99. Anderson, *Durham County*, 260. See also Greene, *Our Separate Ways*, 9.
100. Anderson, *Durham County*, 400, 417–18. See also Leonard Rogoff, *Homelands: Southern Jewish Identity in Durham and Chapel Hill, North Carolina* (Tuscaloosa: University of Alabama Press, 2001), 247.

101. Tim Vercellotti, "Wal-Mart Finds Home on 15–501 between Durham, Chapel Hill," *Raleigh News & Observer*, June 28, 1994, B2; Renée DeGross, "Mall Developers Move to Fulfill Shoppers' Wishes," *Raleigh News & Observer*, May 23, 1999, I102; "Table DP-1. Profile of General Demographic Characteristics: 2000," (Washington, D.C.: U.S. Census Bureau, 2000), 1, http://censtats.census.gov/data/NC/390376640.pdf; "Pop-Facts: Demographic Snapshot Report—Trade Area: 5422 New Hope Commons Dr., Durham, NC 27707–9716," report prepared by Claritas, Inc., for Montgomery Carolina Real Estate Services LLC, January 13, 2005, 1, http://www.montgomerydevelopment.com/llc_pdf/newhope_glance1.pdf.

102. Linda Brown Douglas, "Newcomers Part of New Center," *Raleigh News & Observer*, May 25, 1995, C8.

103. Restaurants in Chapel Hill, for example, are prohibited from using drive-through windows to service customers, a common practice among fast-food chains. The sole exception in the town is a local restaurant, the Sunrise Biscuit Kitchen, which operates exclusively as a drive-through establishment and was grandfathered in. Similarly, a Red Roof Inn hotel is barred by the town of Chapel Hill from installing a red roof. On the matter of income, see note 106.

104. J. Ward Best, "The Shopping Center Nobody Wanted Gets Last Laugh," *Durham Herald*, November 23, 1995, B1.

105. Bonnie Rochman, "Chapel Hill Council Unimpressed with Borders' Proposal," *Raleigh News & Observer*, July 3, 1999, B7.

106. In 2000 Durham's median family income was $51,162, which was just a hair below the national average. Chapel Hill's, by contrast, was $73,483, or almost 147 percent of the national average. It's worth noting, however, that Durham's median household income in 2000 ($41,160) was slightly higher than that of Chapel Hill ($39,140). In terms of education, about 42 percent of Durham's population had earned a bachelor's degree or higher. In Chapel Hill that figure was 74 percent. See http://factfinder.census.gov; http://quickfacts.census.gov.

107. Chris O'Brien, "Orange Finds Temptation Across the Border," *Raleigh News & Observer*, January 1, 1996), B6; Vercellotti, "Wal-Mart Finds Home"; Dwight Martin, "Triangle Bookworms Get a New Superstore," *Herald-Sun*, September 29, 1995, B8; Best, "Shopping Center Nobody Wanted."

108. Vercellotti, "Wal-Mart Finds Home"; Linda Brown Douglas, "Work Begins at New Hope Commons," *Raleigh News & Observer*, July 20, 1994, D1.

109. Anderson, *Durham County*, 400.

110. Ibid., 443–44. See also Greene, *Our Separate Ways*, 173–75. Many of Durham's downtown businesses were still open at the time, and the protesters targeted them as well.

111. Elizabeth Wellington, "Readers Offer a Labor of Love," *Raleigh News & Observer*, August 29, 1998, B7.

112. Ray Gronberg, "Intimate Closes the Book on Final Chapter," *Herald-Sun,* March 11, 1999, A1; Wellington, "Readers Offer a Labor of Love"; Kathleen Kearns, "Intimate Bookshop Owner Wallace Kuralt Dies," *Chapel Hill News*, December 16, 2003, http://www.chapelhillnews.com/front/story/954440p-6851675c.html.

113. *The Intimate Bookshop, Inc.* v. *Barnes & Noble, Inc., Barnesandnoble.com, Inc., Borders Group, Inc., and Walden Acquisition Company*, 98 Civ. 5564, S.D.N.Y. (2003). See also Gronberg, "Intimate Closes the Book"; and Kearns, "Intimate Bookshop Owner Wallace Kuralt Dies."

114. Caucasians are a clear majority in Chapel Hill, comprising more than 75 percent of the population. By contrast, Durham's black and white populations are almost the same size, with each group comprising roughly 45 percent of the city's residents. See http://factfinder.census.gov.

115. Dugan, "The Baron of Books."

3. Bringing Bookland Online

1. Joshua Quittner, "An Eye on the Future," *Time*, December 27, 1999, 63.

2. Quittner, "An Eye on the Future," 60.

3. This or some version of the story of the founding of online bookselling is reiterated in virtually every mainstream account of the history of Amazon.com. See Joshua Cooper Ramo, "The Fast-Moving Internet Economy Has a Jungle of Competitors . . . and Here's the King," *Time*, December 27, 1999, 54; Rebecca Saunders, *Business the Amazon.com Way: Secrets of the World's Most Astonishing Web Business* (Dover, Engl.: Capstone, 1999), 7–10; Michael H. Martin, "The Next Big Thing: A Bookstore?" *Fortune*, December 9, 1996, 169–70; Robert D. Hof, "Amazon.com: The Wild World of E-Commerce," *BusinessWeek*, December 14, 1998, http://www.businessweek.com/1998/50/b3608001.htm; and Robert Spector, *Amazon.com: Get Big Fast* (New York: HarperBusiness, 2000).

4. Janice A. Radway, *Reading the Romance: Women, Patriarchy, and Popular Literature* (Chapel Hill: University of North Carolina Press, 1984), 12.

5. Karl Marx, *Capital*, vol. 1, *A Critique of Political Economy*, trans. Ben Fowkes (London: Penguin Books, 1976), 279.

6. Here I am paraphrasing Marx's famous lines from the conclusion to part 2 of *Capital* (279–80).

7. Michael Denning, *Culture in the Age of Three Worlds* (London: Verso, 2004), 94.

8. John Tebbel, *A History of Book Publishing in the United States*, vol. 3, *The Golden Age Between the Two Wars, 1920–1940* (New York: Bowker, 1978), 428.

9. Ibid., 458.

10. James R. Beniger, *The Control Revolution: Technological and Economic Origins of the Information Society* (Cambridge, Mass.: Harvard University Press, 1986), vii.

11. Tebbel, *A History of Book Publishing in the United States*, 427–39; 458–69.

12. O. H. Cheney, *Economic Survey of the Book Industry, 1930–1931* (New York: Bowker, 1960), 1.

13. Richard Ohmann, *Selling Culture: Magazines, Markets, and Class at the Turn of the Century* (London: Verso, 1996), 162–64.

14. Stuart Ewen, *Captains of Consciousness: Advertising and the Social Roots of the Consumer Culture*, rev. ed. (New York: Basic Books, 2001). Bernays was cognizant

of Cheney and his writings on business competition. Given Bernays's investment in "propaganda," it is unsurprising that he ignored what Cheney had to say about logistics. See Edward L. Bernays, *Propaganda* (Brooklyn, N.Y.: Ig Publishing, 2005), 99–101.

15. O.H. Cheney, "The New Competition," *Nation's Business* (June 1926): 14.

16. Ibid., 13.

17. "Comments on the New Competition," *Nation's Business* (September 1926): 74.

18. O.H. Cheney, "The Answer to the New Competition," *Nation's Business* (October 1927): 15–17, 80–81.

19. "Industry's Control Required in Trade," *New York Times*, April 14, 1929, 52.

20. See, e.g., "Comments on the New Competition," 74–75; Stuart Chase, "New Competition Vexes Business," *New York Times*, October 31, 1926, 6; O.H. Cheney, "It Ain't Gonna Rain No More," *Nation's Business* (December 1926): 13–16; Cheney, "The Answer to the New Competition," 15–17, 80–81; "New Competition Explained," *Washington Post*, December 11, 1927, R1; and O.H. Cheney, "Mind Your Own Business," *Nation's Business* (August 1928): 18–20, 78–81.

21. Quoted in Cheney, "The Answer to the New Competition," 15.

22. "Comments on the New Competition.

23. "Cheney Lays Crash in Stocks to Banks," *New York Times*, March 21, 1930, 25.

24. O.H. Cheney, "The Publishing Industry Discovers Economics," *Publishers Weekly*, June 7, 1930, 2809–12.

25. Frederic G. Melcher, foreword to *The Economic Survey of the Book Industry, 1930–1931*, by O.H. Cheney (New York: Bowker, 1960), vi.

26. Robert Lynd, "The Book Industry," review of *The Economic Survey of the Book Industry, 1930–1931*, by O. H. Cheney, *Saturday Review of Literature*, January 16, 1932, 458.

27. Cheney, *The Economic Survey*, 208, 310.

28. Ibid., 150–52.

29. Ibid., 84, 87.

30. Ibid., 222.

31. Ibid., 30.

32. Ibid., 320.

33. Ibid., 70.

34. Ibid., 224; emphasis added.

35. Ibid., 323–27.

36. Ibid., 322; emphasis added.

37. Ibid., 326.

38. Ibid., 170–71. See also Robert A. Carter, "What's Changed Since Cheney?" *Publishers Weekly*, October 5, 1992, 43.

39. Cheney, *The Economic Survey*, 1.

40. "A Book Business Survey," *New York Times*, January 7, 1932, 22.

41. "Book Trade Denies Cheney Strictures," *New York Times*, January 6, 1932, 19. For more reactions to the Cheney Report, see Tebbel, *A History of Book Publishing*, 438.

42. Quoted in "Hope of Book Trade Put in New Survey," *New York Times*, January 7, 1932, 14.
43. "The Background of the Survey," *Publishers Weekly*, January 2, 1932, 37.
44. "Publishers Advise a Curb on Books," *New York Times*, June 3, 1932,17; "Publishers List Fewer New Books," *New York Times*, February 6, 1932, 15.
45. Lynd, "The Book Industry," 458; Tebbel, *A History of Book Publishing*, 438.
46. Tebbel, *A History of Book Publishing*, 438.
47. Ibid., 439.
48. Carter, "What's Changed Since Cheney?" 44.
49. See, e.g., Joan Shelley Rubin, *The Making of Middlebrow Culture* (Chapel Hill: University of North Carolina Press, 1992): 32, 336 n. 66; and Laura J. Miller, *Reluctant Capitalists: Bookselling and the Culture of Consumption* (Chicago: University of Chicago Press, 2006), 29–30.
50. Tebbel, *A History of Book Publishing in the United States*, 437.
51. *ISBN: International Standard Book Numbering (Incorporating Recommendations of the Publishers Association for Implementing the Standard Book Numbering Scheme)*, 4th rev. ed. (London: Standard Book Numbering Agency, 1978), 5. See also Daniel Melcher, "Standard Book Numbering," *Publishers Weekly*, April 15, 1968, 39.
52. *ISBN*, 5.
53. Ibid.
54. F. G. Foster, "Standard Book Numbering in the Book Trade," http://www.informaticsdevelopmentinstitute.net/isbn1966.rtf.
55. "Standard Book Numbering Approved for U.S.A.," *Publishers Weekly*, September 25, 1967, 76.
56. *ISBN*, 5. Basically the only difference is that the ISBN includes a "group number" to designate the book's language/country/region of origin.
57. "Standard Book Numbering Approved for U.S.A.," 76.
58. "Publicity Committee Promotes ISBN Usage on Several Fronts," *Publishers Weekly*, May 17, 1976, 43. See also George Goldberg and Jeff Goldberg, "The Progress of Bookland EAN," *Publishers Weekly*, October 16, 1987, 55.
59. This example and the preceding explanation are drawn from *ISBN*, 5–6. See also Melcher, "Standard Book Numbering," 39–40.
60. Radway, *A Feeling for Books*, 166.
61. "Complete ISBN Coverage in Latest Books in Print," *Publishers Weekly*, October 29, 1979, 73.
62. Stephen A. Brown, *Revolution at the Checkout Counter* (Cambridge, Mass.: Harvard University Press, 1997), 39–40. See also Benjamin Nelson, *Punched Cards to Bar Codes: A 200 Year Journey* (Peterborough, N.H.: Helmers, 1997), 62.
63. Brown, *Revolution at the Checkout*, 90; Nelson, *Punched Cards to Bar Codes*, 62.
64. "Bar Code History," *Barcode 1*, http://www.adams1.com/pub/russadam/history.html.
65. Sandra K. Paul, "A New Era in Order Fulfillment?" *Publishers Weekly*, April 10, 1978, 36.

66. Paul D. Doebler, "ISBN Task Force Begins Experimental Use of Computerized Book Ordering Methods," *Publishers Weekly*, May 17, 1976, 43.

67. "Progress Is Slow but Sure Toward ISBN Optical Reading," *Publishers Weekly*, June 5, 1981, 56.

68. For example, the ISBN conveys no pricing information. While the basic UPC symbol does provide price, it communicates only minimal data pertaining to the "identity" of a given item.

69. "Later U.P.C. Developments," http://members.aol.com/productupc/upc.work.html. See also "Book Industry Bar Codes," http://www/barcode-us.com/support_desk/booksuppcontent.html; and "Universal Product Code (UPC) and EAN Article Numbering Code (EAN)," *Barcode 1*, http://www.adams1.com/pub/russadam/upc-code.html.

70. "Universal Product Code." See also Sonja Bolle, "The Book Industry Moves Toward a Bar Code Standard," *Publishers Weekly*, May 23, 1986, 77.

71. Bolle, "The Book Industry," 77.

72. "Book Industry Bar Codes."

73. Zoë Wykes, ed., *ISBN-13 for Dummies* (Hoboken, N.J.: Wiley, 2005), electronic book, http://www.bisg.org/isbn-13/ISBN13_For_Dummies.pdf. See also American Booksellers Association, "FAQs about the 13-Digit ISBN and the 2005 Sunrise and GTIN Initiatives," http://www.bookweb.org/graphics/pdfs/13-digit-isbn.pdf.

74. Goldberg and Goldberg, "The Progress of Bookland EAN," 54.

75. Ibid.

76. Ibid., 51–53.

77. Andrew Ross, "Jobs in Cyberspace," in *Real Love: In Pursuit of Cultural Justice* (London: Routledge, 1998), 12.

78. Amazon.com, "2004 Annual Report," 6, http://library.corporate-ir.net/library/97/976/97664/items/144853/2004_Annual_report.pdf.

79. Quoted in Quittner, "An Eye on the Future," 64.

80. By comparison, its offices at the time occupied eleven hundred square feet. See Spector, *Amazon.com*, 66.

81. Martin, "The Next Big Thing," 170.

82. Paul Barton-Davis, quoted in Spector, *Amazon.com*, 68.

83. Spector, *Amazon.com*, 114, 138.

84. Ibid., 135.

85. For example, the company turned over its stock sixteen, eighteen, and nineteen times in 2004, 2003, and 2002, respectively. See Amazon.com, "2004 Annual Report," 27.

86. Spector, *Amazon.com*, 135.

87. Ibid., 115.

88. Saul Hansell, "Amazon Ships to a Sorting Machine's Beat," *New York Times*, January 21, 2002, C3.

89. Steven M. Zeitchik, "Virtual Bookselling, with Bricks and Mortar," *Publishers Weekly*, December 15, 1997, 23.

90. Amazon.com, "Letter to Shareholders, Customers, and Employees (1998)," 1, http://

media.corporate-ir.net/media_files/irol/97/97664/reports/Shareholderletter98.
pdf.

91. "Sales, Losses Jump at Amazon.com," *Publishers Weekly*, May 1, 2000, 16.

92. Spector, *Amazon.com*, 175.

93. Joelle Tessler, "The Real Side of Amazon," *Raleigh News & Observer*, November 25, 1999, D6; Joe Zeff, "From Your Mouse to Your House: What Goes on Behind the Scenes When You Place an Order at Amazon.com," *Time*, December 27, 1999, 72.

94. Tessler, "The Real Side of Amazon," D6; Michael Krantz, "Cruising Inside Amazon," *Time*, December 27, 1999, 71; Joe Zeff, "From Your Mouse to Your House," 72.

95. Tessler, "The Real Side of Amazon," D6 ; Zeff, "From Your Mouse to Your House," 72.

96. Tessler, "The Real Side of Amazon," D6.

97. Hansell, "Amazon Ships to a Sorting Machine's Beat," C3.

98. Spector, *Amazon.com*, 89.

99. Ibid., 89–90. See also Hof, "Amazon.com: The Wild World of E-Commerce."

100. Spector, *Amazon.com*, 90.

101. Ibid., 173.

102. Joseph Turow offers a parallel account, in which he explores how product codes, databases, and other technologies have been used to track and manage consumer behavior. See *Niche Envy: Marketing Discrimination in the Digital Age* (Cambridge, Mass.: MIT Press, 2006).

103. Hansell, "Amazon Ships to a Sorting Machine's Beat," C3.

104. Ibid.

105. Ibid.

106. Marx, *Capital*, vol. 1, 534.

107. Jacques Attali, *Noise: The Political Economy of Music*, trans. Brian Massumi (Minneapolis: University of Minnesota Press, 1985), 66. Cf. Marx: "A single violin player is his own conductor; an orchestra requires a separate one. The work of directing, superintending and adjusting becomes one of the functions of capital, from the moment labour under capital's control becomes co-operative" (*Capital*, vol. 1, 448–49).

108. Jonathan Sterne, "Amazon.com," in *Encyclopedia of New Media: An Essential Reference to Communication and Technology*, ed. Steve Jones (Thousand Oaks, Calif.: Sage, 2002), 5–6; Jim Milliot, "Amazon.com Cuts 1,300 Jobs in Drive for Profitability," *Publishers Weekly*, February 5, 2001, 9; Miguel Helft, "Campaign for Unionization at Amazon Intensifies," http://www.infoworld.com/articles/hn/xml/00/11/23/001123hnamazon.xml; Keith Regan, "Amazon Backtracks on Gag Rule for Layoffs," *E-Commerce Times*, http://ecommercetimes.com/perl/story/7202.html.

109. Cheney, *The Economic Survey*, 322.

110. Miller, *Reluctant Capitalists*, 209.

111. Cheney, *The Economic Survey*, 332. Of course, as a member of the professional managerial class Cheney went on to suggest that others like him—particularly publishers and booksellers—should reap the lion's share of the rewards.

4. Literature as Life on Oprah's Book Club

1. "Oprah's Book Club Anniversary Party," *The Oprah Winfrey Show*, September 22, 1997, 1 (transcript).
2. Paul Streitfeld, "On Oprah: People Who Read," *Washington Post*, September 26, 1996, A1. See also Paul Gray, "Winfrey's Winners," *Time*, December 2, 1996, 84.
3. "Newborn Quintuplets Come Home," *The Oprah Winfrey Show*, October 18, 1996, 15 (transcript).
4. Bridget Kinsella, "The Oprah Effect: How TV's Premier Talk Show Host Puts Books Over the Top," *Publishers Weekly*, January 20, 1997, 276–78.
5. Paul Gray, "Winfrey's Winners," 84; "Touched by an Oprah," *People*, December 20, 1999, 113; "Ticker," *Brill's Content* (April 2000): 84.
6. Cecelia Konchar Farr, *Reading Oprah: How Oprah's Book Club Changed the Way America Reads* (Albany: State University of New York Press, 2005), 2. Farr's statistics only cover titles selected for the book club between 1996 and 2002.
7. "Oprah's Book Club Anniversary Party," 17.
8. Abby Fowler, "Saying No to Oprah," *Newsweek*, November 5, 2001, 21. See also Kathleen Rooney, *Reading with Oprah: The Book Club That Changed America* (Fayetteville: University of Arkansas Press, 2005), 158.
9. See Farr, *Reading Oprah*, 2–3, 41, 66, 145n47. Farr continually draws parallels between her role as a literature professor and Winfrey's leadership of the book club. See also Rooney, *Reading with Oprah*, 145, 159, 205. Rooney chastises Winfrey for being insufficiently professorial and for encouraging "childish" forms of reading.
10. Methodologically this consists of a close reading of transcripts of episodes of *The Oprah Winfrey Show* that have featured Oprah's Book Club.
11. "About Oprah: Global Distribution List for *The Oprah Winfrey Show*," http://www2.oprah.com/about/press/about_press_globelist.jhtml. See also Kinsella, "The Oprah Effect," 277; Gray, "Winfrey's Winners," 84.
12. Luisa Kroll, "The World's Billionaires," *Forbes.com*, March 5, 2008, http://www.forbes.com/2008/03/05/richest-people-billionaires-billionaires08-cx_lk_0305billie_land.html; Matthew Miller, "The Forbe's 400," *Forbes.com*, September 20, 2007, http://www.forbes.com/2007/09/19/richest-americans-forbes-lists-richlist07-cx_mm_0920rich_land.html; Elizabeth MacDonald and Chana R. Schoenberger, "The World's 100 Most Powerful Women," *Forbes.com*, August 30, 2007, http://www.forbes.com/2007/08/30/most-powerful-women-biz-07women-cz_em_cs_0830power_land.html; and Lea Goldman, Monte Burke, and Kiri Blakeley, "The Celebrity 100," *Forbes.com*, June 14, 2007, http://www.forbes.com/2007/06/14/best-paid-celebrities-07celebrities_cz_lg_0614celeb_land.html.
13. The origins of the term are generally attributed to a *Wall Street Journal* editorial in 1997, though I've found an earlier instance in an editorial from 1996 that was published in the same paper. That piece, interestingly, couches the term within the phrase "what's been called the Oprahfication of politics," suggesting that it had already been circulating in the popular imagination for an indeterminate period of time. See the following editorials: "Queen Oprah," *Wall Street Journal*, Septem-

ber 17, 1997, A22; "Bathos and Credibility," *Wall Street Journal*, August 30, 1996, A8. For other uses of the term "Oprahfication," including critical commentary, see Mark Steyn, "Comic Oprah," *National Review*, March 23, 1998, http://www .nationalreview.com/23mar98/steyn032398.html; LaTonya Taylor, "The Church of O," *Christianity Today*, April 1, 2002, http://www.christianitytoday.com/ ct/2002/004/1.38.html; Chuck Colson, "Oprahfication and Its Discontents: Our Mile-Wide, Inch-Deep Religious Culture," *Christian Examiner* (May 2002), http://www .christianexaminer.com/Articles/Chuck%20Colson/Art_May02_Colson.html; Jane M. Shattuc, "The Oprahification of America: Talk Shows and the Public Sphere," in *Television, History, and American Culture: Feminist Critical Essays*, ed. Mary Beth Haralovich and Lauren Rabinovitz (Durham, N.C.: Duke University Press, 1999), 168–80; idem, *The Talking Cure: TV Talk Shows and Women* (New York: Routledge, 1997), 85–109; and Farr, *Reading Oprah*, 53–54; 60–64. See also Eva Illouz, *Oprah Winfrey and the Glamour of Misery: An Essay on Popular Culture* (New York: Columbia University Press, 2003). Although she does not use the word "Oprahfication" explicitly, she seems to invoke the spirit of the term in her critique of the "cultural matrix" of the Oprah Winfrey phenomenon.

14. R. Mark Hall, "The 'Oprahfication' of Literacy: Reading 'Oprah's Book Club,'" *College English* 65, no. 6 (July 2003): 646–67. In contrast to most critics, Hall doesn't use "Oprahfication" in a disparaging sense.

15. See Farr, *Reading Oprah*, 21. See also Rooney, *Reading with Oprah*, 8.

16. Janice A. Radway, *A Feeling for Books: The Book-of-the-Month Club, Literary Taste, and Middle-Class Desire* (Chapel Hill: University of North Carolina Press, 1997), 165.

17. Janice A. Radway, *Reading the Romance: Women, Patriarchy, and Popular Literature* (Chapel Hill: University of North Carolina Press, 1984), 43.

18. On the branding of Oprah, see Gayle Feldman, "Making Book on Oprah," *New York Times Book Review*, February 2, 1997, 31.

19. Kinsella, "The Oprah Effect," 276.

20. Paddy Scannell, *Radio, Television and Modern Life: A Phenomenological Approach* (Oxford: Blackwell, 1996), 12.

21. Quoted in Kinsella, "The Oprah Effect," 276.

22. Scannell, *Radio, Television and Modern Life*, 12.

23. Ibid., 155.

24. The notion of the "talking life" of books is drawn from Farr, *Reading Oprah*, 2.

25. Cynthia Crossen, "Read Them and Weep: Misery, Pain, Catastrophe, Despair . . . and That's Just the First Chapter," *Wall Street Journal*, July 13, 2001, W15.

26. "Oprah's Book Club," *The Oprah Winfrey Show*, June 23, 2000, 17 (transcript).

27. Ibid., 18.

28. "Book Club Finale," *The Oprah Winfrey Show*, June 18, 1997, 1 (transcript).

29. Ibid., 17.

30. "Oprah's Book Club," *The Oprah Winfrey Show*, June 18, 1998, 17 (transcript).

31. "Behind the Scenes at Oprah's Dinner Party," *The Oprah Winfrey Show*, December 3, 1996, 20–21 (transcript).

32. "Newborn Quintuplets Come Home," 16.
33. "Letters to Oprah's Book Club," *The Oprah Winfrey Show*, July 6, 2001, http://www
   .oprah.com (transcript).
34. Ibid. See also "Oprah's Book Club," September 9, 1999, 9.
35. "Letters to Oprah's Book Club."
36. "Oprah's Book Club Anniversary Party," 5.
37. "Letters to Oprah's Book Club."
38. Ibid.
39. Ibid.
40. Scannell, *Radio, Television and Modern Life*, 176.
41. "Oprah's Book Club Anniversary Party," 4.
42. Ibid., 3.
43. Crossen, "Read Them and Weep," W15.
44. "Book Club—Toni Morrison," *The Oprah Winfrey Show*, March 6, 1998, 1 (transcript). Extra time may also have been allotted since Winfrey was engaged in a
   court battle in Amarillo, Texas, at the time. A group of cattle ranchers filed suit
   against Winfrey after a broadcast in April 1996 about beef and the dangers of mad
   cow disease.
45. "Oprah's Book Club," March 31, 1999, 21.
46. "Oprah's Book Club," August 23, 2000, 20.
47. "Oprah's Book Club: *White Oleander,*" *The Oprah Winfrey Show*, June 15, 1999, 14–
   15 (transcript).
48. Ibid., 17.
49. Oprah's Book Club," September 9, 1999, 8.
50. Ibid., 9.
51. Ibid.
52. Ibid.
53. Ibid., 20.
54. "Oprah's Book Club: *We Were the Mulvaneys,*" *The Oprah Winfrey Show*, March 8,
   2001, 1 (transcript).
55. "Oprah's Book Club Anniversary Party," 17.
56. "Oprah's Book Club," *The Oprah Winfrey Show*, January 24, 2001, 2–3 (transcript).
57. Ibid., 11–12.
58. Ibid., 13.
59. "Anne Murray and Her Daughter's Battle with Anorexia," *The Oprah Winfrey Show*,
   November 10, 1999, 11 (transcript).
60. Ibid., 10.
61. "Oprah's Book Club: *Cane River,*" *The Oprah Winfrey Show*, September 24, 2001, 2
   (transcript).
62. Ibid., 3.
63. Ibid., 15. The book not only contains photos of Tademy's relatives but also birth
   certificates, bills of sale between slave owners, and so forth.
64. Three children's books penned by comedian Bill Cosby—*The Best Way to Play, The
   Meanest Thing to Say,* and *The Treasure Hunt*—were also chosen early on as club

selections. Given the fact that no other children's books have been chosen since, their selection seems anomalous.

65. Illouz, *Oprah Winfrey and the Glamour of Misery*, 146. Illouz has borrowed the quoted phrase from Arthur Danto.

66. "Oprah's Book Club Anniversary Party," 2.

67. "Oprah's Book Club," March 21, 1999, 13.

68. According to Illouz, "In conjunction with the [*Oprah Winfrey Show*], the novel is used to reflect on daily life and to transform it." *Oprah Winfrey and the Glamour of Misery*, 145. Illouz here implies that the club focuses solely on novels, which is not the case.

69. "Oprah's Book Club," March 21, 1999, 15, 17.

70. Ibid., 16.

71. Ibid., 15.

72. "Anne Murray and Her Daughter's Battle with Anorexia," 17.

73. Ibid., 1.

74. Ibid., 6.

75. "Oprah's Book Club: *We Were the Mulvaneys*," 6.

76. Ibid., 1–4. Unlike Marianne Mulvaney, Susan committed suicide.

77. Ibid., 7.

78. "Anne Murray and Her Daughter's Battle with Anorexia," 17.

79. Ibid., 18. See also "Oprah's Book Club," December 3, 1999, 19; and Bob Minzesheimer, "Winfrey's Book Talk Wins Publishing Gold," *USA Today*, November 17, 1999, D1.

80. Illouz, *Oprah Winfrey and the Glamour of Misery*, 108.

81. "Oprah's Book Club," November 16, 2000, 21. During the program in which Kingsolver's *Poisonwood Bible* was discussed, Winfrey and several women observed how they felt "transported" to Congo by Kingsolver's prose. I would argue, however, that the book generally tended not to be considered an "escape" by the women featured on the show, since many observed how, upon reading the book, they became increasingly aware of and thankful for such domestic accoutrements as dishwashers, soap, etc. See "Oprah's Book Club," August 23, 2000.

82. This meeting of Oprah's Book Club was one of just a handful that included a male discussant.

83. "Oprah's Book Club: *Cane River*," 1.

84. Ibid., 16–17.

85. Dave Weich, "Jonathan Franzen Uncorrected," *Powells.com*, October 4, 2001, http://www.powells.com/authors/franzen.html.

86. Quoted in Jeff Baker, "Oprah's Stamp of Approval Rubs Writer in Conflicted Ways," *Oregonian*, October 12, 2001, 5.

87. Jonathan Franzen, "Meet Me in St. Louis," *New Yorker*, December 31, 2001, http://www.newyorker.com/archive/2001/12/24/011224fa_FACT1.

88. Terry Gross, "Jonathan Franzen on His Newest Book, *The Corrections*, His Relationship with His Parents and That Connection to the Book," *Fresh Air*, NPR, October 15, 2001, http://www.npr.org/templates/story/story.php?storyId=1131456.

89. Twinges of chauvinism surely inflected his complaint. Yet if we're to believe what he had to say in a piece he contributed to *Harper's* in 1996, it was also grounded in a more affirmative conviction that men, like women, simply should be reading more—a conviction not inconsistent with Winfrey's own project of "getting the whole country reading again." See Jonathan Franzen, "Perchance to Dream: In the Age of Images, a Reason to Write Novels," *Harper's*, April 1996, http://www .harpers.org/archive/1996/04/0007955.

90. Gross, "Jonathan Franzen on His Newest Book."

91. Franzen, "Perchance to Dream."

92. On the biographical impulses behind Oprah's Book Club, see Illouz, *Oprah Winfrey and the Glamour of Misery*, 103.

93. Jeff Giles, "Errors and 'Corrections,'" *Newsweek*, November 5, 2001, 68.

94. David D. Kirkpatrick, "Winfrey Rescinds Offer to Author for Guest Appearance," *New York Times*, October 24, 2001, C4; David D. Kirkpatrick, "'Oprah' Gaffe by Franzen Draws Ire and Sales," *New York Times*, October 29, 2001, E1.

95. Baker, "Oprah's Stamp of Approval," 5.

96. Kirkpatrick, "'Oprah' Gaffe," E1. This comment seems to contradict Franzen's 1996 piece in *Harper's*. There he partially attributes the waning of "good" fiction to popular culture. See Franzen, "Perchance to Dream."

97. Dinitia Smith, "'Corrections' Is Winner of Top Prize for Fiction," *New York Times* November 15, 2001, A29.

98. Todd Gitlin, "The Dumb-Down," *The Nation*, March 17, 1997, 28.

99. Illouz, *Oprah Winfrey and the Glamour of Misery*, 63.

100. "Why Everybody Hates Chris Rock and Special OBC News," *The Oprah Winfrey Show*, September 22, 2005, 22 (transcript).

101. "The Man Who Kept Oprah Awake at Night: *A Million Little Pieces*," *The Oprah Winfrey Show*, October 26, 2005, 4 (transcript).

102. Ibid., 19.

103. "The Man Who Conned Oprah," *Smoking Gun*, January 8, 2006, http://www.the smokinggun.com/jamesfrey/0104061jamesfrey1.html.

104. The periodical noted, though, that because nine of Frey's alleged fourteen arrests had occurred when he was minor, the records would have been sealed.

105. James Frey, *A Million Little Pieces* (New York: Anchor Books, 2003), 94.

106. "The Man Who Conned Oprah."

107. Frey, *A Million Little Pieces*, 250.

108. Ibid., 366–70.

109. "The Man Who Conned Oprah."

110. Ibid. See also "Interview with James Frey," *Larry King Live*, January 11, 2006, http:// transcripts.cnn.com/TRANSCRIPTS/0601/11/lkl.01.html; and Frey, *A Million Little Pieces*, 431–32.

111. "The Man Who Conned Oprah." For an astute discussion of the market pressures driving the recent upsurge in memoirs, see Kathleen Rooney, *Reading with Oprah: The Book Club That Changed America*, 2nd ed. (Fayetteville: University of Arkansas Press, 2008), 225.

112. "The Biggest of 2005: The 200 Bestselling Books of the Year," *Book Standard*, January 4, 2006, http://www.thebookstandard.com/bookstandard/search/article_display.jsp?vnu_content_id=1001804456. See also Dermot McEvoy, "Something Old, Something New," *Publishers Weekly*, March 27, 2006, http://www.publishersweekly.com/article/CA6318931.html.

113. "Interview with James Frey."

114. "*The Oprah Winfrey Show* with James Frey," *The Oprah Winfrey Show*, January 26, 2006, http://www.nytimes.com/ref/books/excerpts-oprah.html.

115. Quoted in Edward Wyatt, "Oprah's Book Club Responding to Writers Who'll Sit and Chat," *New York Times*, September 23, 2005, A1.

116. Illouz, *Oprah Winfrey and the Glamour of Misery*, 144; see also 73–74.

117. Frank Rich of the *New York Times* used this neologism on the January 26, 2006, episode of *The Oprah Winfrey Show* to describe Frey's fictionalization of truthful events. The notion of "truthiness" speaks to feelings or impressions of veracity that flow from information hovering on the border of truth and falsity. Rich borrowed the term from Comedy Central's Stephen Colbert, who introduced it on his tongue-in-cheek current events program *The Colbert Report*. See "*The Oprah Winfrey Show* with James Frey." For a further discussion of "truthiness" as it pertains to the James Frey controversy, see Rooney, *Reading with Oprah*, 220, 232–33. Note that Rooney sees the importance of truth arising on Oprah's Book Club only in the wake of the terrorist attacks of 9/11 and the U.S. government's not altogether truthful (i.e., "truthy") justifications for subsequently waging war against Iraq. Conversely, I see this as a core element of the book club's value system, predating 9/11.

118. See, e.g., Alberto Manguel, *A History of Reading* (New York: Penguin Books, 1996),121; James P. Danky and Wayne A. Wiegand, eds., *Print Cultures in a Diverse America* (Urbana: University of Illinois Press, 1998); Janice A. Radway, "On the Importance of Reading: Book History and the Possibilities for Rethinking the Social" (1999), unpublished manuscript; and Elizabeth Long, *Book Clubs: Women and the Uses of Reading in Everyday Life* (Chicago: University of Chicago Press, 2003), 7, 13.

119. See, e.g., Sven Birkerts, *The Gutenberg Elegies: The Fate of Reading in an Electronic Age* (New York: Fawcett Columbine, 1994). See also Walter Ong, *Orality and Literacy: The Technologizing of the Word* (London: Routledge, 1982); Rooney, *Reading with Oprah*, 109–62. In *The Making of Middlebrow Culture* (Chapel Hill: University of North Carolina Press, 1992) Joan Shelley Rubin explores the synergy books have shared with radio and other media.

120. See Farr, *Reading Oprah*, 42; Rooney, *Reading with Oprah*, 145, 159, 205.

121. Here I am echoing R. Mark Hall, "The 'Oprahfication' of Literacy," 664–65.

122. Franzen, "Meet Me in St. Louis." Franzen quotes an *Oprah* producer as saying: "This [*The Corrections*] is a difficult book for us. I don't think we're going to know how to approach it until we start hearing from our readers."

123. See Farr, *Reading Oprah*, 101, 104.

124. Cf. Long: "In general, contemporary reading groups . . . are not geared toward collective action or politics." *Book Clubs*, 59.

125. Farr, *Reading Oprah*; and Rooney, *Reading with Oprah*. A third book, Illouz's *Oprah Winfrey and the Glamour of Misery*, also discusses the book club at some length.

5. Harry Potter and the Culture of the Copy

1. On the number of Potter books in print, see Motoko Rich, "Harry Potter's Popularity Holds Up in Early Sales, *New York Times*, July 23, 2007, A12, http://www.nytimes.com/2007/07/23/books/23potter.html. On translations of the Harry Potter series, see "Harry Potter in Translation," *Wikipedia*, http://en.wikipedia.org/wiki/Harry_Potter_in_translation.
2. See, e.g., David Baggett and Shawn E. Klein, eds., *Harry Potter and Philosophy: If Aristotle Ran Hogwarts* (Chicago: Open Court, 2004); Andrew Blake, *The Irresistible Rise of Harry Potter* (London: Verso, 2002); Suman Gupta, *Re-reading Harry Potter* (Basingstoke, Engl.: Palgrave Macmillan, 2003); Philip Nel, *J. K. Rowling's Harry Potter Novels: A Reader's Guide* (New York: Continuum, 2001). Some scholarly books lack any disclaimer. See, e.g., Giselle Liza Anatol, ed., *Reading Harry Potter: Critical Essays* (Westport , Conn.: Praeger, 2003); Elizabeth E. Heilman, ed., *Harry Potter's World: Multidisciplinary Critical Perspectives* (New York: Routledge-Falmer, 2003); and Lana A. Whited, ed., *The Ivory Tower and Harry Potter: Perspectives on a Literary Phenomenon* (Columbia: University of Missouri Press, 2002).
3. The title of this chapter is meant as an homage to Hillel Schwartz, *The Culture of the Copy: Striking Likenesses, Unreasonable Facsimiles* (New York: Zone Books, 1998).
4. Dilip Parameshwar Gaonkar and Elizabeth A. Povinelli, "Technologies of Public Forms: Circulation, Transfiguration, Recognition," *Public Culture* 15, no. 3 (Fall 2003): 386.
5. J. K. Rowling, *Harry Potter and the Order of the Phoenix* (New York: Scholastic, 2003), 250–78.
6. In many parts of the world the book carries its original British title, *Harry Potter and the Philosopher's Stone*. The U.K. edition was published by Bloomsbury in 1997. First printing figures appearing in the text refer solely to American editions published by Scholastic.
7. First printing and in-print figures for the Harry Potter series are drawn from Jane Henderson, "Growing Up Harry," *St. Louis Post-Dispatch*, July 13, 2005, A1. See also Bob Thompson, "A Little Wizard Goes a Long Way," *Washington Post*, July 14, 2005, C1; Teresa Mendez, "Tight Security Measures to Guard Harry's Magic," *Christian Science Monitor*, July 11, 2005, 11; "'Deathly' Gets Record Printing," *Publishers Weekly*, March 14, 2007, http://www.publishersweekly.com/article/CA6424402.html.
8. Thompson, "A Little Wizard Goes a Long Way," C1.
9. Edward Wyatt, "Test for Security Efforts: Next Harry Potter Book," *New York Times*, July 5, 2005, E1, http://www.nytimes.com/2005/07/05/books/05pott.html;

Jon Cronin, "The Magic of Selling Harry Potter," *BBC News*, July 14, 2005, http://news.bbc.co.uk/2/hi/business/4679553.stm.

10. Motoko Rich and Julie Bosman, "Harry Potter's Final Act Set for July 21," *New York Times*, February 1, 2007, http://www.nytimes.com/2007/02/01/books/01cnd-harry.html. See also Oliver Bullough, "Boy Wizard Turns Green," *Guardian Unlimited*, March 21, 2007, http://books.guardian.co.uk/harrypotter/story/0,,2039221,00.html. Initial reports set the *Half-Blood Prince's* sales figures considerably lower, at 5.8 million copies in the first week of the book's release. See Steven Zeitchik, "Indies Vexed Over Potter Economics," *Publishers Weekly*, August 8, 2005, http://www.publishersweekly.com/article/CA632779.html. The latter report bases its sales estimate on Nielsen BookScan figures, which are based on somewhat limited data.

11. Steven Zeitchik, "The Potter Effect," *Publishers Weekly*, July 11, 2005, http://www.publishersweekly.com/article/CA624542.html.

12. Zeitchik, "Potter Effect"; Peter Stack, "Harry Potter Casts His Spell," *San Francisco Chronicle*, June 14, 2000, http://www.sfgate.com/cgi-bin/article.cgi?f=/c/a/2000/06/14/DD90776.DTL.

13. André Schiffrin, *The Business of Books: How International Conglomerates Took Over Publishing and Changed the Way We Read* (London: Verso, 2000), 2.

14. Thompson, "A Little Wizard Goes a Long Way," C1.

15. "Scholastic Inc. *Harry Potter and the Half-Blood Prince* Agreement (Supplement to the Scholastic 2005 On-Sale Date Policy Contract)," http://www.scholastic.com/custsupport/booksellers/HalfBloodAgreement.pdf; "2007 Scholastic Inc. On-Sale Date Policy," http://www.scholastic.com/custsupport/booksellers/On_Sale_Date_Policy_2007_Final_Combined.pdf; "Scholastic Inc. *Harry Potter and the Deathly Hallows* Agreement (Retailer) (Supplement to the Scholastic 2007 On-Sale Date Policy Conract)," http://www.scholastic.com/custsupport/booksellers/Deathly_Hallows_On_Sale_Agreement_Retailer_Final.pdf. See also Anna Weinberg, "Harry Potter and the Embargo of Doom," *The Book Standard*, July 14, 2005, http://www.thebookstandard.com/bookstandard/news/retail/article_display.jsp?vnu_content_id=1000979412; Thompson, "A Little Wizard Goes a Long Way," C1; Cathryn Atkinson and John Ezard, "Order of the Gag as Harry Potter Spring a Leak," *The Guardian*, July 13, 2005, 7; Stack, "Harry Potter Casts His Spell."

16. "Scholastic Inc. *Harry Potter and the Deathly Hallows* Agreement (Retailer)."

17. Ibid.

18. According to several press reports, *Harry Potter and the Deathly Hallows* performed as expected during its initial day of sales, despite its contents having been leaked on the Internet several days earlier. See Motoko Rich, "Harry Potter's Popularity Holds Up in First-Day Sales," *New York Times*, July 23, 2007, A12; Steven Zeitchik, "'Deathly Hallows' Sells 8.3 Million," *Variety*, July 22, 2007, http://www.variety.com/article/VR1117968991.html. For his part Steve Riggio, Barnes & Noble's CEO, claimed that if "the ending is revealed prior to midnight Friday [July 20, 2007], it will not result in us selling a single less copy of the book." Quoted in Motoko Rich, "Leak Preview: New Harry Potter Book Appears on Wed (Or Does It?)," *New York Times*, July 18, 2007, A12. An official with publisher Alfred A. Knopf sim-

ilarly stated: "I can't think of a single example from our publishing list where sales were hurt. . . . None of the leaks are going to hurt sales of Potter." Quoted in Hillel Italie, "Leaks and Legal Action Mark Final Days Before Potter Release," *Associated Press State & Local Wire*, July 18, 2007.

19. A message posted on or about July 16, 2007, to the Booksellers' area on Scholastic's Web site read: "Violation of July 21st on-sale date: If you see *Harry Potter and the Deathly Hallows* on sale and/or on display prior to 12:01 a.m. on July 21st, please notify Scholastic immediately by calling 800/242-7737 ext. 2 or 800/558-8341. We would greatly appreciate it if you would purchase the book and provide us with a receipt (you will be reimbursed for the cost of the book). All violations will be taken very seriously. Thank you." http://www.scholastic.com/custsupport/booksellers/harrypotter.htm#contact.

20. Henderson, "Growing Up Harry," A1.

21. Wyatt, "Test for Security Efforts," E1.

22. Roback and Milliot, "Getting to the Witching Hour."

23. Weinberg, "Harry Potter and the Embargo of Doom."

24. Roback and Milliot, "Getting to the Witching Hour."

25. Ibid; Anna Weinberg, "Harry Potter and the Embargo of Doom."

26. Tamer El-Ghobashy, "Hocus-Pocus! We Got Harry," *New York Daily News*, June 18, 2003, 5; Tamer El-Ghobashy and Tracy Common, "Harry Potter Seller Won't Be in Book Bind," *New York Daily News*, June 20, 2003, 4.

27. David Gates, "Keeping the Lid On," *Newsweek*, June 30, 2003, 55; Wyatt, "Test for Security Efforts."

28. Rebecca Rothbaum, "New Potter Book Materializes Early," *Times Union*, July 13, 2005, A2. See also Weinberg, "Harry Potter and the Embargo of Doom."

29. Kelly Kendall, "2 Score Copies of Potter Book," *Indianapolis Star*, July 14, 2005, B1.

30. "Man Admits Stealing Potter Book," *BBC News*, May 14, 2003, http://news.bbc.co.uk/go/pr/fr/-/2/hi/uk_news/england/suffolk/3026993.stm.

31. "Thousands of Potter Books Stolen," *BBC News*, June 17, 2003, http://news.bbc.co.uk/go/pr/fr/-/2/hi/entertainment/2996718.stm; "Protecting the Potter Magic," *BBC News*, June 17, 2003, http://news.bbc.co.uk/go/pr/fr/-/2/hi/entertainment/2966290.stm.

32. "'Stolen' Potter Pair Charged," *BBC News*, June 4, 2005, http://news.bbc.co.uk/go/pr/fr/-/2/hi/uk_news/england/northamptonshire/4608999.stm; "Guard Jailed for Harry Book Theft," *BBC News*, January 19, 2006, http://news.bbc.co.uk/go/pr/fr/-/2/hi/england/northamptonshire/4626988.stm; Weinberg, "Harry Potter and the Embargo of Doom."

33. Quoted in Tabassum Siddiqui, "Potter Purchasers Bound to Secrecy," *Toronto Star*, July 12, 2005, A1.

34. Nicholas Read and Vito Pilieci, "Maximum Security for New Harry Potter," *Ottawa Citizen*, July 12, 2005, A1. See also Atkinson and Ezard, "Order of the Gag" 7; Roback and Milliot, "Getting to the Witching Hour"; and Weinbery, "Harry Potter and the Embargo of Doom."

35. Italie, "Leaks and Legal Action"; Rich, "Leak Preview," A12; Motoko Rich, "'Potter' Peeks Prove to Be Genuine," *New York Times*, July 20, 2007, E10.

36. Monica Hesse, "Spolier Frenzy Follows Early Mailing of 'Hallows,'" *Washington Post*, July 19, 2007, C1; Karen Holt, "Schoastic's Intricate Plan to Guard HP 7 Apparently Undone By Upstart E-Tailer," *Publishers Weekly*, July 18, 2007, http://www.publishersweekly.com/article/CA6461311.html; Motoko Rich, "Suit Follows Reports of Early 'Potter' Shipments," *New York Times*, July 19, 2007, A20. Some reports erroneously pegged the total number of incorrectly shipped copies of *Deathly Hallows* at 120; see, e.g., Italie, "Leaks and Legal Action."

37. Will Collier, "I Was an eBay Voldemort," *National Review Online*, July 19, 2007, http://article.nationalreview.com/?q=OTYxYmE5Y2UzNDMyNWQ2YzFmYTk3NzYiMTkxZGFhNzI=. The day after Collier finalized the sale, eBay removed the auction listing from its site. It did so in response to a letter from the Christopher Little Literary Agency (Rowling's agent) claiming—falsely—that selling the book prior to its official release constituted a violation of the agency's intellectual property rights. See Will Collier, "Fool If You Think It's Over," *Vodkapundit and the Weblog of Tomorrow*, July 19, 2007, http://vodkapundit.com/archives/008960.php.

38. Michiko Kakutani, "An Epic Showdown as Harry Potter Is Initiated into Adulthood," *New York Times*, July 19, 2007, A20, http://www.nytimes.com/2007/07/19/books/19potter.html; Mary Carole McCauley, "An Inevitable Ending to Harry Potter Series," *Baltimore Sun*, July 18, 2007, http://www.baltimoresun.com/entertainment/booksmags/bal-2potter0718,0,2741335.story.

39. Gates, "Keeping the Lid On," 55. See also Henderson, "Growing Up Harry," A1; Siddiqui, "Potter Purchasers Bound to Secrecy," A1.

40. Rob Corddry, "Harry Potter Terror: Could It Happen Here?" *The Daily Show with Jon Stewart*, July 14, 2005.

41. For an excellent account of the neoliberal underpinnings of surveillance and security in the United States today, see Mark Andrejevic, *iSpy: Surveillance and Power in the Interactive Era* (Lawrence: University of Kansas Press, 2007).

42. "*Harry Potter and the Half-Blood Prince:* First Author-Signed U.S. Edition Journey to America," http://www.scholastic.com/harrypotter/funstuff/video/index.htm.

43. Ibid. The quotation comes from the Web page accompanying the video.

44. Ibid. See also Roback and Milliot, "Getting to the Witching Hour."

45. Walter Benjamin, "The Work of Art in the Age of Mechanical Reproduction," in *Illuminations: Essays and Reflections*, ed. Hannah Arendt, trans. Harry Zohn (New York: Shocken Books, 1968): 221.

46. J. K. Rowling, *Harry Potter and the Chamber of Secrets* (New York: Scholastic, 1999), 86–103, 190.

47. Ibid., 297–98.

48. Adrian Johns, *The Nature of the Book: Print and Knowledge in the Making* (Chicago: University of Chicago Press, 1998); Susan Stewart, *Crimes of Writing: Problems in the Containment of Representation* (Durham, N.C.: Duke University Press, 1994); and Siva Vaidhyanathan, *Copyrights and Copywrongs: The Rise of Intellectual Property and How It Threatens Creativity* (New York: NYU Press, 2001).

49. "Fake Harry Potter Book Released in China," *USA Today*, July 5, 2002, http://www.usatoday.com/news/world/2002/07/05/harry-potter-china.htm; Brooke Glad-

stone, "China's Harry Potter," *On the Media*, July 19, 2002, http://www.onthemedia.org/transcripts/transcripts_071902_china.html.

50. "Harry and the Frauds" *Hobart Mercury*, April 19, 2003, 34.

51. John Pomfret, "Chinese Pirates Rob 'Harry' of Magic, and Fees," *Washington Post*, October 31, 2002, A1.

52. Pomfret, "Chinese Pirates," A1. See also Oliver August and Jack Malverm, "Legal Magic Spells Win for Harry in China," *The Times*, November 2, 2002, 14; "Fake Harry Potter Novel Hits China," *BBC News*, July 4, 2002, http://news.bbc.co.uk/2/hi/entertainment/2092661.stm; Joseph Kahn, "The Pinch of Piracy Wakes China Up on Copyright Issue," *New York Times*, November 1, 2002, C1; "Fake Harry Potter Book"; and Gladstone, "China's Harry Potter."

53. See Stephanie Grunier and John Lippman, "Warner Bros. Claims Harry Potter Sites," *Wall Street Journal*, December 20, 2000, http://zdnet.com.com/2100-11-503255.html. See also Rebecca Sutherland Borah, "Apprentice Wizards Welcome: Fan Communities and the Culture of Harry Potter," in *The Ivory Tower and Harry Potter: Perspectives on a Literary Phenomenon*, ed. Lana A. Whited (Columbia: University of Missouri Press, 2002), 353–55.

54. Xing Yuhao, "The Chinese Harry Potter Epidemic," *China Today*, December 2003, http://www.chinatoday.com.cn/English/p50.htm.

55. Ibid.

56. Andrew Wang, "Harry to Cast His Magic in Hindi," *The Age*, November 9, 2003, http://www.theage.com.au/articles/2003/11/08/1068243304732.html.

57. Tim Wu, "Harry Potter and the International Order of Copyright," *Slate*, June 27, 2003, http://www.slate.com/id/2084960/.

58. Steve Gutterman, "Harry Potter Calls in His Lawyers," *CBS News.com*, November 6, 2002, http://www.cbsnews.com/stories/2002/11/06/entertainment/main528433.shtml. See also Wu, "International Order of Copyright."

59. Gutterman, "Harry Potter Calls in His Lawyers"; Alex Rodriguez, "Russian Parody of 'Harry Potter' Books Vexes British Author," *San Diego Union-Tribune*, December 22, 2002, A25.

60. Robyn Dixon, "Harry Potter Battles Attack of the Clones," *Los Angeles Times*, April 13, 2002, 41.

61. O'Flynn, "Potter Spawns Parody Part II," *St. Petersburg Times*, November 29, 2002, http://www.sptimes.ru/index.php?action_id=2&story_id=8705; Rodriguez, "Russian Parody Vexes British Author," A25; Wu, "International Order of Copyright." The Russian version of the title represents my best attempt to transliterate it into the Roman alphabet.

62. The names are taken from an unauthorized translation of *Porri Gatter and the Stone Philosopher*, published by Ivan Mytko and Andrei Zhvalevsky, *Porridge Gutter and the Stone Philosopher*, trans. Mat Sver Mecca, http://zhurnal.lib.ru/m/mekallx_m_s/pga01.shtml.

63. Mytko and Zhvalevsky, *Porridge Gutter and the Stone Philosopher*.

64. O'Flynn, "Potter Spawns Parody Part II."

65. Rodriguez, "Russian Parody Vexes British Author," A25.

66. See, e.g., Vaidhyanathan, *Copyrights and Copywrongs*, 37–55; and Eva Hemmungs Wirtén, *No Trespassing: Authorship, Intellectual Property Rights, and the Boundaries of Globalization* (Toronto: University of Toronto Press, 2004), 14–37.

67. *Uitgeverij Byblos, B.V.* v. *Joanne Kathleen Rowling, Uitgeverij de Harmonie, B.V., and Time Warner Entertainment Company, L.P.*, 844/03 SKG (Court of Appeal of Amsterdam, Fourth Three-Judge Civil Section 2003), sec. 4.1c.

68. Ibid, sec. 1. See also Dixon, "Harry Potter Battles Attack of the Clones," 41.

69. *Uitgeverij Byblos, B.V.* v. *Joanne Kathleen Rowling, Uitgeverij de Harmonie, B.V., and Time Warner Entertainment Company, L.P.*, sec. 4.7.7.

70. Ibid., sec. 4.7.8. For Rowling's literary influences and appropriations see the following: Anne Hiebert Alton, "Generic Fusion and the Mosaic of *Harry Potter*," in *Harry Potter's World: Multidisciplinary Critical Perspectives*, ed. Elizabeth A. Heliman (New York: Routledge-Falmer, 2003), 141–62; Blake, *The Irresistible Rise of Harry Potter*, 18–19; Nancy Gibbs, "The Real Magic of Harry Potter" *Time*, June 23, 2003, 64–65; Nel, *J. K. Rowling's Harry Potter Novels*, 9–11; and Karen Manners Smith, "Harry Potter's Schooldays: J. K. Rowling and the British Boarding School Novel," in *Reading Harry Potter: Critical Essays*, ed. Giselle Liza Anatol (Westport, Conn.: Praeger, 2003), 69–87.

71. *Uitgeverij Byblos, B.V.* v. *Joanne Kathleen Rowling, Uitgeverij de Harmonie, B.V., and Time Warner Entertainment Company, L.P.*, sec. 4.7.6.

72. Ibid., sec. 4.7.4.

73. Ibid., sec. 4.7.7.

74. Ibid., sec. 4.7.9.1. The internal quotation presumably is drawn from a brief filed by Byblos's attorneys or possibly from its attorneys' oral arguments.

75. Ibid., sec. 4.7.9.3.

76. For example, Michael Gerber, *Barry Trotter and the Unauthorized Parody* (New York: Fireside, 2002).

77. Ibid., sec. 4.7.10.

78. Burton Bollag, "Don't Steal This Book," *Chronicle of Higher Education*, April 2, 2004, A38.

79. Mark Phillips, "Publishing Pirates Are Robbing Legitimate Publishers Blind Worldwide," *CBS Evening News*, June 5, 2003 (transcript).

80. Quoted in Shujen Wang, *Framing Piracy: Globalization and Film Distribution in Greater China* (Lanham, Md.: Rowman and Littlefield, 2003), 73.

81. Bollag, "Don't Steal This Book," A38.

82. Jen Lin-Liu, "Textbook Pirates Find a Huge Market in China," *Chronicle of Higher Education*, April 2, 2004, A44.

83. Quoted in Phillips, "Publishing Pirates Are Robbing Publishers."

84. Ravi Sundaram, "Recycling Modernity: Pirate Electronic Cultures in India," in *Internationalizing Cultural Studies: An Anthology*, ed. Ackbar Abbas and John Nguyet Erni (Malden, Mass.: Blackwell, 2005), 45.

85. "The Crash," *Frontline*, PBS, June 29, 2002, http://www.pbs.org/wgbh/pages/frontline/shows/crash/.

86. Wang, *Framing Piracy*, 180.

87. Ziauddin Sardar, "On the Political Economy of the Fake," in *Internationalizing Cultural Studies: An Anthology*, ed. Ackbar Abbas and John Nguyet Erni (Malden, Mass.: Blackwell, 2005), 660.

88. Ibid., 659–60.

89. Ibid., 658.

90. Ibid., 661.

91. See, e.g., Bollag, "Don't Steal This Book"; Martha Overland, "Publishers Battle Pirates in India with Little Success," *Chronicle of Higher Education*, April 2, 2004, A40–41.

92. Wang, *Framing Piracy*, 74.

93. Sardar, "On the Political Economy of the Fake," 661.

94. Some book publishers maintain a "dual pricing system," according to which they offer discounted books to economically less enfranchised countries. Often the motivation for such a program is grounded less in a commitment to economic equity or distributive justice than a desire to compete with the local publishing "pirates" who threaten to undersell them. See Overland, "Publishers Battle Pirates in China," A40.

95. Wang, *Framing Piracy*, 26.

96. As Ivan Mytko and Andrei Zhvalevsky, authors of *Porri Gatter and the Stone Philosopher*, suggested, "We're giving them [Harry Potter] free promotion." Quoted in O'Flynn, "Potter Spawns Parody Part II."

97. "Harry Potter Bewitches E-books," *Taipei Times*, July 15, 2003, http://www. taipeitimescom/News/feat/archives/2003/07/15/2003059551.

98. Rowling, *Harry Potter and the Chamber of Secrets*, 44.

99. Maurice Blanchot, "Everyday Speech," in *The Infinite Conversation*, trans. Susan Hanson (Minneapolis: University of Minnesota Press), 240. There Blanchot writes: "The everyday escapes."

100. The quotations about social life are drawn from Gaonkar and Povinelli, "Technologies of Public Forms," 387. On the idea of "putting culture into motion," see Renato Rosaldo, *Culture and Truth: The Remaking of Social Analysis* (Boston: Beacon Press, 1993), 91–108.

101. "When Harry Met Money," *Newsweek*, June 30, 2003, 53; "Save Muggle Forests," July 7, 2005, http://www.greenpeace.org/usa/news/save-muggle-forests; Oliver Bullough, "Boy Wizard Turns Green."

102. Quoted in Wyatt, "Test for Security Efforts," E1.

103. J. K. Rowling, *Harry Potter and the Sorcerer's Stone* (New York: Scholastic, 1997), 298.

Conclusion: From Consumerism to Control

1. Elizabeth Eisenstein, "The End of the Book? Some Perspectives on Media Change," *The American Scholar* 64, no. 4 (Autumn 1995): 555.

2. Laura J. Miller, *Reluctant Capitalists: Bookselling and the Culture of Consumption* (Chicago: University of Chicago Press, 2006), 20.

3. James Carey, "Afterword: The Culture in Question," in *James Carey: A Critical Reader*, ed. Eve Stryker Munson and Catherine A. Wilson (Minneapolis: University of Minnesota Press, 1997), 324.

4. See, e.g., Roy Rosenzweig, *Eight Hours for What We Will: Workers and Leisure in an Industrial City, 1870–1920* (Cambridge: Cambridge University Press, 1983). For discussions of the ways in which consumerism helped to mitigate labor unrest, see Gary Cross, *An All-Consuming Century: Why Commercialism Won in Modern America* (New York: Columbia University Press, 2000); and Stuart Ewen, *Captains of Consciousness: Advertising and the Social Roots of the Consumer Culture*, rev. ed. (New York: Basic Books, 2001), 7.

5. Lizabeth Cohen, *A Consumers' Republic: The Politics of Mass Consumption in Postwar America* (New York: Knopf, 2003), 155.

6. Cohen, *A Consumers' Republic*, 84–85. See also Cross, *An All-Consuming Century*, 139; Ewen, *Captains of Consciousness*, 91, 215; Lawrence Grossberg, *We Gotta Get Out of This Place: Popular Conservatism and Postmodern Culture* (New York: Routledge, 1992), 139; and Stuart Hall, "Notes on Deconstructing 'the Popular,'" in *Cultural Theory and Popular Culture: A Reader*, 2nd ed., ed. John Storey (Athens: University of Georgia Press, 1998), 442–53.

7. Raymond Williams, "Culture Is Ordinary," in *Resources of Hope: Culture, Democracy, Socialism*, ed. Robin Gale (London: Verso, 1989), 10.

8. Michel de Certeau, *The Practice of Everyday Life*, trans. Steven Rendall (Berkeley: University of California Press, 1984), xii–xiii.

9. Henri Lefebvre, *Everyday Life in the Modern World*, trans. Sacha Rabinovitch (New Brunswick, N.J.: Transaction Publishers, 1984), 60, 68–109. Lefebvre uses the phrase "bureaucratic society of controlled consumption." I've opted to jettison the bureaucratic aspect since I'm not altogether convinced that consumption is controlled in as centralized or bureaucratic a fashion as Lefebvre—writing in 1967—believed. For more on the concept of control, see Gilles Deleuze, *Negotiations, 1972–1990*, trans. Martin Joughin (New York: Columbia University Press, 1995), 169–82.

10. Lefebvre, *Everyday Life*, 45–54.

11. Ibid., 56.

12. Ibid., 60, 64.

13. Ibid., 55.

14. Raymond Williams, *Marxism and Literature* (Oxford: Oxford University Press, 1977), 126.

15. Lefebvre, *Everyday Life*, 64.

16. Norbert Wiener, *The Human Use of Human Beings: Cybernetics and Society* (Cambridge, Mass.: Da Capo, 1954), 15. For an astute discussion of this etymology and its politico-technical implications, see Mark Andrejevic, *iSpy: Surveillance and Power in the Interactive Era* (Lawrence: University of Kansas Press, 2007), 19.

17. Lefebvre, *Everyday Life*, 64, 72. Lawrence Lessig draws a parallel to Lefebvre's idea of programming in his discussion of regulation through code: "If in the middle of the nineteenth century the threat to liberty was norms, and at the start of the twentieth it was state power, and during much of the middle twentieth it was the market, then my argument is that we must come to understand how in the twenty-first century it is a different regulator—code—that should be our current concern." Lawrence Lessig, *Code Version 2.0* (New York: Basic Books, 2006), 121.

18. Quoted in Joseph Turow, *Niche Envy: Marketing Discrimination in the Digital Age* (Cambridge, Mass.: MIT Press, 2006), 21. The adage is often attributed to department store magnate John Wannamaker.

19. Lefebvre, *Everyday Life*, 82.

20. See Giles Slade, *Made to Break: Technology and Obsolescence in America* (Cambridge, Mass.: Harvard University Press, 2006), 4–5.

21. Lefebvre, *Everyday Life*, 59–60, 72.

22. For more on this reversal of the logic of branding, see Naomi Klein, *No Logo: No Space, No Choice, No Jobs* (New York: Picador, 2002), 22–26. See also Christine Harold, *OurSpace: Resisting the Corporate Control of Culture* (Minneapolis: University of Minnesota Press, 2007), xxii.

23. See, e.g., Cross, *An All-Consuming Century*, 18; Ewen, *Captains of Consciousness*, 53; and Rosenzweig, *Eight Hours for What We Will*, 35–64.

24. Cross, *An All-Consuming Century*, 15.

25. See, e.g., Andrejevic, *iSpy*.

26. My analysis here shares a certain resonance with that of Laura J. Miller, who explores how bookstores have been implicated in the production of what she alternatively calls "standardized" and "rationalized" consumers. See Miller, *Reluctant Capitalists*, 17–18.

27. Michel Foucault, "The Birth of Biopolitics," in *Ethics: Subjectivity and Truth*, ed. Paul Rabinow, trans. Robert Hurley et al. (New York: The New Press, 1997), 73–79; idem, *Security, Territory, Population: Lectures at the Collège de France, 1977–1978*, ed. Michel Senellart, trans. Graham Burchell (New York: Palgrave Macmillan, 2007). For some of the best examples of the uptake of this work, see Graham Burchell, Colin Gordon, and Peter Miller, eds., *The Foucault Effect: Studies in Governmentality* (Chicago: University of Chicago Press, 1991). See also Nikolas Rose, *Powers of Freedom: Reframing Political Thought* (Cambridge: Cambridge University Press, 1999); Andrejevic, *iSpy*; and James Hay and Mark Andrejevic, "Introduction—Toward an Analytic of Governmental Experiments in These Times: Homeland Security as the New Social Security," *Cultural Studies* 20, nos. 4–5 (July–September 2006): 331–48.

28. Andrejevic, *iSpy*, 161–86.

29. Ibid., 144.

30. Foucault, *Security, Territory, Population*, 107–8.

31. Will Collier, "Fool If You Think It's Over," *Vodkapundit and the Weblog of Tomorrow*, July 19, 2007, http://vodkapundit.com/archives/008960.php. The first-sale doctrine, which was codified in the U.S. Copyright Act of 1976 (17 U.S.C. sec. 109),

stipulates that once a copyright holder has sold a particular work, she or he no longer possesses the right to dictate its resale or redistribution terms. The relevant passage reads: "Notwithstanding the provisions of section 106 (3), the owner of a particular copy or phonorecord lawfully made under this title, or any person authorized by such owner, is entitled, without the authority of the copyright owner, to sell or otherwise dispose of the possession of that copy or phonorecord."

32. Tarleton Gillespie, *Wired Shut: Copyright and the Shape of Digital Culture* (Cambridge, Mass.: MIT Press, 2007), 169.

33. Alexander R. Galloway, *Protocol: How Control Exists after Decentralization* (Cambridge, Mass.: MIT Press, 2004), 172; McKenzie Wark, *A Hacker's Manifesto* (Cambridge, Mass.: Harvard University Press, 2004), 74–78, 158.

34. James Carey, "The Paradox of the Book," *Library Trends* 33 (1984): 105.

35. Among the most important and engaging works are the following: Cecelia Konchar Farr, *Reading Oprah: How Oprah's Book Club Changed the Way America Reads* (Albany: State University of New York Press, 2005); Elizabeth Long, *Book Clubs: Women and the Uses of Reading in Everyday Life* (Chicago: University of Chicago Press, 2003); Miller, *Reluctant Capitalists*; Janice A. Radway, *Reading the Romance: Women, Patriarchy, and Popular Literature* (Chapel Hill: University of North Carolina Press, 1984); idem, *A Feeling for Books: The Book-of-the-Month Club, Literary Taste, and Middle-Class Desire* (Chapel Hill: University of North Carolina Press, 1997); Kathleen Rooney, *Reading with Oprah: The Book Club That Changed America* (Fayetteville: University of Arkansas Press, 2005); Joan Shelley Rubin, *The Making of Middlebrow Culture* (Chapel Hill: University of North Carolina Press, 1992); John Tebbel, *A History of Book Publishing in the United States*, vol. 2, *The Expansion of an Industry, 1865–1919* (New York: Bowker, 1975); idem, *A History of Book Publishing in the United States*, vol. 3, *The Golden Age Between Two Wars, 1920–1940* (New York: Bowker, 1978); idem, *A History of Book Publishing in the United States*, vol. 4: *The Great Change, 1940–1980* (New York: Bowker, 1981). Although I'm less fond of these books owing to their nostalgic overtones, see also Jason Epstein, *Book Business: Publishing Past, Present, and Future* (New York: Norton, 2001); and André Schiffrin, *The Business of Books: How International Conglomerates Took Over Publishing and Changed the Way We Read* (London: Verso, 2000).

36. National Endowment for the Arts, *Reading at Risk: A Survey of Literary Reading in America*, Research Division Report no. 46 (Washington, D.C.: National Endowment for the Arts, 2004), xii.

37. Rubin has explored this synergy with respect to radio in the mid-twentieth century. See *The Making of Middlebrow Culture*, 266–329.

Index

Begos, Jr., Kevin, 40

Beniger, James R., 84

Bernays, Edward L., 27, 28, 29, 35, 37, 84, 182, 200*n*60, 209*n*14

best-seller(s): lists, 112; *New York Times*, 112; Oprah's Book Club selections and, 115

Bezos, Jeffrey Preston, 20, 81, 101, 102

bibliographic taste, 137–38, 139

bibliomania, 4

big-box bookstores, 49; book culture and, 50; books and, 50; bookselling and, 50, 78; chains, 51, 53–55, 77; culture and, 50; economic inequality and, 50; economics and, 50, 51–55; everyday book culture and, 51; history of, 56; independent bookstores and, 50, 51–55, 75, 76–77, 208*n*1; lawsuits against, 76; local communities and, 77–78; mass culture and, 78; morality and, 50; racial inequality and, 50, 77; senses of place and, 77. *See also* Barnes & Noble; *specific big-box bookstores*

Birkerts, Sven, 24–25, 26, 197*n*16

Bloomington, Indiana, 51

Bloomsbury, 145, 146, 155

Bolter, Jay David, 3, 15

book(s): advertising, 89, 90, 99; big-box bookstores and, 50; about books, 4, 187–88, 229*n*35; capitalism and, 7, 8, 183, 188; as closed entities, 11, 195*n*48; as commodities, 9, 44, 99; consumerism and, 5, 8; credit and, 8; crisis discourses about, 3, 188; cultural study of, 13–14, 195*n*57, 196*n*62; culture of, 112; decline *vs.* thriving of, 2; economics and, 6, 7; edges, 11, 12; gift, 7–8, 193*n*32; industrial organization and, 3; mimic, 28–29, 31, 67; new media *vs.*, 2, 188; Oprah's Book Club and standards for, 117, 139; *The Oprah Winfrey Show* and, 116; production, 82, 91; reading and, 12, 109; recurrent patterns of discussion of, 15; romance novels, 12, 32, 194*n*45; as "sacred products," 9; scholarship, 187; social infrastructure of, 14; television and, 17, 138; television personalities and,

3; terminology of, 11; used, 41; uses of, 12–13; value of, 6; vitality in late age of print, 188; work/leisure patterns and, 3. *See also* e-books; Harry Potter books; printed books

Book 2.0, 23

bookbacks. *See* mimic books

book borrowers: book industry *vs.*, 35–36. *See also* book sneaks

bookcases. *See* bookshelves

book circulation, 12; book industry and, 37–38; consumer capitalism and, 39; everyday book culture and, 13; Harry Potter books and, 17–18, 143, 171–72; international copyright treaties and, 34, 39; IP politics and, 17–18; politics of, 13; poll on, 37. *See also* book borrowers; lending rights

book clubs, 57. *See also* Oprah's Book Club

book coding, 91, 99; computerized, 92; machine based, 89, 98; numerical, 92–93. *See also* bar codes; International Standard Book Number; OCR-A; Standard Book Number

book consumption, 82

book culture: big-box bookstores and, 50; book technologies and, 46; commodities *vs.* sacred objects and, 9; crisis, 2–3, 6, 188–89; cultural studies of, 13–14, 195*n*57, 196*n*62; economics and, 6, 7; history of, 187; modern changes in, 2–3, 4; myths of, 6; product codes and, 107–8; sites as facets of contemporary, 14–15; today, 5, 10. *See also* everyday book culture

book distribution, 82, 95; Amazon.com and, 102, 103–4, 106, 107; book industry organization and, 89, 91, 99, 179; Cheney on, 88, 89, 91, 100; labor and, 100; online bookselling and, 83, 100, 101. *See also* book coding

book history, 4, 13, 192*n*17; books about, 188, 229*n*35; books today and, 5; crisis in, 175; fakes/piracy in, 158–59; scholarly, 187; technology and, 11. *See also* late age of print book industry: book borrowers *vs.*, 35–36; book circulation and, 37–38; bottom line and, 6; branding and, 115; commercialization, 91; competition in, 34–35; controlled consumption and, 185; economics and, 6–7, 88, 90, 193*n*27; grocery industry and, 95, 96; growth of, 17; history in U.S., 26–27, 32–33, 34, 35, 56–79, 81, 82, 83, 84–109, 199*n*54, 209*n*3; labor and, 100, 108–9; mass culture and U.S., 33, 78; product codes and, 107–8; tragedy of, 84, 88. *See also* bookselling; book trade; Cheney Report; food selling; publishing

book industry organization, 99; book distribution and, 89, 91, 99, 179; Cheney on, 89, 91. *See also* book coding

Bookland EAN, 97, 98, 100; Amazon.com and, 101, 102, 104, 105, 106, 108

book market: higher education and, 58, 205*n*32; middlebrow cultural goods and, 58

Book of Tea (Okakura), 23

Book-of-the-Month Club, 31, 57, 115, 199*n*54

book ownership. *See* printed book ownership

book piracy, 168–69; in book history, 158–59; China and, 159, *160*, 161–62, 167; dual pricing systems and, 226*n*94; global, 167; intellectual property and, 170; in U.S., 32; Western imperialism and, 169–71. *See also* Harry Potter book piracy

book publishing. *See* publishing

book reproduction, 36, 200*n*62; *Agrippa vs.*, 41; international copyright treaties and, 34

Book Search. *See* Google

booksellers: economics and, 16–17; independent *vs.* corporate, 16, 51–52

bookselling: asynchronous, 145, 146, 155; big-box bookstores and, 50, 78; food selling and, 58, 64–65, 67, 95; growth of, 17; Harry Potter books and, 144–47, 221*n*10; politics of, 16, 17; techniques, 59; in U.S., 16, 50, 51, 52–56. *See also* book

industry; educational bookselling; grocery industry; online bookselling; retail bookselling

books, future of, 41; books today and, 5; disappearing text and, 40–41; printed book ownership in, 39–40

bookshelves, 27, 182; campaign for built-in, 28, 29, 30, 31, 32, 33; home construction of, 28, 29; middle class and, 31; mimic books and, 28–29. *See also* home bookshelf construction; home book shelving

book shelving. *See* home book shelving

Booksnap, 43

book sneak(s), 31, 35, 37, 200*n*60

books today: book history and, 5; books, future of and, 5; prevalent/pedestrian character of, 5

bookstore(s): modern changes in, 3; small towns and, 48–49, 203*n*2. *See also* big-box bookstores; campus bookstores; chain bookstores; independent bookstores; *specific bookstores*

bookstore design, 205*n*34; Barnes & Noble, 62–63; supermarkets and, 58

book technologies: book culture and, 46. *See also* digital rights management technology

book trade: economics of, 6–7; globalization of, 146; integration, 99; Oprah's Book Club and, 114, 124; pass-along, 37, 38, 41, 201*n*82; used, 41. *See also* book industry

Boorstin, Daniel, 176

Borders, 50, 55, 186, 206*n*73; customer loyalty cards, 184–85

Borders Group, 52, 76

Borders, Louis, 206*n*73

Borders, Tom, 206*n*73

borrowers, of books. *See* book borrowers; book sneaks

bottom line: book industry, 6; corporate publishing, 6

Bourdieu, Pierre, 93, 193*n*27

Bowlby, Rachel, 58

branding: book industry and, 115; Oprah, 115; Oprah's Book Club and, 113, 115, 182

British Publishers Association (BPA), 92, 93

Byblos (publisher), 165–66

campus bookstores, 58, 59, 62–63, 64–65, 66, 67, 69

Cane River (Tademy), 126–27, 216*n*63

capitalism, 86; books and, 7, 8, 183, 188. *See also* conspicuous consumption; consumer capitalism; print capitalism

Carey, James, 176, 187, 188

Carlson, Chester, 36

case-cutting, 59

CCC. *See* Copyright Clearance Center

celebrity, 114; commerce and, 112; culture and, 112

de Certeau, Michel, 179

chain bookstores, 56, 70; big-box, 51, 53–55, 77; corporate retail, 49; large-scale retail, 78; mass culture and large-scale retail, 78; smaller mall-based, 48

"Chain Reaction: As Mega-Bookstores Move into Their Neighborhoods, Independents Worry About the Future," 53

Chapel Hill, North Carolina, 51, 71, 73, 74–75, 178, 207*n*90, 208*n*103, 208*n*106, 209*n*114. *See also* Durham, North Carolina

Chaplin, Charlie, 104

Cheney, Dick, 156

Cheney, Orion Howard, 84, *85*, 99, 108, 109, 209*n*14, 213*n*111; on book distribution, 88, 89, 91, 100; on book industry organization, 89, 91; other writings of, 86–87

Cheney Report, 83, 87–89, 90–91

China, People's Republic of (PRC): book piracy and, 159, *160*, 161–62, 167; Harry Potter piracy in, 159, *160*, 161–62

Christmas: consumerism and, 8; gift books and, 7–8, 193*n*32

circulation. *See* book circulation

Clarke, Breena, 126

class: conspicuous consumption and working, 199*n*41; in Durham, North

Carolina, 72, 74, 77; racial inequality and, 72, 77

codes. *See* bar codes; commodity codes; product codes

coding, of books. *See* book coding; International Standard Book Number; OCR-A; Standard Book Number

Cohen, Lizabeth, 177

Colbert, Steven, 219*n*17

college bookstores. *See* campus bookstores

Collier, Will, 153, 186, 228*n*31

Comedy Central, 154

The Coming of the Book (Febvre and Martin), 6–7

commerce: celebrity and, 112; culture and, 112

commodities: books as, 9, 44, 99; laws and books, 3; ownership, 39, 45; *vs.* sacred objects and book culture, 9

commodity codes, 99; labor and, 106, 213*n*102. *See also* bar codes; product codes

competition, 86, 87

conspicuous consumption: middle class and, 30–31; race and, 199*n*41; working class and, 199*n*41

consumer(s): culture, 31, 199*n*41; in societies of controlled consumption, 183

consumer capitalism, 183; book circulation and, 39; controlled consumption and, 180, 183–84, 185; cultural politics and, 177–79, 183, 185; e-books and, 16, 23, 45; obsolescence in, 181; post, 182; printed books and, 23, 57; three core principles of, 45; white professional middle class, 30–31. *See also* conspicuous consumption

consumerism, 175; books and, 5, 8; Christmas and, 8; control and, 175, 176; credit and, 8; U.S. and mass, 176–77

consumption, 86. *See also* book consumption; conspicuous consumption; controlled consumption

control: alternatives and, 186; consumerism and, 175, 176; intellectual property rights holders and information, 23;

e-book readers, 20, 23

e-books, 5; consumer capitalism and, 16, 23, 45; copying, 42–43, 202*n*86; digital rights management technology and, 41–42, 43–44, 179; disappearing text and, 40, 41, 179, 182; economics and, 19–20, 196*n*1; emergence of, 22–23; politics of, 24; printed books *vs.*, 16, 21–22, 23–24, 26, 197*n*8; problems with, *21*, 22, 23–24, 26

economic(s): big-box bookstores and, 50, 51–55; book culture and, 6, 7; book industry and, 6–7, 88, 90, 193*n*27; books and, 6, 7; booksellers and, 16–17; book trade and, 6–7; e-books and, 19–20, 196*n*1; Harry Potter book piracy and, 170; independent bookstores and, 51–56; pricing, 60–61; publishing and, 7, 87; reading and, 31; U.S. and, 176–77

economic inequality, and big-box bookstores, 50, 77

Economic Survey of the Book Industry, 1930–1931 (Cheney). *See* Cheney Report

education: book market and higher, 58, 205*n*32; Oprah's Book Club and literary, 113, 138, 214*n*9. *See also* campus bookstores

educational bookselling, 58, 59; Barnes & Noble, 62–63, 64–65, 66, 67, 69

Eisenstein, Elizabeth, 175

ElcomSoft, 42, 202*n*86

electronic books. *See* e-books

electronic media: home bookshelf construction and, 30; printed books *vs.*, 188; reading and, 2, 188

Epstein, Jason, 204*n*31, 229*n*35

European Article Number (EAN): bar codes, *98*, 108; ISBN and, 97. *See also* Bookland EAN

everyday, 9–11, 194*n*45

everyday book culture, 9, 109, 194*n*45; big-box *vs.* independent bookstores and, 51; book circulation and, 13; changing conditions of, 46; entitlement of, 11; inner workings of, 10–11; labor politics and, 83; in late age of print, 112, 176;

Oprah's Book Club and, 111–12, 113, 115; research, 14, 15

everyday lives: Oprah's Book Club and, 113, 114, 116, 117, 118, 121, 125, 128, 138, 139; Oprah's Book Club selections and, 125–26, 127–29, 130, 139, 217*n*68; *The Oprah Winfrey Show* and, 119; reading and, 119–20, 121; in societies of controlled consumption, 182; Winfrey and, 114; of women, 119–21, 128–29

fair use, 43, 186, 202*n*91. *See also* copyright; intellectual property

fakery, in Harry Potter piracy, 159, *160*, 161–62, 167

Farr, Cecelia Konchar, 214*n*6, 214*n*9, 214*n*13

Febvre, Lucien, 6–7

Felski, Rita, 10

first-sale doctrine, 43, 186, 202*n*91, 228*n*31

food selling: bookselling and, 58, 64–65, 67, 95; ISBN and, 95. *See also* grocery industry

Forbes, 114

Foster, F. Gordon, 93

Foucault, Michel, 47, 184, 185

Franzen, Jonathan, 113, 130–33, 218*n*89, 218*n*96

Fresh Air, 131

Frey, James, 113, 133–37, 218*n*104, 219*n*17

future, of books. *See* books, future of

Gaonkar, Dilip Parameshwar, 143

Gibson, William, 40, 41

gift books, Christmas, 7–8, 193*n*32

Gillespie, Tarleton, 186

Gitlin, Todd, 133

globalization, of book trade, 146

global lay-down date, 146–47, 148, 149, 150, 151, 156, 158; as publicity, 154

Gnomon Corporation, 37, 201*n*69

Google: Book Search, 20, 44, 45; Library, 44; publishers lawsuit against, 44–45, 203*n*92

grocery industry: bar codes, 95, 96; book industry and, 95, 96. *See also* food selling

Grossberg, Lawrence, 196n59
Gross, Terry, 131
Gutenberg Elegies: The Fate of Reading in an Electronic Age (Birkerts), 24

hacking, 186
Hamilton, Mary, 194n45
handwriting, *vs.* mechanical writing, 25
Harcourt Brace, 34
Harper Brothers, 33, 35
Harry Potter: creators/rights holders, 141, 142, 144, 145–46, 157, 161, 164–65, 171, 179; fans, 142, 145, 182; movies, 141; popularity, 141, 142; product franchises, 141; proliferation, 141, 171; transfiguration, 143, 161, 171, 173
Harry Potter and Leopard Walk Up to Dragon (impostor volume), 159, *160*, 161
Harry Potter and the Chamber of Secrets (Rowling), 144, 145, 157–58, 171
"Harry Potter and the Culture of Copy," 141, 142, 171, 174
Harry Potter and the Deathly Hallows (Rowling), 141, 144, 147, 148, 152, *153*, 172, 186, 221n18, 222n19
Harry Potter and the Goblet of Fire (Rowling), 144, 146
Harry Potter and the Half-Blood Prince (Rowling), 144, 145, 149, 150, 151–52, 154, 155, 172, 173, 221n10
Harry Potter and the Order of the Phoenix (Rowling), 143–44, 150, 151, 159, 172
Harry Potter and the Philosopher's Stone (Rowling), 141, 162, 163, 220n6. *See also Harry Potter and the Sorcerer's Stone*
Harry Potter and the Prisoner of Azkaban (Rowling), 144
Harry Potter and the Sorcerer's Stone (Rowling), 144, 145, 174, 220n6. *See also Harry Potter and the Philosopher's Stone*
Harry Potter book piracy, 157, 173, 186; Byblos (publisher) and, 165–66; in China, 159, *160*, 161–62; copies and, 167; economics of, 170; fakery in, 159, *160*, 161–62, 167; global incidents of, 159; intellectual property rights and, 17–18,

142, 165–66, 170; lawsuits and, 165–66; in Netherlands, 165–66; parody and, 166; Porri Gatter books and, 163–64; Russia and, 162–64, 224n61; in South Asia, 162; Tanya Grotter books and, 162, *163*, 164, 165–66; unauthorized reproductions in, 141, 142, 143, 144
Harry Potter books, 5, 135, 140, 176; book circulation and, 17–18; bookselling and, 144–47, 221n10; printings of, 144; releases of, 143, 144–45; success of, 172–73
Harry Potter books, control of, 172, 174, 179, 186; book releases, 146–54, *155*, 156–57, 182, 221n18, 222n19, 223n36; cultural politics and, 183; leaks and, 152, 153, 221n18; mass production of scarcity and, 157; security measures/failures in, 147–54, *155*, 156–57, 181, 186, 223n41, 223nn36–37, 228n31; unauthorized products and, 141, 142
Haynes, Melinda, 122–24
Heidegger, Martin, 25, 26
Henry Holt publishing house, 33
Higgins, Dick, 15
Hinds, Arthur, 61
history. *See* book history
home bookshelf construction, 28; electronic media and, 30; home redefinition and, 29–30; white professional middle class and, 30
home book shelving, accumulating printed books and, 27–28, 29, 30
home redefinition, and home book shelving, 29–30
House of Sand and Fog (Dubus III), 126, 129–30
"Housing Your Books," 27–28

IBM: Selectric typewriter, 24, 25; Universal Product Code, 96
Illouz, Eva, 129, 217n68
imperialism, and book piracy, 169–71
independent bookstores: ABA and, 52, 55, 56; big-box bookstores and, 50, 51–55, 75, 76–77, 208n1; driven out of business, 51–56; economics and, 51–56;

independent bookstores: *(continued)*
everyday book culture and, 51; well-
stocked, 47–48
inequality. *See* economic inequality; racial
inequality
information control, by intellectual
property rights holders, 23
infrastructure: social, of books, 14; technical,
180–81
intellectual property (IP), 202*n*89; book
piracy and, 170; law, 43, 202*n*89; politics
and book circulation, 17–18; rights and
Harry Potter book piracy, 17–18, 142,
165–66, 170; rights holders and
information control, 23; U.S. and, 32.
See also copyright; fair use; trademark
intermediation, 15, 16, 188
international copyright treaties: book
circulation and, 34, 39; book reproduction and, 34; U.S. and, 32, 33–34
International ISBN Agency, 97, 98
International Standard Book Number
(ISBN), 17, 83, 92, 93, 94, 99, 179, 211*n*56,
212*n*68; Amazon.com and,
101, 104, 105, 106, 108; bar codes,
97, *98*, 108; EAN and, 97; food selling
and, 95, 96; labor and, 100, 108
International Standards Organization
(ISO), 93
Internet bookselling. *See* online bookselling
IP. *See* intellectual property
ISBN. *See* International Standard Book
Number
ISO. *See* International Standards Organiza-
tion

jobbers (wholesalers), 60

Kindle, 20
Kingsolver, Barbara, 118, 122, 203*n*2
King, Stephen, 19, 20, 196*n*1
Kinko's, 37, 201*n*69
Knopf, 57
Kuralt, Wallace, 76–77

labor, 99, 109; Amazon.com and, 104,
105, 106–7, 108, 186, 213*n*107; bar
codes and, 100, 108; book distribution
and, 100; book industry and, 100, 108–9;
commodity codes and, 106, 213*n*102;
ISBN and, 100, 108; politics and
everyday book culture, 83
Larry King Live, 136
late age of print, 3, 4, 5, 9, 13, 14, 17, 44,
83, 185–86; book vitality in, 188;
consumerism in, 178; crises in,
175–76; cultural politics in, 178, 183, 189;
everyday book culture in, 112,
176; forward/backward movement
of, 176; ownership in, 45; politics in, 18,
186; on the verge, 176, 188, 189
lawsuits: against big-box bookstores, 76;
against Google Book Search, 44, 203*n*92;
against Harry Potter book piracy,
165–66; against photocopying, 37,
201*n*69
Lefebvre, Henri, 5, 10, 180–81, 183, 227*n*9,
227*n*17
lending rights, public: international, 38,
201*n*73; in U.S., 38, 201*n*72
Lessig, Lawrence, 34, 202*n*91, 227*n*17
libraries, 38, 41, 200*n*65, 201*n*80
Lippincott, Joseph Wharton, 28, 29
literacy, of Oprah's Book Club selections,
117–18, 138
Local Literacies (Barton and Hamilton),
194*n*45
LockStream Corporation, 41–42
logistics, 84, 89, 95, 100, 142, 156. *See also*
control
Los Angeles Times, 53
Lynd, Robert, 87, 90

malls, 70–71, 75, 77
market. *See* book market
marketplace, public, 59, 60
Martin, Henri-Jean, 6–7
Marx, Karl, 9, 82, 95, 101, 107, 185
mass culture: back office of, 82, 99, 157;
big-box bookstores and, 78; history

of, 51, 178; large-scale retail chain bookstores and, 78; politics of, 50; U.S. book industry and, 33, 78

mass production: of printed books, 8, 34, 82; publishing and, 7, 8

McGraw-Hill, 42

media: politics of writing, 24–25, 197*n*16. *See also* electronic media; intermediation; new media

men, and Oprah's Book Club, 131, 218*n*89

middlebrow cultural goods, 57; book market and, 58

middle class: bookshelves and, 31; conspicuous consumption and, 30–31; printed books and, 31. *See also* white professional middle class

Miller, Laura J., 176, 228*n*26

A Million Little Pieces (Frey), 127, 133–37

mimic books, 28–29, 31, 67

Mitchard, Jacquelyn, 111, 119

Modern Times, 104

morality: big-box bookstores and, 50; on Oprah's Book Club, 137, 139; pricing, 60–61

Morris, Mary McGarry, 118, 125

Morris, Meaghan, 47, 56

Morrison, Toni, 112, 122, 216*n*44

Mother of Pearl (Haynes), 122–24

Muzak, 64

Mytko, Ivan, 164, 226*n*96

NABP. *See* National Association of Book Publishers

Napster, 43

National Association of Book Publishers (NABP), 84, 87, 88, 89

National Endowment for the Arts (NEA), 1–2, 188, 191*n*2, 191*n*8

NEA. *See* National Endowment for the Arts

neoliberal governmentality, 184, 185

Netherlands, 165–66

new competition. *See* competition

new media: books *vs.*, 2; printed books *vs.*, 3, 4

New South, 71, 207*n*90

Newsweek, 112, 154

New York Review of Books, 57

New York Times, 28, 42, 52, 53, 54, 55, 86, 89, 107, 111, 153, 219*n*17; best-sellers, 112

Nissenbaum, Stephen, 8, 193*n*32

Noble, G. Clifford, 61, 62

Noble, Lloyd Adams, 61

North Carolina. *See* Chapel Hill, North Carolina; Durham, North Carolina

Norton, W. W., 89

Oates, Joyce Carol, 125, 129

obsolescence: in consumer capitalism, 181; in societies of controlled consumption, 181–82

OCR-A, 96, 97

Odegard Books, 53, 54–55

Ohmann, Richard, 30, 32, 33

Okakura, Kakuzo, 23

Ong, Walter J., 195*n*48

online bookselling, 5, 56, 99, 203*n*2; book distribution and, 83, 100, 101; history of, 81, 82, 83, 100, 101, 108, 209*n*3; politics of, 82; product codes and, 108. *See also* Amazon.com

Oprah: branding, 115; effect, 111, 112. *See also* Winfrey, Oprah

Oprah books, 115; talking life of, 117, 138

Oprahfication, 114, 214*n*13

Oprah's Book Club, 5, 17, 109, 176, 186; bibliographic taste and, 137–38, 139; book standards and, 117; book trade and, 114, 124; branding and, 113, 115, 182; discussions, 121, 123, 125, 128, 129, 130, 216*n*63; everyday book culture and, 111–12, 113, 115; everyday lives and, 113, 114, 116, 117, 118, 121, 125, 128, 138, 139; influence of, 114, 115, 137–38; literary education and, 113, 138, 214*n*9; men and, 131, 218*n*89; *The Oprah Winfrey Show* and, 116–17, 118, 119, 120, 121, 122–24, 125, 126–27, 128, 129, 138–39, 216*n*44; participants, 113, 119–20, 121, 122–24, 138–39, 140, 214*n*10; politics of, 113, 117, 139–40, 219*n*124;

publishing: bottom line corporate, 6; economics and, 7, 87; mass production and, 7, 8; modern changes in, 3. *See also* book industry

publishing house history, in U.S., 33, 34, 35, 199n54

publishing piracy. *See* book piracy

race, and conspicuous consumption, 199n41

racial inequality: big-box bookstores and, 50, 77; class and, 72, 77; in Durham, North Carolina, 71–73, 75, 77, 178, 208n110, 209n114

Radway, Janice A., 12, 31, 57, 82, 94, 115, 194n45

Raincoast, 146, 151–52, 155

Random House, 57, 100

RCA bull's-eye bar code, 95, *96*

reading: achievement and, 1–2; books and, 12, 109; cultural crisis of, 1–2, 6, 191n2, 191n8; culture, 112; decline of, 2, 188; economics and, 31; electronic media and, 188; everyday lives and, 119–20, 121; in interwar years, 31; media and politics, 24; Oprah's Book Club and, 113, 115, 121–24, 128, 138; *The Oprah Winfrey Show* and, 115, 120; technologies and intellectual history, 26; in U.S., 1–2, 31, 191n2, 191n8; Winfrey and, 111, 113, 114, 115, 120, 128; women and, 119–20, 121–22

Reading at Risk (NEA), 1, 2, 188, 191n2, 191n8

Reading the Romance, 194n45

reproduction, of books. *See* book reproduction

research: everyday book culture, 14, 15; intermediation and, 15–16

retail bookselling, 2, 17, 50, 52, 62; effect of educational bookselling on, 66, 67; large-scale, 50, 59, 66, 78, 83, 91, 99; Miller study of, 176. *See also* annex bookselling

retailers, 60

retail shopping, 59, 60

Rich, Frank, 219n117

Riding the Bullet (King), 19, 196n1

Riggio, Leonard, 65–66, 69, 206n73

Riggio, Steve, 173, 221n18

rights. *See* lending rights, public

rights management software. *See* digital rights management technology

River, Cross My Heart (Clarke), 126

romance novels, 12, 32, 194n45

RosettaBooks, 42

Ross, Andrew, 101

Rowling, J. K., 135, 141, 142, 144, 148, 155, 156, 161, 164, 166, 167. *See also* Harry Potter

Russia, 162–64, 224n61

Sardar, Ziauddin, 168–69

SBN. *See* Standard Book Number

Scannell, Paddy, 10–11, 116, 120

Schiffrin, André, 55–56, 204n31, 229n35

Scholastic, 144, 145, 146, 147, 148, 149, 150, 152, 155, 156, 172, 181, 222n19

school bookstores. *See* campus bookstores

Schroeder, Pat, 44, 197n8

Schwartz, Hillel, 200n62

shelving, of books. *See* home book shelving

shopping centers. *See* malls

Silberman, Steve, 23

Simon & Schuster, 19, 34, 57

sites, as contemporary book culture facets, 14–15, 18

Sklyarov, Dmitry, 42

Slack, Jennifer Daryl, 196n59

slavery, 71–72, 126–27, 216n63

Smoking Gun, 134, 136, 218n104

societies of controlled consumption: consumers in, 183; control and, 180–82; everyday lives in, 182; infrastructure in, 180–81; neoliberal governmentality and, 184, 185; obsolescence in, 181–82; programming in, 181, 227n17

Songs in Ordinary Time (Morris), 118, 125, 127

South Asia, 143, 162, 169–70

speech, *vs.* writing, 26, 198n21

Standard Book Number (SBN), 93, 211n56

Stoddard, Paul W., 35, 36

superstores. *See* big-box bookstores